RAND Education

Who Is Leading Our Schools?

An Overview of School Administrators and Their Careers

Susan M. Gates
Jeanne S. Ringel
Lucrecia Santibañez
Karen E. Ross
Catherine H. Chung

Prepared for the
Wallace-Reader's Digest Funds

The research described in this report was supported by the Wallace-Reader's Digest Funds.

Library of Congress Cataloging-in-Publication Data

Gates, Susan M., 1968–
Who is leading our schools? : an overview of school administrators and their careers / Susan M. Gates, Jeanne Ringel, Lucrecia Santibanez, with Catherine Chung and Karen Ross.
p. cm.
"MR-1679."
Includes bibliographical references.
ISBN 0-8330-3353-0 (alk. paper)
1. School administrators—United States. 2. Educational leadership—United States. I. Ringel, Jeanne S. II. Santibanez, Lucrecia. III. Title.

LB2831.82.G39 2003
371.2'011—dc21

2003002130

Published 2003 by RAND
1700 Main Street, P.O. Box 2138, Santa Monica, CA 90407-2138
1200 South Hayes Street, Arlington, VA 22202-5050
201 North Craig Street, Suite 202, Pittsburgh, PA 15213-1516
RAND URL: http://www.rand.org/
To order RAND documents or to obtain additional information, contact Distribution Services: Telephone: (310) 451-7002; Fax: (310) 451-6915; Email: order@rand.org

PREFACE

Some policymakers are concerned that just as state and federal governments are increasing school accountability requirements and relying on school administrators to promote improvement, schools and districts are finding it increasingly difficult to attract and retain people to fill school administrative positions and to do the job well. Several remedies for this perceived problem have been proposed, most of them grounded on little concrete information on the nature of the labor market for school administrators.

As part of the Wallace-Readers Digest Funds LEADERS Count initiative, RAND undertook a study to examine what the existing research and empirical data can reveal about the careers of school administrators. This was seen as a way to begin building a solid understanding of school administrative career paths and the challenges facing schools that employ these administrators.

This report develops a conceptual structure for understanding the careers of school administrators. Focusing on school principalships and superintendencies as important and readily identifiable positions, it emphasizes the fact that a career in school administration involves many steps and that it is important to consider the different paths people take to these high-visibility positions. The authors describe what is known about the individuals who hold administrative positions and how their characteristics have changed over time. They also describe what is known about the factors expected to influence individuals' decisions to seek particular administrative positions, focusing particularly on wages, working conditions, and barriers. The report should be of interest to education policymakers at the national, state, and local levels, as well as to educational researchers and practitioners.

Future RAND research will build on this base, examining the careers of school administrators in several states in greater detail.

This research was funded by the Wallace Funds and was conducted within RAND Education. This effort reflects RAND Education's mission to bring accurate data and careful, objective analysis to the national debate on education policy.

CONTENTS

FIGURES

TABLES

SUMMARY

The recently passed No Child Left Behind legislation reflects the increasing visibility and importance of school administration in the larger education reform effort. But just when the role of school administrators is being emphasized, policymakers and the public are becoming increasingly concerned that there is or soon will be a shortage of qualified individuals to fill formal school and district management positions. This concern stems primarily from the perception that a large number of people are leaving school administrative positions, that districts are having a hard time replacing those who leave, and that replacements often lack the skills necessary to succeed in school administration.

To know whether the United States is indeed facing a crisis in the recruitment and retention of school administrators, the Wallace-Readers Digest Funds asked RAND to conduct a systematic analysis of the career patterns of school administrators, including the moves they make into and out of the profession and the factors that might be expected to influence those moves.

WHAT IS KNOWN ABOUT THE CAREERS OF SCHOOL ADMINISTRATORS

Our study provides descriptive information about school administrators and their careers. We examined

- The characteristics of school administrators.
- Movement into, out of, and within the school administrative career field.
- Incentives for movement into, out of, and between school administrative positions.

We looked at current conditions as well as changes over time. We also examined how the observable characteristics of schools relate to the careers of school administrators. Our study does not constitute a complete analysis of the potential shortage of capable school administrators, however, since it focuses solely on supply, and a complete analysis must consider supply, demand, and the relationship between the two. A related report, also sponsored by the Wallace Funds (Roza et al., 2002), links supply and demand in an analysis of principal shortages in specific districts.

In this report, we present the conceptual framework we developed to describe the careers of school administrators. We then use this framework as a structure for discussing both the research that has been conducted on the subject and our original analyses of existing national data.

Although the existing data provide a useful starting point for developing an understanding of school administrative careers, they do not provide a long-run look at the careers of individual administrators. Better, longitudinal data are needed to conduct a more robust and complete assessment of these careers.

THE NUMBER OF SCHOOL ADMINISTRATORS IS STABLE BUT THE PROFESSION IS AGING

Our examination of the characteristics of school administrators revealed a professional area experiencing neither tremendous growth nor tremendous decline. This finding is evident in the trends among principals, who represent nearly half of all school administrators. According to the most recent National Center for Education Statistics (NCES) Schools and Staffing Survey (SASS), the number of principals grew by over 7 percent for public schools and by over 3 percent for private schools between the 1987–1988 and 1999–2000 school years. The national trends obscure some important regional variations, however; and high rates of growth in the numbers of schools and administrative positions in the West may be putting pressure on labor markets in some states.[1] The 1990s also saw dramatic progress in the representation of women in the principalship, as well as somewhat less dramatic progress in the representation of racial/ethnic minorities.

Perhaps the most striking finding of our analysis is that the nation's principals are growing older as a group. From 1987–1988 to 1999–2000, the average age of principals increased from 47.8 to 49.3 in the public sector and from 46.0 to 49.9 in the private sector. Moreover, not only are principals aging overall, but those entering the principalship for the first time are getting older. In 1987–1988, 38 percent of new public school principals were 40 or younger; by 1999–2000, only 12 percent were in this age group. A similar though less dramatic shift in age distribution occurred for new private school principals.

Our analysis also suggests that school and district hiring decisions with regard to new principals and the retirement programs that are in place may be contributing to this aging trend. Schools, particularly public schools, are now less likely to hire people under 40 into a principalship than they were a decade ago. These new principals thus will spend fewer years in the labor force before reaching retirement age. This finding is of particular concern in the public sector, where principals appear to be much less likely to remain on the job after 55.

---

[1]The number of principals alone has increased by 18 percent in public schools and 13.8 percent in private schools in this area of the country.

THERE IS LITTLE EVIDENCE THAT SCHOOL ADMINISTRATORS ARE BEING LURED INTO OTHER CAREER FIELDS

A review of the rates at which school administrators leave their professional field provided no evidence of a recent exodus. Over the sample period (1983–1999), exit rates ranged from 15 to 33 percent per year, with no evident time trend. A similarly large fraction of individuals, 19 to 29 percent, entered school administration each year. Nor was there evidence that administrators left to take jobs in other sectors of the economy. On average, those leaving school administration experienced a decrease in the average number of hours worked per week and in average wage. These trends do not support the contention that people are being lured away from school administration into other careers.

There also appears to have been no major shift in the factors one would expect to influence entry into and exit from the school administration field. For example, we found that the compensation of school administrators kept pace with that of other managerial professions in the public and private sectors.

Moreover, we found that while private school administrators, and principals in particular, still earn less than their public school counterparts, the earnings gap has decreased. In addition, the average experience of private school principals has increased by over two years since 1987–1988, while that of public school principals has declined. It is thus possible that in the future, traditional public schools may face greater competition from private schools for school administrators.

Possible Administrative Career Barriers and Incentives

Some policymakers have wondered whether state-level certification requirements deter people, particularly those without teaching backgrounds, from entering the field of school administration. This issue becomes particularly salient if there are not enough people to fill school administrative positions, but it may also be of general interest. Most states have detailed education and experience requirements for public school administrators, but many states are contemplating changes to their requirements and/or alternative certification routes because they are concerned about a shortage of people qualified to assume administrative positions. Certification requirements can indeed pose a barrier that inhibits movement into the field, but we found that the number of people *certified* for, and thus officially qualified to fill, existing school administrative positions appears to be adequate.

Overall, individuals appear to have financial incentives to move into and through the school administrative field. Teaching is the most common gateway into most administrative positions: Over 99 percent of public school principals and nearly 90 percent of public school superintendents and private school principals have some teaching experience. In general, the financial incentives for individuals to move from teaching to administration appear to be moderate. And although the financial rewards of school administration relative to those of teaching have varied over time and declined slightly through the 1990s, we found (after controlling for the number of months worked per year) that public school principals earned on average about 33 percent more per year than experienced teachers in the same school did. Private school principals earned 44 percent more. Moreover, our literature review showed that the average salary of principals was greater than that of assistant principals, and that superintendents and senior district administrators earned more than principals did.

Salary Variations Across Schools and States

Nothing we have said denies that an individual teacher might have to take a pay cut to move into the principalship. The average salary differential between principals and experienced teachers obscures some important variations across schools and states. We found schools where principals earned less than experienced teachers did, and we found schools where principals earned twice as much or more. However, overall, principals seemed to earn more than experienced teachers in the same school did, and we found no *systematic* patterns suggesting that certain types of schools offer principals more than they offer teachers.

PRINCIPALS ARE NOT FLEEING SCHOOLS SERVING DISADVANTAGED STUDENTS

We found no evidence that the more-experienced principals were systematically choosing not to work in urban schools serving larger populations of disadvantaged students—i.e., minority, low-income,[2] or limited English proficient (LEP) students. On average, principals at schools with observable characteristics typically assumed to pose greater challenges were found to have the same level of experience as principals at other schools did.

This lack of variation in principals' experience by school characteristics, or sorting, is particularly interesting in view of another one of our findings: Principals' perceptions of school problems varied in systematic ways according to a school's observable characteristics. Principals reported more school problems when they worked in public schools, in schools with a higher proportion of low-income students, in high schools, and in schools with larger enrollments.

We also found that salaries were adjusted to pay principals more highly for working in schools with observable characteristics often associated with more problems. In addition, principals' salaries varied in systematic ways with other observable school characteristics: Public school principals earned substantially more than private school principals did, high school principals earned more than elementary school principals did, and principals of larger schools tended to earn more than principals of smaller schools did.

---

[2]Low-income students are defined as those qualifying for free or reduced-price lunch programs.

POLICY IMPLICATIONS

Our analysis provides no evidence to support the idea that there is a nationwide crisis in the ability of schools to attract and retain school administrators, and thus does not argue for nationwide policies aimed at attracting more people into the field of school administration. Nevertheless, it does raise some important issues for policymakers and education administrators to consider.

Public School Systems Should Look for Ways to Respond to Aging Trends in the Principalship

The principalship is an aging profession, and many states, schools, and districts are concerned about the proportion of principals they will have to replace due to retirement in the next five years. Our analysis suggests that the aggregation of local hiring decisions that typically place a premium on experience may be contributing to the situation. The profession is aging not just because people hired into administrative positions 25 years ago are getting ready to retire, but also because many schools are hiring first-time principals who are already close to retirement age. Schools, districts, and states may benefit from thinking of how to reach out to younger people as a way to create a group of administrators whose careers can be longer. At the same time, public school systems could look at their retirement systems, which appear to create incentives for individuals to retire or leave the education system at a relatively young age.

Local-Level Data and Analyses of the Careers of School Administrators Are Needed

While the data provide no evidence of a nationwide crisis, they do not dispute the notion that individual schools and districts may be having difficulty finding or retaining administrators. A comparison of schools and districts that have similar observable characteristics but differ as to whether they are struggling to attract and retain school administrators may be particularly useful. Our analysis suggests that there are important differences in the challenges faced by different states and provides support for a detailed state-level analysis of the careers of school administrators. Such an analysis is the best way to understand local variation and to continuously monitor the challenges. In our view, solutions must be devised and implemented at the local or, perhaps, the state level.

Policymakers Should Further Examine the Forms of Entry into the School Administrative Field

Since teaching is the main gateway to school administration, schools and districts need to attract high-quality potential administrators into the teaching pool and to ensure that some teachers have an incentive to move into school administration. To this end, policymakers should further examine the relationship between the labor market for teachers and that for school administrators. Given that all school administrators together are a small group relative to all teachers, only a small fraction of teachers need to make the move to school administration to ensure adequate supply. In addition, formal barriers, such as certification requirements, and informal district hiring practices all but exclude those without teaching experience from consideration for administrative positions. Therefore, if policymakers are serious about drawing people from outside education into school administration, they must address these barriers to the profession as well.

ACKNOWLEDGMENTS

We would like to thank the Wallace-Readers Digest Funds for supporting this research and for bringing together a community of scholars, policymakers, and practitioners committed to improving school leadership. Our research effort benefited greatly from interactions with other Wallace Funds grantees too numerous to mention here.

We thank Dominic Brewer for the guidance he provided as director of the program under which this report was produced, as well as RAND colleague Tom Glennan for his helpful guidance at several stages of the research. We benefited from conversations and collaborations with Jim Wyckoff, Frank Papa, Hamilton Lankford, Raymond Kesper, and James Kadamus, and from extensive interaction with University of Washington researchers who are also conducting research on school leadership issues.

Susan Bodilly, Eric Eide, Cassandra Guarino, and Sheila Kirby provided helpful reviews of an earlier version of this report. Our earlier versions also benefited from comments of seminar participants at RAND, the University of Washington, and the Education Commission of the States, as well as from Marguerite Roza. Donna White provided helpful secretarial support; Kristin Leuschner helped revise sections of the document to improve the presentation; Jeri O'Donnell carefully edited the final copy.

Ed Pauly, Kim Jinnett, Peter Kleinbard, Lee Mitgang, and Judith Johnson of the Wallace Funds gave us useful feedback on the research leading up to this report and on drafts of the report.

ACRONYMS AND ABBREVIATIONS

AASA	American Association of School Administrators
BIA	Bureau of Indian Affairs
BLS	Bureau of Labor Statistics
BRR	Balance Repeated Replication
CEO	chief executive officer
CPI	consumer price index
CPS	Current Population Survey
DoD	Department of Defense
ESEA	Elementary and Secondary Education Act
GS	General Schedule
LEP	Limited English Proficient
NCES	National Center for Education Statistics
ORG	Outgoing Rotation Group
PEP	Principals' Executive Program
SASS	Schools and Staffing Survey

Chapter One

INTRODUCTION

Policymakers and the public are becoming increasingly concerned that there is or soon will be a shortage of qualified individuals to fill formal management positions in our nation's school districts (Colvin, 2000). This concern has several important and distinct dimensions:

- A large number of people are leaving school administrative positions.[1]
- Districts have a hard time finding people to replace those who leave.
- The replacements often lack the skills required to succeed in school administrative positions.

Press reports paint a picture of an exodus of principals, highlighting annual turnover rates as high as 20 percent among principals in several states, including Vermont, Washington, Kentucky, and Texas (Steinberg, 2000). Although school administrators leave their positions for many reasons (including retirement), schools and districts are particularly worried by testimonials from former principals who decided to return to teaching because the modest pay increase accompanying their administrative role did not offset the increased time requirements, stress, and other demands of the job (Steinberg, 2000).

Not only do administrators seem to be leaving at alarming rates, but schools appear to be having a hard time replacing them. In Vermont, several retired principals agreed to return on an interim basis until a permanent principal could be found. In New York City schools, where the turnover rate can exceed 25 percent over a two-year period, the 2000–2001 school year began with 163 temporary principals (Steinberg, 2000), and over half of the city's principals had three or fewer years of experience (Archer, 2002a). In Los Angeles, a threatened shortage of principals led the Los Angeles Unified School District to call on retired principals to temporarily fill the gaps (Sahagun, 2000). State certification requirements might be posing a barrier for teachers who would like to become administrators, but the evidence shows that teachers who already have administrative credentials sometimes choose to remain in

[1]School administrators are those filling a variety of school-, district-, and state-level management positions in the K–12 school system. Principals and district superintendents are the most visible administrators, but there are many others as well, such as assistant principals, district business managers, and regional superintendents.

the classroom rather than assume the burden of an administrative position. Teachers reportedly are deterred by the comparatively longer hours and administrative activities involved in the job (Steinberg, 2000).

The third concern is that schools, faced with a shrinking pool of qualified people from which to select administrators for increasing numbers of vacancies, will end up filling positions with people of lesser quality, thus jeopardizing quality (Houston, 2000).

Policymakers at the national, state, and local levels have been working on ways to address the perceived recruiting and retention challenges in various ways. Nationally, the Council of Chief State School Officers has emphasized quality and preparation issues. It has been pushing for adoption of a set of professional standards to link attributes of school administrators to improved student outcomes (Council of Chief State School Officers, 1996), and the Education Testing Service has developed two assessments—one for principals and one for superintendents.[2] Nine states and the District of Columbia require the first test as part of the licensure process for principals. The National Board for Professional Teaching Standards is spearheading an effort to create a system of advanced certification for school administrators based on the existing national teacher certification effort (Archer, 2002b).

At the state level, there are calls to change administrative certification requirements in hopes of attracting new people into the field (e.g., by offering an "alternative route to certification" for those with non-educational career backgrounds). Some states are also trying to improve the quality of training that principals receive or to make it easier for people to acquire the training. For example, in 1984 the North Carolina General Assembly established the Principals' Executive Program (PEP), a professional development program for principals, assistant principals, and other administrative personnel in North Carolina's public schools. Nearly all of the program costs are covered by state funds; in the 2001–2002 fiscal year, PEP received a state appropriation of $1.6 million (Principals' Executive Program, 2002).

At the local level, many districts—particularly large urban districts—are trying to facilitate recruiting by increasing the supply of people interested in and qualified for school administrative positions through mentoring programs (Colvin, 2000). Some districts, such as New York City, have principal institutes that identify excellent teachers and encourage and prepare them to become successful administrators (Crow, Mecklowitz, and Weekes, 1992). Grow-your-own programs (Johnson and Douglas, 1990) allow districts to develop a pool of potential administrators over time from the pool of current teachers. In addition, some districts have increased their administrative salaries, often in targeted ways.

While efforts at all levels appear to be reasonable, each makes a different claim with regard to the underlying causes of the challenges schools and districts face in trying to recruit and retain school administrators. Some responses suggest that low pay is a

---

[2]Available at http://www.ets.org/sls/index.html.

key issue, others that working conditions are problematic, and others that certification is a barrier to recruitment.

An empirically based understanding of the career patterns of school administrators, the moves they make, and the factors that might be expected to influence those moves can provide some understanding of the supply side of the labor market for school administrators. This can be a first step toward ascertaining whether the nation is truly facing a crisis in recruitment and retention and, if it is, what the potential causes of the crisis are. It can also contribute to the overall policy debate. Our study establishes an empirical baseline both for considering the claims about causes underlying the challenges in recruiting and retaining school administrators and for evaluating potential solutions for those challenges.

STUDY OBJECTIVE AND APPROACH

Our study's goal was to answer four key questions about the careers of school administrators:

- What are the characteristics of school administrators, and how have they changed over time?
- What kinds of movement into and out of the school administrative career field are occurring, and what factors are likely to affect these movements?
- What kinds of movement between the different types of positions within the administrative career path are occurring?
- What kinds of movement are occurring within the principalship, and what do they reveal about the relationship between position turnover and observable school characteristics?

We began our study by developing a conceptual framework for understanding the careers of school administrators. We then used the framework to summarize what is currently known about school administrators and their careers and to address the four key questions listed above. Our summary draws on a broad review of the existing literature as well as our analyses of such career-related issues as salary, career paths, and attitudes using the National Center for Education Statistics (NCES) Schools and Staffing Survey (SASS) data from the U.S. Department of Education and the Current Population Survey (CPS) from the U.S. Census Bureau.

SCOPE OF STUDY

The Wallace-Readers Digest Funds LEADERS Count initiative focuses on promoting the improvement of school leadership, broadly defined. Our study focused more narrowly, on understanding the careers of those who currently hold traditionally defined positions of responsibility and authority in primary and secondary schools (mainly principals and superintendents). While such individuals are an important aspect of school leadership, current discussions on ways to improve school leadership focus on the roles played by people throughout the school system (Resnick and

Glennan, 2002) and on redefining the role of the principal and/or superintendent (Portin et al., 2003).

Our research was directed at understanding what existing data and research can tell us about the individuals who hold formal positions of responsibility and authority, as currently defined, in schools. Thus, this study should be viewed as a complement to current research on the role of principals and the role of school leadership in education reform.

In press reports and policy debates, there is much discussion about the "shortage" of principals and school administrators. Our study is related to and can inform a discussion of this shortage, but a complete analysis of a shortage must consider supply, demand, and the relationship between the two. By focusing on the careers of school administrators, we have analyzed the supply but not the demand. A related report, also sponsored by the Wallace Funds (Roza et al., 2002), links supply and demand in an analysis of principal shortages in specific districts.

REPORT OVERVIEW

Chapter Two presents a conceptual framework of the career flow of school administrators that can aid in understanding the key factors that may contribute to the perception that there is or will be a crisis in recruiting and retaining school administrators. Chapter Three provides a descriptive overview of current school administrators based on empirical data; it also points out major national trends and differences between the public and private sectors. Chapters Four, Five, and Six focus on the moves administrators make over the course of their careers and the factors likely to influence those moves. Chapter Four describes what is known about movement into and out of the school administrative career field; Chapter Five addresses how school administrators progress through positions within the career field; Chapter Six looks specifically at the moves school principals make. Chapter Seven then presents our conclusions and provides suggestions for future research.

The main body of this report highlights the key results of our analyses without delving into technical detail. This information should be of interest to a wide audience, including policymakers concerned about school leadership issues, school administrators at various levels, and education researchers. Readers interested in more detail—researchers and those concerned with specific issues—are directed to Appendices A through D, where they will find a full description of the research methodology, including a description of the databases and a full set of regression results. Appendix A gives an overview of the SASS, summarizing the information related to administrative careers that is available from the survey's different waves. Appendix B presents regression analyses using the SASS database. Appendix C contains an analysis of the relationship between observable school characteristics and principals' reports of school problems, using principals' responses to questions about school problems contained in the SASS. Appendix D covers an analysis we did using the CPS to examine salary trends of school administrators relative to those of other, similar professionals.

Chapter Two

UNDERSTANDING THE CAREER FLOW OF SCHOOL ADMINISTRATORS

Formal leadership positions in K–12 education are assumed by people with experience—usually in the education system, but sometimes in other settings as well. It is impossible to consider concerns about the ability of schools to hire school administrators without recognizing the paths people take to those positions. Teaching is considered to be a valuable experience for school administrators, which is why most school administrators are teachers before beginning their administrative careers. Only a minority of school administrators enter the field directly, without working as teachers first.

This chapter discusses the careers of school administrators, starting with a framework and then turning to entries into and exits out of the field. Movement within the field itself is discussed in Chapter Five.

ADMINISTRATIVE CAREER FLOW FRAMEWORK

Figure 2.1 describes our conceptualization of the overall career flow for school administrators. As shown in the diagram, the flow is not unidirectional—people move into and out of different positions for different reasons at different stages of their career. Also shown is that the administrative career field includes not only the principalship and superintendency, but other administrative positions at both the school and the district level (such as assistant principal, business manager, and public affairs specialist). We use this figure to structure our discussion of what we found about the careers of school administrators.

We found no published research that considers the career flow of school administrators in its entirety. Instead, the literature focuses on specific pieces of the whole. For example, there is a large body of literature on the careers of teachers that tries to understand entry into, progression within, and exit from the teacher labor force. This research demonstrates that compensation is an important component of teachers' entry and exit decisions (see, e.g., Murnane and Olsen, 1989; Murnane et al., 1991). However, this literature treats all exits from teaching positions in the same way, ignoring the fact that it would be quite natural for successful teachers to move into the administrative career field at some point. Moreover, while the data on teachers are good, as are those on principals and, to some extent, superintendents, the data on other school administrators are extremely limited.

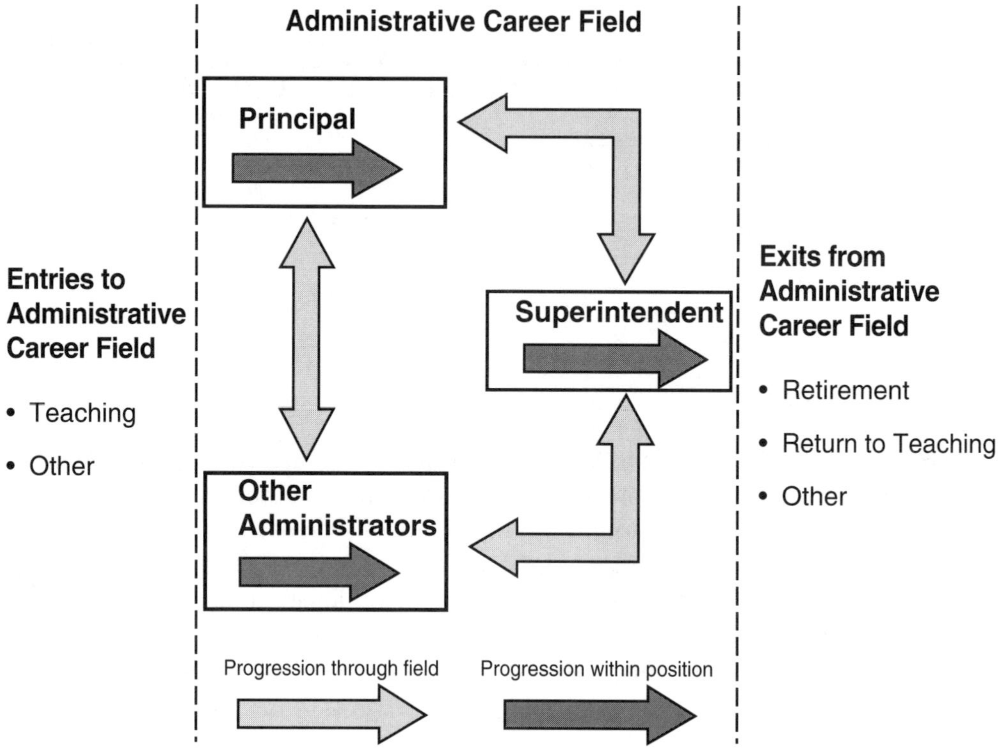

Figure 2.1—Career Flow of School Administrators

Entries into and exits from the administrative career field reflect individuals' decisions to enter or leave, respectively, any position within that field. The career field boundary draws a line between positions in that career field and other activities—e.g., teaching, retirement, unemployment, or employment in any position outside the career field.

When examining career flow, it is important to consider the scope of the career field. For example, if one studies career flow at the national level and considers only movements into and out of the administrative career field at that level, one may overlook important differences across states or districts. If one focuses on the district level only, one may find a very high level of exit or turnover when people are, in fact, not leaving the school administrative field but, rather, just moving across districts. We chose to use existing literature and data to say as much as possible about administrative career paths from a national, state, and local perspective.

Public policymakers may want to determine whether public school administrators are leaving their jobs for similar positions in private schools. To do so, they would have to define the career field in terms of public school administration only and treat moves from the public to the private sector as movement out of the career field. Similarly, policymakers interested in the extent to which individuals are crossing state or district lines would have to think of the career field in terms of the state or district.

USING THE FRAMEWORK TO SYNTHESIZE INFORMATION ON THE CAREERS OF SCHOOL ADMINISTRATORS

We use our administrative career flow framework (see Figure 2.1) to summarize what we currently know about school administrators and their careers. Our discussion of the moves administrators make is divided into three parts: moves into and out of the school administrative career field, moves within the administrative career field, and, finally, moves within one of the positions, the principalship. Each type of move sheds light on different elements of the recruiting and retention issue, as follows:

- *Movement into and out of the school administrative career field* may be influenced by how attractive school administration is relative to teaching, positions outside of education, and leisure/retirement. Examination of this topic helps inform the question of whether school administrators are being lured away from careers in education by more-attractive alternatives, and whether there is an incentive for teachers to move into administration.
- *Movement within the administrative career field* may be influenced by the incentives individuals are offered to move into different positions.
- *Movement within the principalship* may be influenced by the relative attractiveness of different jobs. Examination of this topic allows us to consider whether some schools are at an advantage or disadvantage in attracting and retaining principals and whether there may a "crisis" for particular types of schools even if there is no nationwide crisis.

We examine two types of evidence related to the moves individuals make: straightforward information on the moves themselves—i.e., the number of people moving into and out of particular positions and trends over time—and the factors that would be expected to influence these moves based on a simple labor market perspective that assumes individuals choose whether or not to accept positions.[1]

The three key factors that would be expected to influence individual choices about different jobs are monetary compensation, working conditions, and entry barriers (both formal and informal). Monetary compensation is an obvious factor to consider in evaluating a job's relative attractiveness. All other things being equal, we would expect people to gravitate toward jobs that pay more. But all other things usually are not equal, and different jobs are often associated with different amenities and disamenities.

[1]One may be concerned that reality does not correspond with this "choice" model of administrative labor markets, corresponding to a queuing/assignment model instead. In the latter, administrative jobs are attractive, there are more people seeking them than there are positions available, and the hiring entity (in this case, the district) is able to assign individuals to jobs. While we acknowledge that some districts do adopt an assignment approach, such districts still face competition from other districts in the sense that an administrator can choose to move to a neighboring district rather than accept an unwanted assignment. In that sense, then, an individual administrator can exercise employment choice even in a queuing/assignment model, except when there is a general oversupply of those who want to be administrators at current salaries across all districts in an area.

The theory of compensating differentials argues that individuals consider both monetary and non-monetary benefits and costs associated with different jobs when choosing whether and where to work (Rosen, 1986). In other words, people think of their "real wage" as a combination of what they are paid and the working conditions (both positive and negative) they experience in performing their job. They attribute a positive value to a job's desirable characteristics and a negative value to its undesirable characteristics and then essentially add the positives to and subtract the negatives from what they are paid when comparing different job opportunities. The more other options individuals have, the more they need to be paid to accept undesirable work characteristics, such as on-the-job stress, health and safety risks, an unpleasant work location, an inflexible or unattractive work schedule (such as night-shift work), a lack of autonomy, and a lack of job security.

Generally speaking, employers do not create unfavorable working conditions to torture employees; certain undesirable characteristics just go along with particular jobs. The theory of compensating differentials supposes that employers have some latitude to improve working conditions at a cost and that they make a financial tradeoff between paying higher wages and providing better working conditions. If labor markets are competitive, the theory predicts that wages will be higher for jobs with poorer working conditions.[2] However, this general result can be confounded by unionization and collective bargaining (Daniel and Sofer, 1998). For example, if some companies have unions with greater bargaining strength and if a strong union is able to negotiate both better working conditions and better wages for its members, we might expect to see a positive relationship between working conditions and wages.

In sum, the theory of compensating differentials suggests that the more demanding the job in terms of time required, skills needed, job stress, etc., the higher the compensation individuals will demand to do the job.[3] Conversely, the intrinsic rewards of a job, such as feeling that one is doing interesting work or contributing to society, or the prestige associated with leading a successful school, can reduce the required monetary compensation.[4] The literature on compensating differentials informed our analyses of moves into and out of the administrative career field, within the field itself, and across schools.

---

[2]This simplistic overview of the theory assumes that all workers are of the same quality or have the same skills. Extensions of the basic theory allow for variation in quality across workers and cause employers to make tradeoffs between wages, working conditions, and worker quality. For example, an employer may choose to offer both lower wages and worse working conditions and simply accept the fact that the workers he gets will be of lower quality.

[3]For example, teachers might be willing to trade salary increases for smaller class sizes.

[4]Herzberg (1987) makes a distinction between job satisfaction and job dissatisfaction, emphasizing that one is not simply the opposite of the other. Job satisfaction typically stems from factors intrinsic to the job, such as achievement, recognition of achievement, the work itself, responsibility, and advancement. Job dissatisfaction tends to be caused primarily by factors extrinsic to the job, such as company policy and administration, supervision, interpersonal relationships, working conditions, salary, status, and security. Herzberg argues that the presence of negative extrinsic factors can make a job unpleasant, but that the absence of such factors or the presence of positive extrinsic factors does not necessarily make a job pleasant. Instead, people typically find a job pleasant when positive intrinsic factors exist.

In addition to monetary compensation and working conditions, we also consider barriers, such as certification requirements that limit an individual's ability to move into school administration from teaching or other career fields, cultural barriers that may deter teachers from moving into school administration, and structural barriers, such as the effect a move has on tenure, retirement eligibility, etc.

DISEQUILIBRIUM IN THE LABOR MARKET

Because we examine only the supply side of the labor market, we cannot conclude that there is or is not a shortage of school administrators. However, we can say whether the information on school administrators reveals symptoms of a labor market in crisis or disequilibrium.

First, do the data suggest that the incentives to induce people to move into school administration are adequate? Problems with incentives can be reflected in different ways: negative changes in principals' characteristics that suggest schools are relaxing their standards (e.g., less experience), small or nonexistent compensation differentials between positions with less- and more-demanding working conditions, and an inadequate salary differential between teachers and administrators.

Second, do the data suggest that people are being lured away from administrative careers by other, more attractive job opportunities? Evidence of this would include high or increasing exit rates among school administrators and substantial reductions in the compensation of school administrators relative to that of other professionals.

Last, does the market seem to support an inequitable distribution of principal "quality" across schools of different types? If we assume that schools and districts have some flexibility to vary compensation across schools and that administrators have some flexibility to change jobs and move to different schools or districts, then, if market conditions are driving principals away from certain types of schools, we would expect to see some evidence that the more highly qualified principals are concentrated in schools with certain characteristics.

DATA SOURCES

The empirical overview presented here draws on existing research and the results of our analyses of existing data.

The National Center for Education Statistics (NCES) Schools and Staffing Survey (SASS) is a nationally representative survey of current public and private school principals (see Appendix A) that generates a portrait of the national principalship at specific points in time. The survey requests career information from principals and matches it with data on the schools and districts where they work. We used the survey data to examine differences among principals by sector (public, private), state, and school characteristics. However, the survey's usefulness in providing information on the flow of school administrative careers is limited in several respects.

First, the SASS focuses on teachers and principals, so we learned little about other administrative positions. Second, because the SASS is a cross-sectional rather than a longitudinal survey, it does not purposefully survey the same people in different survey years. Thus, we could compare differences over time in the population as a whole but could not tackle questions related to turnover or hiring. Third, the survey does not focus on career issues, and, indeed, the most recent survey wave even dropped many of the career-related questions that had previously been included (see Appendix A, Table A.1, for more information).

Another useful data source is the Current Population Survey (CPS), a monthly survey of approximately 60,000 households conducted by the U.S. Bureau of Labor Statistics. This survey includes data on demographics, labor force participation, industry and occupation, and earnings. Through the occupation field in this survey, we identified elementary and secondary school administrators, and we were able to create a short-panel data set (see Appendix D for more information) that, although limited by the number of school administrators included and by the small number of observations of respondents, offered us a unique opportunity not only to examine movement into and out of school administration, but also to compare the salaries and work hours of school administrators with those of other professionals. However, because the occupational codes the survey uses to classify people's jobs are fairly general, we were unable to focus specifically on principals and superintendents, and had to instead look at all individuals holding an administrative position in a primary or secondary school or school system. To put it in terms of our administrative career flow diagram (Figure 2.1), the CPS allowed us to look at the arrows coming out of the principal, superintendent, and other administration boxes taken together. The reader should bear in mind that when we use the term "school administrator," we are thus referring to that general categorization rather than to principals in particular.

Chapter Three

OVERVIEW OF CURRENT SCHOOL ADMINISTRATORS

The first step in understanding the careers of school administrators is to describe the numbers and characteristics of those currently filling these positions. We looked at the numbers and, in particular, at salary, age, experience, gender, and race/ethnicity. Our overview is based on a literature review and data analyses; it indicates whether the characteristics of administrators have changed in ways that might raise concern about the labor market for school administrators.

This chapter begins with a discussion of how many school administrators there are in the United States. We then discuss the earning and demographic characteristics of school administrators and how these have changed over time.

NUMBER OF ADMINISTRATORS

National data provide comprehensive information on principals and, to a lesser extent, superintendents. National-level information on other administrative positions[1] is, however, not available. Figure 3.1 summarizes what we know about the number of people within the administrative career field in both the private and the public sectors.[2] Our counts for principals are accurate, but our counts for superintendents and other administrators are not, because there is no comprehensive national survey similar to the Schools and Staffing Survey (SASS) for these positions. To facilitate discussion, the figure also shows the number of teachers in both sectors.

Figure 3.1 clearly shows that school administrators are a small group compared to teachers. The number of principals is only 2.5 percent of the number of teachers in public schools and 6 percent of the number of teachers in private schools. The number of all administrators (principals, superintendents, and other administrators) is

---

[1]This category includes assistant principals and assistant superintendents, district administrators, regional office staff, deans, and other central office staff such as business managers. It does not include subject area coordinators and other certified school staff such as counselors and nurses.

[2]The italicized numbers reflect rounded estimates. The estimate for superintendents is based on information from the American Association of School Administrators (AASA) (Glass, Bjork, and Brunner, 2000). For other administrators, the estimates are much rougher and represent an extrapolation based on the SASS-reported number of teachers and principals in which relationships between the numbers of teachers, principals, and other administrators observed in the state of Illinois were used. The percentages are also consistent with education workforce data from the state of New York when we impose similar definitions of administrative positions.

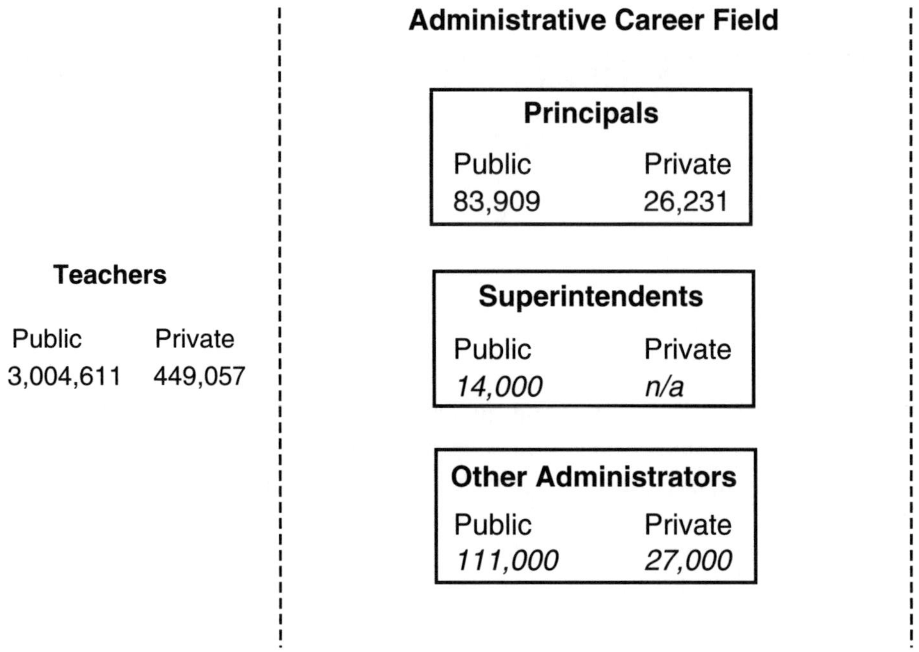

NOTE: Numbers for principals and teachers are from 1999–2000 SASS; other numbers (italicized) are rounded estimates.

Figure 3.1—Number of School Administrators, 1999–2000

6.5 percent of the number of teachers in public schools and 12 percent in private schools.

OVERVIEW OF PRINCIPALS

Table 3.1 describes all principals.[3] In 1999–2000, there were about 110,000 principals, 76 percent of whom worked in public schools.[4] School administration was not a rapidly growing career field in the late 1980s and 1990s. Between 1987–1988 and 1999–2000, the number of principals grew by over 7 percent for public schools and by over 3 percent for private schools. However, these national averages obscure substantial regional and sectoral differences. As Table 3.2 shows, the public sector saw growth in each region, but the growth was substantially higher in the West. The private sector saw declines in the number of principals in the Northeast and Midwest, and increases in the South and West.

Elementary school principals made up a majority (58 percent) of public school principals but only 32 percent of private school principals (see Appendix A, Tables A.4

[3]When we speak of "public school principals," we are including principals of charter and Bureau of Indian Affairs (BIA) schools.

[4]The SASS contains rich information on our nation's principals, including information linked to data on the school and district in which principals serve. Detailed information on the survey, sources of information, and our data analysis are in Appendix A.

Table 3.1

Description of All School Principals, 1999–2000

	Public	Private
Number of principals	83,909	26,231
Average age	49.3	49.9
Average annual salary[a]	$66,487	$41,656
Average years of experience as principal	9.0	10.2
Average years of teaching experience	14.0	14.5
Percent women	43.7	54.6
Percent minority	17.8	11.1

SOURCE: SASS.

[a]In real 2000 dollars.

Table 3.2

Growth in Number of Principals by Census Region, 1988–2000

Census Region	Public (%)	Private (%)
Northeast	1.0	–2.7
Midwest	5.6	–7.6
South	6.9	13.9
West	18.0	13.8
Total	7.7	3.3

SOURCE: SASS.

and A.5). A majority (57 percent) of private school principals worked in combined schools (i.e., K–8 and K–12 schools) compared with only 8 percent of public school principals. Middle school principals represented 14 percent of public school principals but only 1 percent of private school principals; and high school principals made up 20 and 10 percent of public and private school principals, respectively.

In 1999–2000, there were 988 charter school principals, and their characteristics as a group differed markedly from those of all public school principals, as reflected in Table 3.3 and discussed below.[5]

Table 3.3

Description of Charter School Principals, 1999–2000

	Charter
Number of principals	988
Average age	48.3
Average annual salary[a]	$53,920
Average years of experience as principal	6.9
Average years of teaching experience	12.0
Percent women	54.0
Percent minority	29.4

SOURCE: SASS.

[a]In real 2000 dollars.

[5]Highlighted differences between all public school principals and charter school principals are significant at the 5 percent level.

SALARY

Principals

Compensation has more than kept pace with inflation since 1987–1988. After we adjusted for changes in the consumer price index (CPI),[6] the average salary of public school principals was seen to have increased by 9 percent and the average salary of private school principals by nearly 40 percent. Despite the higher rate of salary growth in the private sector, public school principals still earned substantially more than private school principals did (on average, just over $65,000 per year, versus $40,000 for private school principals). The average salary of charter school principals (see Table 3.3) was just under $54,000 and was substantially lower than the average public school salary of over $66,000.[7]

Assistant principals earned slightly less than principals did. A survey by the Educational Research Service revealed that the average annual salaries for assistant principals were $56,306 in elementary schools, $59,238 in middle schools, and $62,691 in high schools in 1999–2000. These are 15 to 19 percent lower than the average salaries reported for principals by grade level (Educational Research Service, 2002). The survey found that the rates of salary growth for assistant principals were similar to those for principals over the past 10 years.

Superintendents

The estimated average salary for all superintendents for 2000–2001 was $118,811, and that increased to $121,794 in 2001–2002. Adjusted for inflation, the average superintendent salary has increased by 14 percent since 1991–1992 (Educational Research Service, 2002). Salaries offered to superintendents of major urban school districts in 2000–2001 ranged from $113,000 to $298,000, with an average of $165,144. In addition, most principals of major urban districts earned bonuses, pay-for-performance supplements, and other benefits, with an average value of $44,954 per year (Council of the Great City Schools, 2001).

Other district-level administrators earned less than superintendents did but typically more than principals did. The average salary in 2001–2002 for deputy or associate superintendents was $104,048; for assistant superintendents, it was $94,137. Average salaries for other administrators (e.g., finance and business, public relations, and staff services) ranged from $65,505 to $82,725.

---

[6]To adjust the salary figures for different years, we used the CPI inflation adjustment calculator available at http://www.bls.gov/cpi/#overview.

[7]For information on average principal salary by grade level, see Table A.4 in Appendix A.

AGE AND EXPERIENCE

Principals

As indicated in Table 3.1, the average principal is in his or her late 40s, and between 1988 and 2000, that average age increased slightly—from 47.8 to 49.3 in the public sector and from 46 to 49.9 in the private sector (see Appendix A, Table A.2). Except in the case of private middle schools (a small group, for which the average age of principals is very high), there appears to be little difference in the average age of principals in schools serving different grade levels (see Appendix A, Tables A.4 and A.5) or in charter versus other public schools (see Appendix A, Table A.2).

These averages conceal the fact that the age distribution of principals in the public sector differs in interesting ways from that in the private sector.[8] Figures 3.2 and 3.3 illustrate this point. Whereas private school principals appear to be distributed fairly evenly across a wide age range, from 35 to 65, a majority (53 percent) of public school principals fall in the 10-year window from 46 to 55. Another striking difference is that only 17 percent (a small proportion) of public school principals are over age 55, compared with 27 percent of private school principals.

These differences in age distribution between the public and private sectors suggest some potentially important differences in principal careers for the two sectors that are worth exploring in greater detail. For example, private school principals may be more likely than their public school counterparts to enter the principalship at earlier ages and to retire or leave the principalship later in life. Such differences would not be surprising, given differences in the retirement incentives of public relative to private school principals, as well as differences in the recruitment strategies of the two types of schools. It may also be that public principals are "retiring" into the private sector. Further exploration of these issues at the state and local levels can provide insights useful to policymakers.

Figures 3.2 and 3.3 also suggest that the age profiles of both public and private school principals shifted between 1987–1988 and 1999–2000. In the public sector, the shift increased the concentration of principals in the 46 to 55 range and diminished the representation of younger individuals, particularly those between 40 and 45. In the private sector, similar shifts diminished the representation of younger individuals.

Such a shift in age distribution could be caused by a spike in hiring during a certain period in the past and the aging of that cohort of principals. However, examination of the age distribution of new principals—which we define as those with three or fewer years of experience—revealed that the age increases were not simply due to the aging of a particular cohort. In 1987–1988, the average age of new principals was 43 for public schools and 42.5 for private schools. By 1999–2000, it had increased to over 45 in public schools and to over 44 in private schools (see Appendix A, Table A.6).

---

[8]See Appendix A for a detailed discussion of the differences in the age distribution.

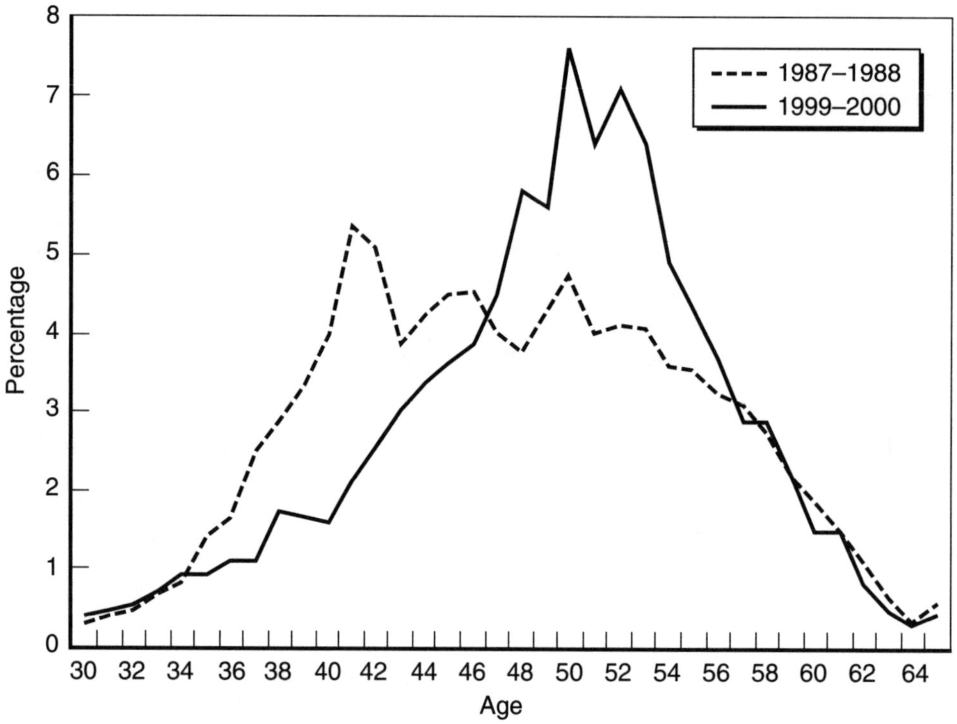

Figure 3.2—Age Distribution of Public School Principals

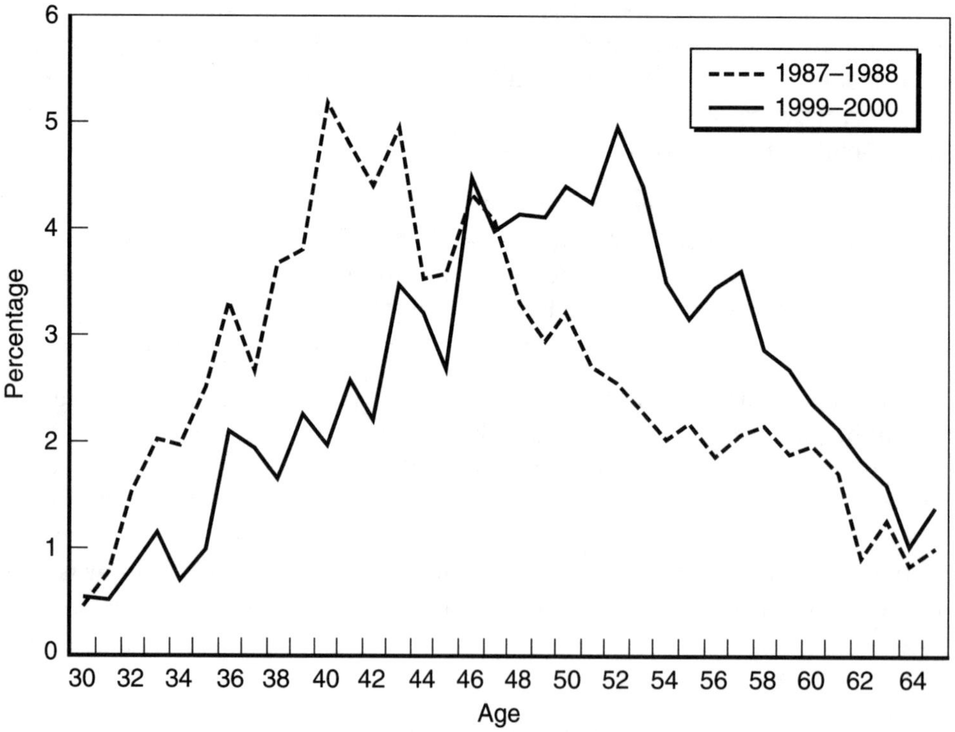

Figure 3.3—Age Distribution of Private School Principals

Between 1987–1988 and 1999–2000, the proportion of new principals under 40, 45, and even 50 years of age decreased markedly in the public sector. Whereas 38 percent of new public school principals were 40 or younger in 1987–1988, by 1999–2000, only 12 percent were. A similar but less dramatic shift in age distribution occurred for new private school principals as well.

Information on the distribution of principals' experience as a principal suggests that the increase in age among private but not public school principals stems from a tendency to stay on the job longer. Figures 3.4 and 3.5 illustrate that private school principals were more experienced in 1999–2000 than in 1987–1988, and that public school principals were less experienced. To put it another way, the increase in age witnessed in the 1990s brought with it an increase in experience among private but not public school principals (see Appendix A for more details).

Overall, the data suggest that principals are an aging population. But although the age increase shows up in both the public and the private sector, it appears to take a different form in each sector. We found that both types of schools were hiring increasingly older new principals. In the public sector, principals tended not to remain in the principalship much beyond age 55, suggesting that those who enter the position later in life have shorter administrative careers. In the private sector, however, it was far more common for principals to stay on the job to age 60 or 65.

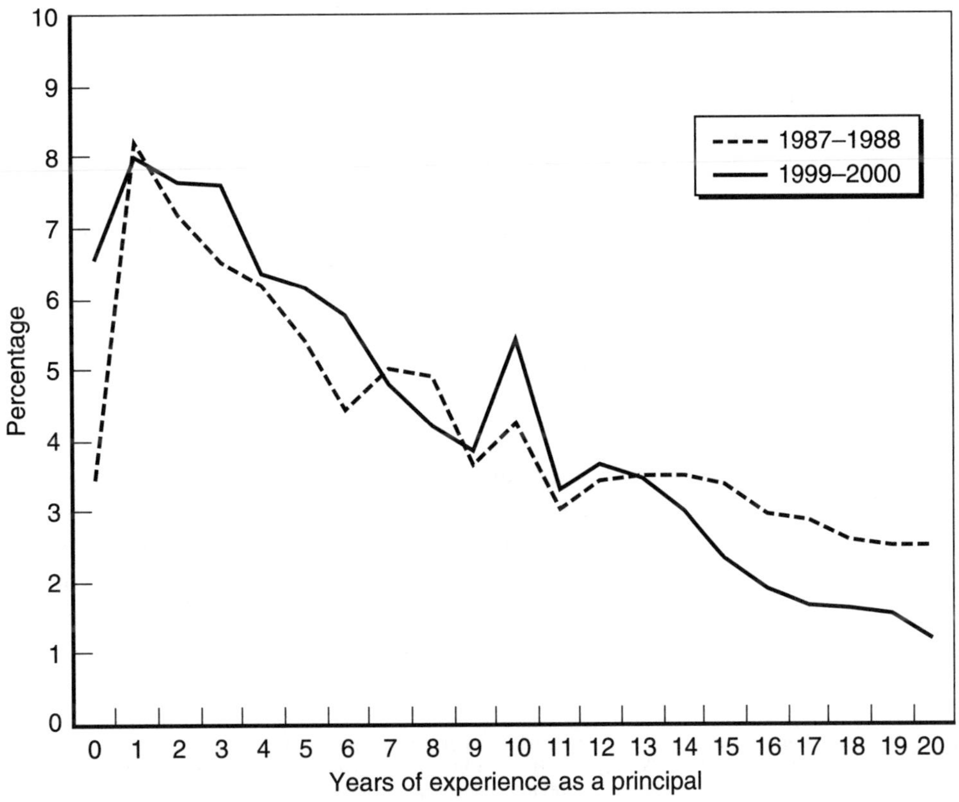

Figure 3.4—Experience Distribution of Public School Principals

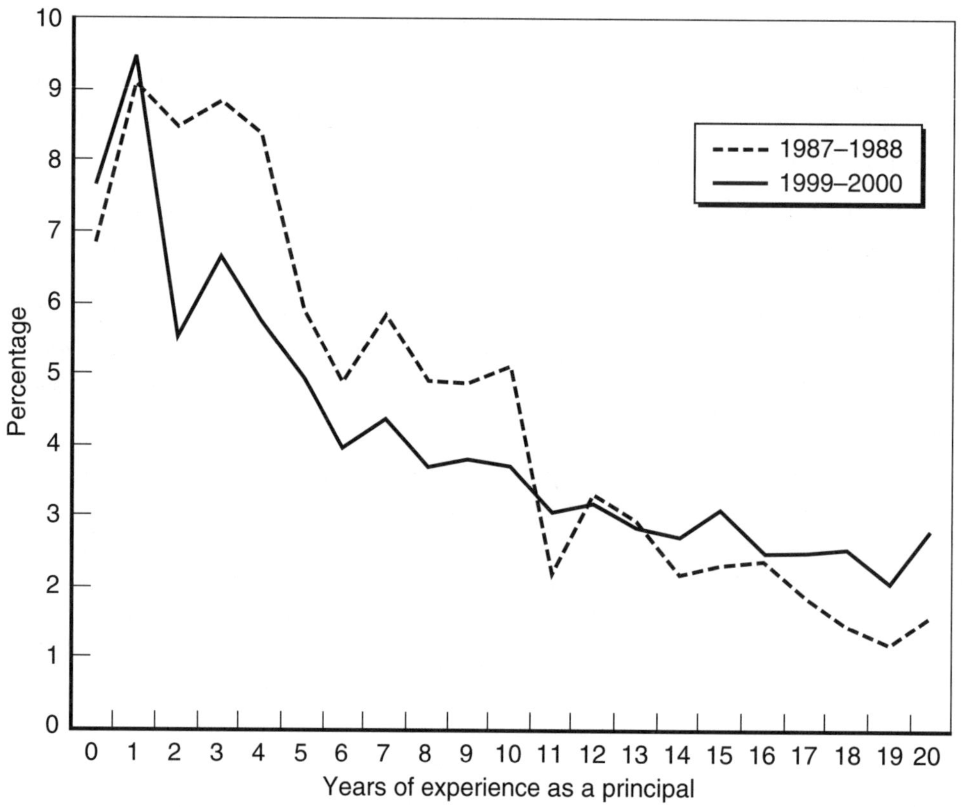

Figure 3.5—Experience Distribution of Private School Principals

It is also worth noting that the average charter school principal had two fewer years of both teaching experience and experience as a principal compared with public school principals generally. Moreover, nearly 50 percent of charter school principals were new by our definition (having three or fewer years of experience), whereas only 30 percent of all public school principals were.

Superintendents

The 1999–2000 American Association of School Administrators (AASA) survey of superintendents confirms that the school administrative workforce is aging in this position as well. The median age of superintendents responding to the survey was 52.5—the oldest median age ever recorded in the survey, which is conducted approximately every 10 years. This increase in age was particularly striking in the smallest districts.[9]

[9]The survey report divides districts into categories based on student enrollment. Group A comprises districts with enrollments over 25,000; group B, districts with enrollments between 3,000 and 24,999; group C, districts with enrollments between 300 and 2,999; and group D, districts with enrollments under 300.

These individuals bring with them a good deal of experience in the superintendency—an average of 8.75 years (Glass, Bjork, and Brunner, 2000), which is similar to the average tenure in 2000 of chief executive officers (CEOs)—seven years (Neff and Ogden, 2001). The corporate world appears to differ from the school administrative field in terms of senior managers' age, however: the average age of corporate CEOs declined from 59 in 1980 to 56 in 2000 (Neff and Ogden, 2001).

GENDER AND RACE/ETHNICITY

Principals

The education literature has paid substantial attention to the gender composition of principals because of concerns that the proportion of female principals is low relative to that of female teachers (Hammer and Rohr, 1994; Bell and Chase, 1993; Biklen and Brannigan, 1980; Joy, 1998; Riehl and Byrd, 1997). In 1999–2000, 44 percent of all public school principals were women (see Table 3.1), up from 35 percent in 1993–1994 and from 25 percent in 1987–1988 (see Appendix A, Table A.2). At 54 percent, women were well represented among charter school principals in 1999–2000 (see Table 3.3), but men still made up a majority of the secondary school principals in both the public and the private sector (see Appendix A, Tables A.4 and A.5). As noted earlier, high school principals are the most highly paid. In 1999–2000, women made up 55 percent of public elementary school principals but just 21 percent of public high school principals (Appendix A, Table A.4). In private schools, women made up a majority of all elementary and combined school principals and were 38 percent of high school principals (Appendix A, Table A.5).

Given that women have been making up an increasingly greater portion of the teaching force,[10] researchers have been emphasizing the fact that the average male teacher is still much more likely than the average female teacher to become a principal (Riehl and Byrd, 1997). The representation of women in 1999–2000 was substantially higher among new principals (those with three or fewer years of principal experience). When only public schools were considered, 54 percent of new principals were found to be women; for private schools, well over half (60 percent) were (Appendix A, Table A.6).

Compared to changes in the gender composition of school principals, changes in the racial/ethnic mix were more limited. We found that only a small proportion of principals were members of an ethnic/racial minority, particularly compared to the proportion of minorities in the student population. Minority representation was higher in the public than in the private sector. Nearly 18 percent of public school principals were members of a racial/ethnic minority, compared with 11 percent of private school principals (see Table 3.1). However, in charter schools, 29 percent were members of racial/ethnic minority groups (see Table 3.3).

---

[10]According to the 1999–2000 SASS, 74.9 percent of teachers in public schools are female (standard error of 0.3 percent), and 76.1 percent of teachers in private schools are female (standard error of 0.5 percent).

We analyzed data to determine whether there was salary discrimination based on gender or race/ethnicity in school administration (see Appendix B). The analysis entailed examining the relationship between salary, school characteristics, and individual characteristics of principals. We found that gender was not related to salary in the public sector after we controlled for other factors, which suggests that females receive comparable pay for comparable work in the public sector. However, our private sector regression revealed that female principals earned nearly $6,000 per year less than their male counterparts in that sector (after accounting for other factors). We found that race was not related to salary in either sector, except in the case of Native American principals, who, in public schools, earned nearly $3,000 per year less than white principals did.[11]

Superintendents

During the 1990s, female and minority representation increased among superintendents as well. The 2000 AASA survey (Glass, Bjork, and Brunner, 2000) indicates that women made up 13 percent of superintendents in 2000, double their proportion in the 1992 survey. According to the 2000 survey, 5.1 percent of superintendents were members of a racial/ethnic minority, and the number of minority superintendents had increased by over 30 percent since 1992. Minority superintendents were found to be much better represented in the largest districts (those with enrollments over 25,000), where they accounted for 23 percent of all superintendents. Overall, the survey suggests that most minority superintendents serve in either large urban districts or rural districts.[12] Another survey, of the superintendents of districts that are part of the Council of the Great City Schools, revealed that as of 2000, a majority of these superintendents were members of a racial/ethnic minority (37.5 percent African American and 14.3 percent Hispanic) and over 30 percent were female (Council of the Great City Schools, 2001).

QUALITY

One of today's concerns is that schools are not or will not be able to find well-qualified people to assume administrative positions. Unfortunately, there is little information for evaluating the overall quality of school administrators in any systematic way. For example, there is no database of principal performance evaluations that would allow performance trends to be tracked. It might be possible to measure student test score growth and attribute that to the quality of the principal, but countless confounding factors make this approach difficult on a practical level and of questionable validity on a theoretical level. Current efforts by the Education Testing Service and the Council of Chief State School Officers to define and measure the

[11]This is a change from 1993–1994, when, compared to white principals, black principals earned nearly $1,800 per year more and Hispanic principals earned $1,300 less. The difference between white and Native American principals was not significant.

[12]However, the survey sample was not nationally representative. Because it oversampled large (and therefore more-urban) districts, the proportions of women and minorities may be higher in this sample than they would be in a national average. The reported survey results were not weighted.

required competencies of school administrators may make it possible to consider the issue of quality more fully in the future.[13]

Analyses that try to address the issue of quality typically look to certification or educational attainment as a measure, or they simply rely on the perceptions of superintendents or district hiring offices. As discussed by Roza et al. (2002), certification and educational attainment are the characteristics emphasized by district hiring offices, but they are poor proxies for the political and leadership skills superintendents claim principals need.

The empirical evidence based on perceptions of quality raises some cause for concern. For example, two-thirds of respondents to a 1998 survey of 3,000 elementary and middle school principals expressed concerns about public education's ability to attract quality people to the principalship in the future (Doud and Keller, 1998). And a survey of superintendents about the hiring of principals echoes these concerns (National Association of Elementary School Principals and National Association of Secondary School Principals, 1998). The latter survey found that about half of the superintendents who had recently filled principal vacancies felt there was a shortage of qualified candidates. However, the respondents also indicated satisfaction with the individuals they hired and reported that the new principals had proved to be adequately prepared for the position.[14]

SUMMARY

Overall, our examination reveals remarkable stability in the characteristics of school administrators and that any changes that did occur were not consistent with a national labor market in crisis. The descriptive overview paints a picture of school administration as a career field that has experienced only modest growth overall in the past decade, with some important national variation. Whereas there was substantial growth in the West, other regions of the country, particularly the Northeast, experienced more moderate growth. The West's relatively high rates of growth, particularly in the public schools, might be expected to be burdensome as schools try to recruit and retain administrators, unless the supply of administrators is also growing.

The compensation of school administrators outpaced inflation across the board. Although the growth rate was modest for public school principals, it was substantial for private school principals.

After years of concern about the representation of women in the principalship, the 1990s saw dramatic progress. By 1999–2000, female representation in the principalship had still not reached the level of female representation in the teaching profession, but nearly half of all public school principals were women, as were over half of all new public school principals and all private school principals. Representation of members of racial/ethnic minorities had also increased, but less dramatically.

---

[13]Information on these efforts is available at http://www.ets.org/sls/index.html.

[14]One-third responded that the new principals' preparation was excellent, and only 8 percent reported that it was inadequate.

We saw no evidence of salary discrimination by race/ethnicity or gender in the public sector. The data do, however, suggest that female principals are underpaid relative to their male counterparts in the private sector.

Perhaps our most striking finding is that the nation's principals are growing older as a group and that people entering the principalship for the first time are doing so later in life. The differences in the age distribution of both new and all principals and in the experience distribution of principals in the public and private sectors raise interesting issues that could be explored in greater detail through a comparative study of employment practices in the two sectors. The data suggest that the retirement patterns of the two sectors may differ significantly. At a time when many people in the United States are working well into their 60s,[15] a surprisingly small fraction (17 percent) of public school principals are over 55.

---

[15]Research on retirement indicates a spike in the retirement rate at ages 62 and 65. Simulations based on the nationally representative Health and Retirement Survey suggest that about 85 percent of individuals who were working at age 52 are still in the labor force at age 56, and over half work beyond age 62. Retirement eligibility under a defined benefit pension plan has a large effect on the probability that an individual will retire, increasing it by 15 percent (Hurd, Smith, and Zissimopoulos, 2002).

Chapter Four

MOVEMENT INTO AND OUT OF THE SCHOOL ADMINISTRATIVE CAREER FIELD

Existing national data allow one to examine whether individuals are turning away from careers in education in general and from public education in particular. In our case, they allow us to consider movement into and out of the school administrative career field (viewing the private and public sectors together or the public sector by itself) and the factors influencing that movement. This chapter presents the results of our analyses of these types of moves, which are illustrated in Figure 4.1.

The national data do not, however, prove useful if one wants to explore the narrower definitions of the career field. To ask the more-focused questions, those about career-field moves that individuals make across schools and districts, one must tap into state-level administrative records. These questions are also discussed here, near the end of the chapter.

OVERVIEW OF ENTRIES AND EXITS

As the career flow conceptual framework suggests, individuals can enter or leave the administrative career field at different points: the principalship, the superinten-

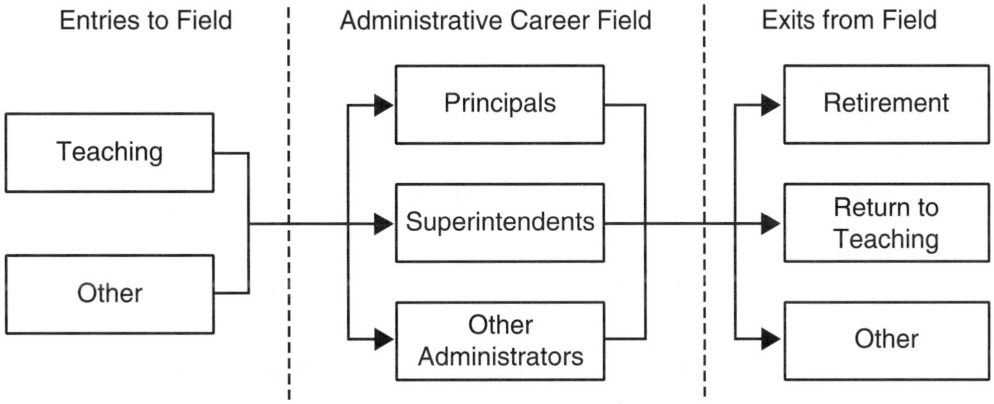

Figure 4.1—Movement Into and Out of Administrative Career Field

dency, and the other administrative positions. Existing research and data provide some insight on these moves, but little research specifically examines the entry and exit of school administrators. We used the Current Population Survey (CPS) to analyze the characteristics of people who moved into or out of school administration positions over the course of one year (details are provided in Appendix D). School administration is defined generally in this analysis to include not only principals and superintendents, but all individuals who perform management functions in primary or secondary schools or school districts.[1]

School administration entry and exit rates ranged from 15 to 33 percent per year during the sample period (1983–1999), with no evident time trend. The entry rate varied significantly from year to year, ranging from 19 to 29 percent (see Appendix D, Figure D.8). The largest share of entrants—nearly 50 percent—had been teachers in the previous year. Of those classified as "other" in Figure 4.1, people entering from managerial occupations in other professions/industries made up about 20 percent of all new entrants, and those moving into the labor force to take a position in school administration made up only about 7 percent. The distribution of age across this latter group was very wide.[2] Just as a large proportion of people entered school administration positions each year, so did a large proportion leave them. Movement out of the labor force accounted for slightly over 18 percent of exits; the average age across this group was 60 (median age, 63). Of those leaving school administration for a new occupation, 22 percent moved into a management position in another profession/industry, and 37 percent moved into a teaching occupation.[3] Approximately 23 percent of exits were to a wide array of other occupations, none of which accounted for more than 1 or 2 percent by itself. On average, those leaving school administration experienced a decrease in the average number of hours they worked per week and in their average wage.

Moving from Teaching to Administration

An overwhelming majority of school principals—over 99 percent in the public sector and nearly 90 percent in the private—had teaching experience. As of 1999–2000, public school principals had an average of 14 years of teaching experience, and private school principals had an average of 14.5 (see Table 3.1). This reflects a dramatic increase from 1994, when the averages were 11 and 9.5 years, respectively (Fiore and Curtin, 1997). Superintendents responding to a 2000 survey reported a similar tendency to have spent time in the classroom, with approximately 90 percent having taught (Glass, Bjork, and Brunner, 2000). This transition from teaching to

[1]For example, financial managers, personnel and labor relations managers, purchasing managers, and accountants and auditors.

[2]The mean age was 54, with a standard deviation of 16. Moreover, the interquartile range was 25. These descriptive statistics indicate that the distribution of age across this group was relatively wide.

[3]Teaching occupations are defined as prekindergarten, kindergarten, elementary, and secondary education teachers and school-based counselors.

school administration is an exceedingly common step for school administrators. Because it has received little attention from education researchers, however, very little is known about how, when, and why the transition occurs.

Analyses of teacher labor markets typically treat a transfer to administration as an exit from teaching (Stinebrickner, 1998; Haffner and Owings, 1991; Bobbitt et al., 1994; Grissmer and Kirby, 1992; Murnane, Singer, and Willett, 1988). Brewer (1996) analyzes the quit decisions of teachers from a broader perspective, explicitly considering how administrative compensation affects teachers' decisions to stay within a district. The logic behind Brewer's analysis is that teachers think not only about their current salary in making decisions about where to work, but also about their future earning potential. Because most administrators first spend time as teachers, administrative compensation factors into estimates of future earning potential for some individuals. Brewer finds some evidence of a relationship between teacher retention and administrative compensation, suggesting that teachers do consider their promotion opportunities in deciding whether to remain in the education field. Among other things, the research shows that after controlling for teacher salary, districts with lower administrative salaries have higher teacher turnover.

Our analysis of movement into and out of school administration (details in Appendix D) suggests that a healthy proportion of that movement involves teachers. Nearly 50 percent of entrants into school administration had worked in teaching occupations the previous year, and, somewhat surprisingly, 37 percent of those who had left school administration did so to return to teaching. These data suggest that there is a strong revolving door between teaching and school administration generally, if not between teaching and the principalship in particular. Papa, Lankford, and Wyckoff (2002) did not find a strong tendency for principals in New York state to return to teaching. This finding may reflect the fact that because the principalship is fairly high up on the administrative career path, people who decide they are not interested in administration do so long before they reach that level.

For those who became superintendents, the decision to leave teaching and enter school administration seems to have come early (Glass, Bjork, and Brunner, 2000). A majority (76 percent) of the superintendents responding to the 2000 AASA survey assumed their first administrative position before age 35; 14 percent became administrators between 36 and 40, 7 percent between 41 and 45, and only 3 percent at 46 or older. Of all superintendents, those in the largest districts appear to have been more likely to enter administration before age 30 (64 percent in large districts, compared with 49 percent overall). This observation is somewhat surprising in view of the fact that the average age of new public school principals (i.e., those with three or fewer years as a principal) in 2000 was nearly 46.

Entry into the teaching profession is clearly an important issue for those concerned about the quality of school administrators, because teachers are the major pool from which school administrators are drawn. Research has suggested that college graduates with the stronger academic backgrounds are less likely to go into teaching and, when they do, are less likely to remain there (Murnane et al., 1991). A recent study (Henke et al., 2000) found that college graduates with scores on college entrance exams in the highest quartile were half as likely to teach as were their peers whose test scores fell in the lowest quartile (9 percent, compared with 18 percent). Of those who did teach, those with the higher test scores were more likely to teach in private or secondary schools and less likely to teach in elementary schools or schools with a high concentration of low-income students. In addition, a pattern of high exit rates early in the career and low exit rates in mid-career has been documented in several longitudinal studies of teachers (e.g., Kirby and Grissmer, 1993; Kirby, Berends, and Naftel, 1999; Murnane, Singer, and Willett, 1988, 1989).

Relative Compensation Between School Administrators and Professionals Other Than Teachers

Level of compensation is a primary determinant of the amount of labor supplied. Changes in compensation over time for a particular professional occupation relative to those for other professional occupations can help to explain variations in the number of people willing to work in an area. If the wage associated with school administrators falls relative to (i.e., grows less than) that of such other professionals as lawyers, medical professionals, or managers, there will be cause for concern about the ability to attract and retain school administrators.

As Figure 4.2 indicates, the real hourly wage of school administrators saw little change between 1984 and 1999 and remained close to that of managers more generally.[4]

These trends do not support the notion that school administrators are being lured away from their field by dramatically better wages in other fields. Although earnings for school administrators have not kept pace with earnings in some other professional occupations (such as lawyers and medical professionals), the average weekly earnings of school administrators relative to those of other managers have remained constant.

Of the other professional occupations considered, manager seems to be the most relevant for the choices made by potential school administrators. We also included medical professionals and lawyers, because these are similar to school administrators in that they typically require certification and certification entails formal education. However, while the compensation for school administrators relative to that for medical professionals and lawyers likely affects an individual's choice of occupation early on (e.g., in high school or college), the fact that the preparation requirements are so different makes it unlikely that many school administrators would leave their position for a career in medicine or law. In contrast, the skills and training required for school administration and for other managerial occupations are quite similar. As a result, it would be relatively easy to move between these two occupations, which

[4]We calculated hourly wage by dividing weekly salary by number of hours worked per week. Hourly wage may change because of changes in salary and/or hours worked.

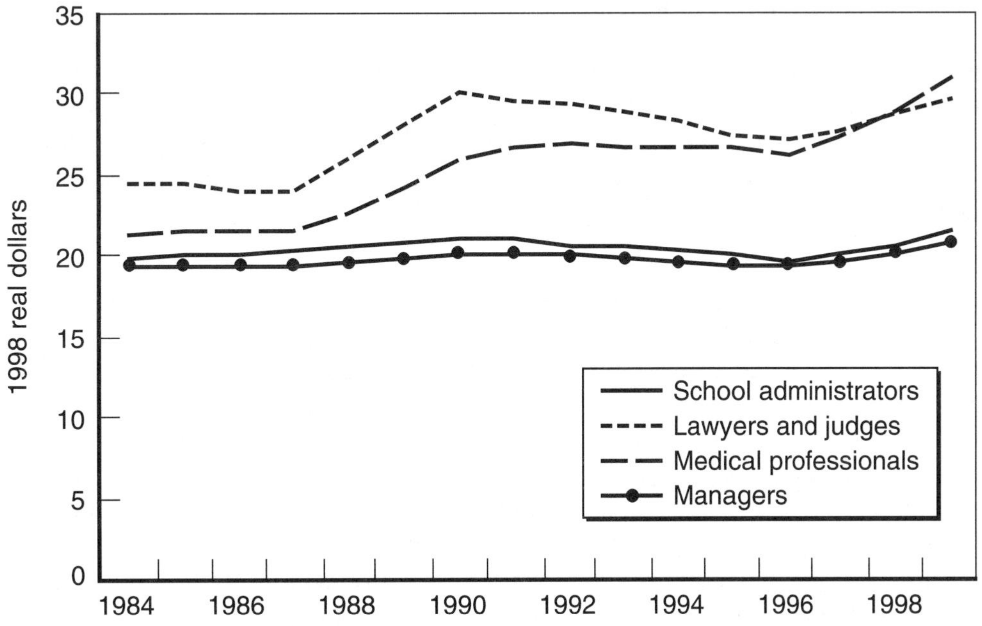

Figure 4.2—Average Real Hourly Wage Across Professions, 1984–1999

means relative compensation becomes an important consideration in any decision to make such a move.

Another useful point of comparison is principals' salaries and the salaries of federal government managers. The federal salary schedule (General Schedule, or GS) associates mid- to upper-managerial positions with grade levels GS-13 through GS-15. In fiscal year 1999–2000, the annual base salary for these positions ranged from $56,000 to $101,000 per year.[5]

In addition, it is interesting to look at how superintendents' compensation stacks up against the compensation for other types of senior managers. We noted in Chapter Three that the estimated average salary for all superintendents for 2001 was $118,811 and that superintendent salaries of major urban school districts ranged from $113,000 to $298,000. This compares favorably with the salaries paid to executives in the federal government. Federal civil servants on the executive service pay schedule earned between $121,600 and $166,700 in the 2001–2002 fiscal year;[6] the most-senior military officers earned a base pay of about $148,000.[7]

---

[5]In addition to annual base pay, federal civil servants receive a locality pay adjustment based on the cost of living in the area where they work. This adjustment added up to 16 percent to an individual's annual salary.

[6]This pay schedule includes the highest-level civil servants in the executive branch (aside from the president and vice president), such as department secretaries and undersecretaries and heads of major offices (such as the Office of Management and Budget). See www.opm.gov/oca/02tables/ex.htm.

[7]According to the *Business Week* 2001 survey of corporate executive compensation, the average CEO pay in that year was $11 million (*Business Week*, 2002). By this measure, superintendents (and most other people) appear to be grossly underpaid.

Relative Compensation Between School Administrators and Teachers

Recently, policymakers have expressed concern that teachers are increasingly reluctant to move into school administration (Education Writers Association, 2002). Observers frequently mention that school administrative jobs are much more difficult than teaching, and that the salary difference does not compensate for the increased demands.

Changes in relative compensation between school administrators and teachers over time may alter the motivation teachers have to move into school administration. Although school administrators earned more than teachers did from 1984 to 1999, the differential varied, as Figure 4.3 shows. In 1984, the real weekly earnings of school administrators were 31 percent higher than those of teachers, a gap that then narrowed until 1996, when it hit 15 percent. Because the salary differential between administration and teaching narrowed from 1984 to 1996, school administration may have become less attractive (at least financially) relative to teaching. After 1996, the trend turned, and school administrators' earnings grew relative to those of teachers. By 1999, the gap had grown enough that school administrators were earning 24 percent more than teachers were.

On average, school administrators reported working more hours per week than teachers did. The difference in reported hours between the two groups fluctuated within a narrow range—from 2.5 to 1.8 hours per week.

To look specifically at the financial incentive teachers might have to move into the principalship, we examined the differential between the compensation of principals and that of experienced teachers at the same school.

Although policymakers are concerned that salary differences between principals and teachers are not large enough to encourage teachers to enter and, if they do enter, to remain in school administration (Education Writers Association, 2002), our calculations based on the 1999–2000 SASS data indicate that public school principals earned roughly 33 percent more per year on an annualized basis than did teachers in the same school with 10 or more years of experience.[8] The same pattern held in private schools, where principals earned on average 44 percent more than experienced teachers did.

Our results are entirely consistent with those of a recent salary survey that compared the average daily rate of experienced teachers (defined as the median teacher salary) with the daily rate of relatively new principals (defined as the 25th percentile princi-

---

[8]Salary figures for teachers and principals are adjusted for contract length in calculating this ratio. This is akin to comparing daily rates of pay, adjusting for the number of months worked per year. Because principals typically work more months per year than teachers do, the adjustment for contract length makes administrators look worse off than they do in a simple comparison of annual salary. Unadjusted figures are 52 percent in the public sector and 63 percent in the private sector. (See Appendix B for a detailed discussion of how we adjusted for contract length. The 1999–2000 SASS did not include a question on principal-contract length, so we imputed a contract length based on data from the 1993–1994 survey.)

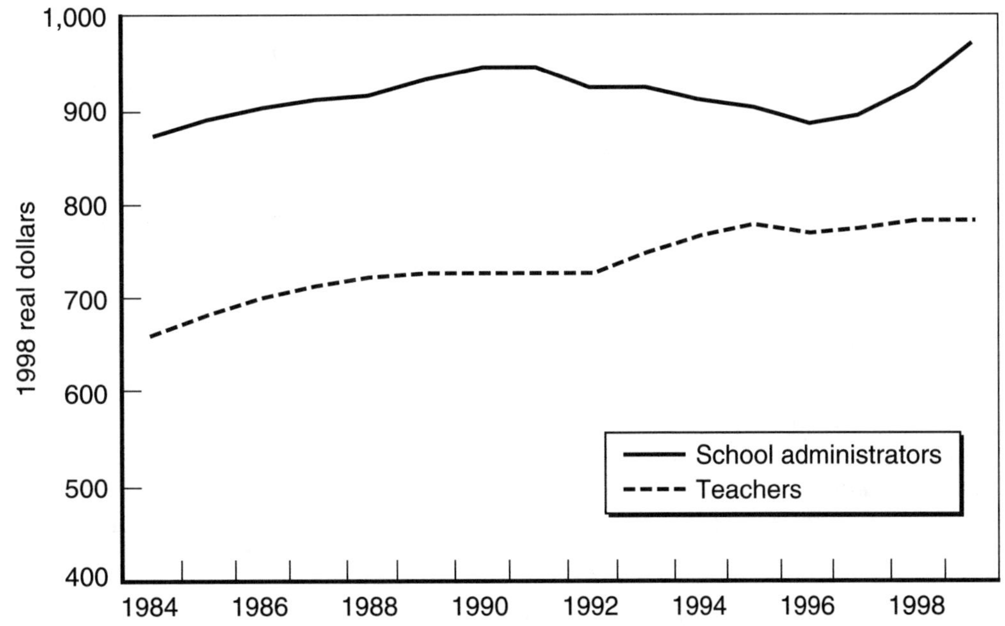

Figure 4.3—Average Real Weekly Earnings of School Administrators and Teachers, 1984–1999

pal in terms of salary). The survey found that compared with experienced teachers, elementary school principals earned 23 percent more and high school principals earned 36 percent more (Educational Research Service, 2002).

Our calculations exclude the salaries of teachers with fewer than 10 years of experience. The average number of years of experience among our "experienced" teachers was 21.5 for public schools and 21.0 for private schools. Thus, we compared principals' salaries to the salaries of a relatively experienced group. We found substantial variation in the ratios of principal to teacher salary—to the point where some principals earned less than experienced teachers in the same school did, and others earned twice as much as experienced teachers did. This validates the concern that the pay increment for principals at some schools may not be enough to encourage teachers to move into administration. However, we also found that the pay increment at some schools was substantial.

A key policy question is whether there are any systematic patterns in the pay differences of schools with different observable characteristics. In other words, do certain types of schools systematically offer principals less, or is this issue really just a local one? To address this question, we conducted a regression analysis to study the relationship of the within-school ratio of principal to teacher salary to school characteristics and the individual characteristics of principals. The analyses revealed that little of the variation in salary ratio was systematically related to student-body demographic characteristics in either the public or the private sector.

Other characteristics of the school and some characteristics of the community were found to be related to the salary ratio (see Appendix B). School grade level mattered in public but not private schools, with principals of public high schools seeing a larger (by five percentage points) salary differential than principals of middle or elementary schools did. The salary differential was six percentage points lower in rural compared with urban schools in the public sector; in the private sector, however, urbanicity did not matter. Enrollment related to the salary differential in a nonlinear way in the private sector, and the differential was lower for charter schools.

In private schools, the salary ratio was substantially lower in Catholic and other religiously affiliated schools. The differential was larger for more-experienced principals, as would be expected. There appears to be no relationship between a principal's race/ethnicity and the salary ratio for principals and teachers, but the regression results do suggest that the differential is less for female principals, even after the school's grade level and the principal's experience are controlled for. The gender effect was minor (three percentage points) in public schools but substantial (over 20 percentage points) in private schools.

For public schools, the salary differential appears to vary substantially by state. Principals in California (which was the omitted category in our regression) and in Alabama, Indiana, Michigan, Pennsylvania, Utah, Washington DC, and West Virginia had a small pay differential compared with that of principals in Hawaii, Iowa, Kansas, Missouri, Nebraska, Nevada, Vermont, Wyoming, the Dakotas, and some other states.

In an analysis of New York state data, Papa, Lankford, and Wyckoff (2002) found that the salary ratio varied dramatically with respect to time and place. In particular, in urban schools in New York City and Yonkers, the salary ratio exhibited tremendous year-to-year variation, along with a striking overall downward trend between 1975 and 1999. This means that the difference (in percentage terms) between principal and teacher salaries in these schools declined, possibly reducing the financial attractiveness of the principalship. This was due to decreases in the real salary of principals over this period, as well as to increases in the real salary of teachers. Schools in suburban New York City and Yonkers exhibited similar overall trends in salary ratio, but the decline in this case primarily stemmed from increases in the real salary of teachers. For schools in the rest of the state, the salary ratio remained fairly stable on average, although some individual schools and districts faced increases and some experienced decreases.

Of course, compensation is only one determinant of labor supply. If working conditions in the two jobs changed over time as well, the effects of compensation changes on teachers' incentives to move into administration might not be observed. Some people assert that school administrative positions have become more difficult over time because of, among other things, increased demands for accountability (Education Writers Association, 2002). If the job has become more difficult relative to the job of teaching, the increases in the labor supply associated with the compensation increases of the late 1990s could be canceled out by decreases in the labor supply because of worsening working conditions.

Overall, it appears that principals do earn more than experienced teachers, but that the financial incentive for a teacher to become a principal is large in some schools and small or nonexistent in others. In 7 percent of public schools, the salary ratio was negative, implying that the principals earned less than experienced teachers in the same school. Meanwhile, the salary ratio was over 100 percent in nearly 3 percent of public schools, indicating that the principal earned more than twice what experienced teachers in the same school did.

The variation in salary ratios was even greater among private schools: nearly one-quarter of principals earned less than experienced teachers in the same schools did, while 14 percent earned more than twice what experienced teachers in the same school did. The question not yet directly addressed in the literature is how much of a difference is "enough" to get teachers to switch to school administration.

Certification as a Barrier to Entering School Administration

Policymakers have begun to wonder whether state-level certification requirements deter people from becoming school administrators. In a review of state-level policies, we found that 49 of 50 states require a special certification for administrative positions in public schools.[9] Twenty-one states offer a general administrative credential that applies across a variety of positions; 28 others have specific credentials for different positions, such as principal and superintendent. A master's degree, often from a state-approved program in educational administration, is required for certification in all but a handful of states. All but nine states require those seeking an administrative credential to have experience in primary or secondary education—up to five years for principals and seven years for superintendents. Other common certification requirements include completion of specific course content, a teaching certificate, and a passing grade on national or state examinations (Tryneski, 2000).

This list of requirements may deter aspiring school administrators, particularly those who are not teachers. In a recent survey of public school district hiring officials, Roza et al. (2002) found that applicants for positions as principals who were not certified were not considered for the job and not included in the reported number of applicants. The survey found that even when considering certified applicants, district hiring offices looked for individuals with as much experience as possible in public education in general and in the hiring district in particular. Thus, district hiring practices may pose an additional barrier to those seeking to enter school administration from other career fields in that they reduce the chance of being hired even when one is certified.

In an analysis of the characteristics of teachers and principals in New York state, Papa, Lankford, and Wyckoff (2002) found a substantial number of people—nearly

[9]Michigan eliminated its administrative certification requirement in 1994.

7,000—under age 45 who were certified to be principals but were not working as principals. Of these, more than 4,000 were working in the state education system, and many of the more than 4,000 had some type of administrative experience. Since there were just over 3,700 principalships in New York state in 2000, there were almost enough certified individuals under age 45 to replace all the current principals twice over. These data indicate that there is a substantial pool of people in the system who have the credentials required to assume a principalship. They do not, however, shed light on whether these people are actually interested in becoming principals.[10]

Additional Barriers Specific to the Transition from Teaching

Some teachers face additional barriers in deciding to move into administration in that they can lose their tenure and job security. We found no hard and fast rules regarding when teachers must give up their tenure. Tenure rules vary by state and district; in many states, a teacher retains tenure as a teacher when he or she moves into an administrative job only if that job is within the district he or she worked in as a teacher.

There is a strong parallel between the decision a teacher makes to move into school administration and the decisions other professionals (e.g., engineers, lawyers, physicians) make to move into corporate administration. In these other professional contexts, managers are typically drawn from the ranks of the corporation's professionals because their technical skills are viewed as an essential component of management (Hoff, 1999). However, individuals are often reluctant to make a career switch from technical practice to management, and those who do may face significant challenges (Biddle and Roberts, 1994; Hoff, 1999; Succi and Alexander, 1999; Dewhirst, 1991). Dewhirst (1991) categorizes these challenges as (1) understanding and operating in a more complex environment, (2) dealing with people, and (3) relinquishing the specialty. These challenges hold true for those contemplating a switch from teaching to school administration as well. The environment in which a school administrator operates is certainly more complex than that of a teacher. Administrators face scrutiny and demands from a wider array of people than teachers do; they also have to interact with school board members, local business leaders, union representatives, public agency officials, and the like—something teachers rarely have to do. And school administrators typically must give up the specialty, teaching.

Professional organizations typically have a need for both managers and experienced practitioners. Dewhirst (1991) suggests that there are different types of professionals—those who seek out a transition to management, those who do not but can adapt

[10]In New York state, certification requires completion of a master's degree program in educational administration. There are two main reasons why teachers who have gone to the trouble of completing such a program might not be interested in a principalship. First, teachers benefit from having a master's degree—even if they remain teachers—through higher pay and other administrative opportunities. A teacher thus may enroll in and complete an educational administration program without ever intending to assume a principalship. Second, teachers may have a potential interest in administration but become disillusioned either in the course of completing the program or some time afterward.

to the new role, and those who actively dislike the idea of management. He argues that organizations must be able to offer career opportunities to all three types and to provide support to those who may not be terribly eager but are nonetheless willing to serve in managerial positions. Dual-ladder career systems, which offer a management track and a specialized technical track, are a common way for organizations to address the need for both managers and specialists.

These general insights on a dual-ladder system are particularly relevant to the entry of teachers into school administration. It is likely that some teachers are eager to become administrators, some are reluctant but could make the transition if encouraged, and some will never make the switch but will make valuable contributions in their role as a teacher. The existence of these different groups is natural, and it should caution against reading too much into anecdotal reports that teachers do not want to become principals. Indeed, Riehl and Byrd (1997, p. 55) found that "there seems to have been a certain amount of 'drift' into school administration, since a vast majority of new administrators had prepared for their career moves but did not express particularly strong feelings about leaving teaching in the near future."

Dewhirst (1991) found that the desire of technical specialists to become managers is related to how much the organizational culture values the managerial role. Interestingly, the question put to superintendents and principals by the Public Agenda survey (Farkas et al., 2001) was whether increasing the pay *and prestige* of school administrative positions would help improve school leadership. We emphasized the compensation aspect of such a strategy earlier, but prestige, too, may play its own, independent role.

MOVEMENT BETWEEN THE PUBLIC AND PRIVATE SECTORS

Just as people can enter into and exit from the school administration field at several points, they can also move between the public and private sectors at different points. As noted in Chapter Two, policymakers may wish to focus on careers in public school administration as distinct from those in private school administration and consider movement between the two sectors.

Movement Between Public and Private School Administrative Positions

Our analysis of CPS data revealed that from 1983 to 1999, public school administrators left public schools for private schools at an annual rate of 2.2 percent and came to public schools from private schools at an annual rate of 2.0 percent. In other words, little movement between the private and public sectors occurred, and the number of people moving in either direction was roughly equal.

Unfortunately, the sample of people moving between the two sectors is too small to generate statistically significant results about trends over time. However, a comparison of public and private school compensation suggests that some possible changes may have been key factors motivating people to work in one sector rather than the other.

Relative Compensation in Public and Private Schools

Public school administrators have consistently earned more than their counterparts in private schools, but the differential has fallen significantly over the past two decades. Figure 4.4 shows that in 1984, public school administrators earned on average approximately 40 percent more per week than private school administrators did. By 1999, however, this gap had narrowed to 12 percent.[11] A similar pattern is seen for average real hourly earnings. If we assume that working conditions in the two sectors remained relatively constant, these findings suggest that private school administration may have become more attractive relative to public school administration. Consequently, we might expect to see more people moving out of public and into private school administrative positions.

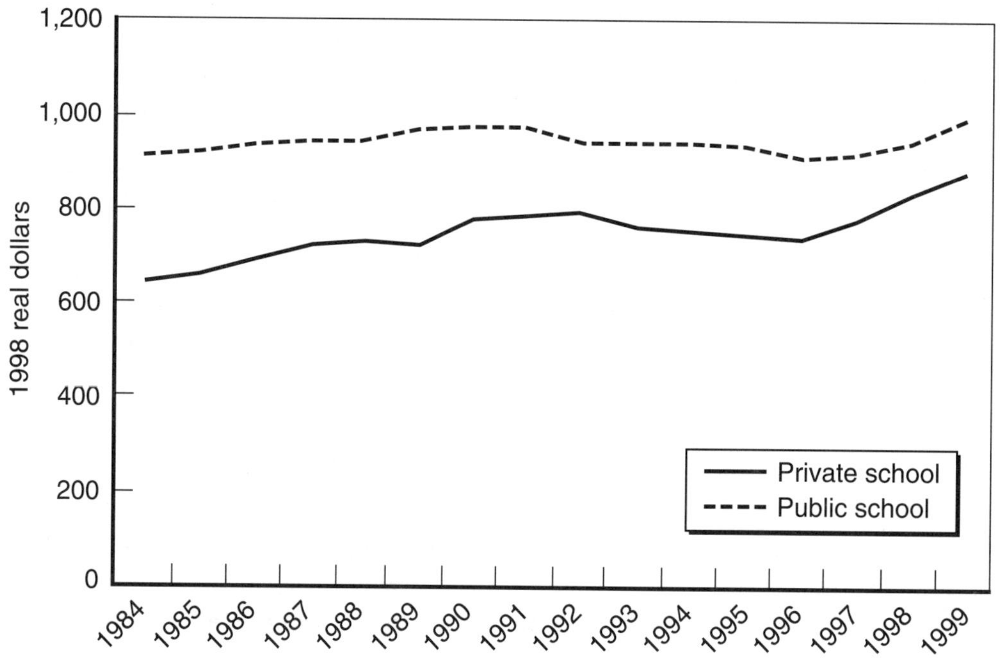

Figure 4.4—Average Real Weekly Earnings of Public and Private School Administrators, 1984–1999

[11]Notice that while the trends reflected here for the diminishing differential between public and private school administrative salaries are similar to those noted in Chapter Three, the magnitude of the difference is much smaller in this analysis. We do not have a definitive answer for what caused this difference, but we note that the definition of school administrator is broad and suggest that public schools may have larger staffs of administrators who are paid less than principals are. A detailed comparative analysis of school administration in the public versus private sector might shed some light on these issues, but such an analysis was beyond the scope of our study.

Movement of Principals Between Public and Private Schools

As mentioned earlier, our analysis of school administrators considered movement into and out of a wide range of administrative positions. What can we say specifically about the movement of school principals? We could not examine movement into and out of the education sector using the SASS data, because they capture information only from people currently working as principals. However, the SASS data did shed light on the movement of school principals between the public and private sectors.

The 1993–1994 SASS asked principals who had held a principalship prior to their current position to describe the school in which they had previously served.[12] Responses to this question suggest that the movement of principals between the two sectors is similar to the movement of school administrators in general—it is uncommon, but it does occur. Of these public school principals, only 2 percent had moved most recently from a private school. In contrast, of the private school principals, 9 percent had moved most recently from a public school. In other words, about 780 current public school principals had moved from a private school principalship, and 878 current private school principals had moved from a public school principalship.

As with the CPS analysis of school administrators, this analysis indicates a roughly equal transfer of principals between the private and public sectors, rather than mass exodus from the private to the public sector. However, because there are roughly threefold more public school principals, the equal transfer implies that, at least as of 1994, private school principals were more likely than public school principals to move to the other sector.

Principalship Differences in the Two Sectors

The SASS data allowed us to look at trends in certain factors that might be expected to affect the movement of principals between the public and private sectors.

There are two important differences between principals' jobs in the two sectors. First, public schools offer higher pay. In 1987–1988, private school principals earned on average only 49 percent of what public school principals earned; by 1999–2000, that percentage had risen to 62 percent. But one must also consider that according to the 1993–1994 SASS, private school administrators were far less likely than their public school counterparts to receive fringe benefits, such as medical care, dental care, and retirement.[13] Moreover, as reflected in Table 4.1, the proportion of private school principals receiving medical and other benefits actually declined between 1988 and 1994, whereas the proportion of public school principals receiving such benefits increased.

---

[12]This question was not included in the 1999–2000 survey.

[13]Benefits questions were omitted from the 1999–2000 survey, so we could not update this information.

Table 4.1

Percentage of Principals Receiving Benefits, by Sector

	Public		Private	
Type of Benefit	1987–88	1993–94	1987–88	1993–94
Medical	86.0	91.8	68.5	64.0
Dental	60.9	66.1	32.5	35.0
Life insurance	67.0	70.7	33.6	35.2
Retirement	58.4	70.4	41.8	46.3
In-kind[a]	41.1	46.2	64.3	55.1

SOURCE: SASS.
[a]In-kind benefits include housing, meals, tuition, and transportation.

A second important way in which public and private school principalships differ is how principals perceive the problems at their school. Public schools are larger, and the average public school principal reports significantly more problems of all types than the average private school principal does (see Appendix C, Tables C.1 and C.2).[14] To the extent that principals prefer to work in schools with fewer problems, we would expect private school principalships to be the more attractive of the two. Principals may also have more flexibility/freedom in private schools.

In terms of experience, private school principals became more experienced in the 1990s, while public school principals became less so.[15] In 1999–2000, the average private school principal had 10.2 years of experience as a principal—1.2 years more than the average public school principal. In 1987–1988, the reverse was true. At that time, the average private school principal had eight years of experience as a principal—two years fewer than the average public school principal.

RETIREMENT: AN IMPORTANT FORM OF EXIT

As we emphasized in Chapter Three, all principals appear to be getting older on average, and the average age at entry into the principalship has increased. If increasingly older people are chosen to replace those who leave the position, schools may face an increased retirement rate and hence an increased overall turnover, unless efforts are made to bring people into the principalship at younger ages.

However, retirement eligibility is not retirement. Retirement eligibility means that individuals have access to full retirement benefits if they choose to retire, but it need not translate into immediate retirement. People can and do choose to continue working upon reaching retirement eligibility.

Retirement decisions involve many factors. Asch and Warner (1999) address this issue in depth in a report examining the optimal retirement age for Department of

[14]The SASS asks principals to report the extent to which about 30 issues are a problem in their school, the issues being such things as verbal abuse of teachers, student apathy, and lack of parental involvement. Table C.1, in Appendix C, lists all the issues included in the survey.

[15]These differences between sectors and across survey waves are statistically significant at the 5 percent level.

Defense (DoD) civil service workers. A person may become eligible for retirement at a certain age but be able to increase his or her retirement benefits by continuing to work. Detailed information on retirement plans at the state and local levels and on principals' ages and years of experience is required to determine whether there is an incentive for individuals to retire immediately upon eligibility. Conclusions may differ by state or even district.[16] However, the difference in the age distribution of principals in the private and public sectors suggests that the two sectors' retirement benefits may affect retirement behavior.

Available information on career intentions and retirement plans is less current, but it suggests that the differences in private and public school principals' attitudes toward retirement may not be entirely driven by differences in retirement plans.[17] In 1994, 32 percent of public and 52 percent of private school principals reported that they would remain at their job as long as they were able; 23 percent and 9 percent, respectively, said they would remain only until they achieved retirement eligibility (Fiore and Curtin, 1997).

According to the 2000 AASA survey, superintendents were generally satisfied with the career they had chosen and did not plan to leave anytime soon. Sixty percent reported that they planned to stay in their current position until they retired (Glass, Bjork, and Brunner, 2000), and only 14 percent planned to leave as soon as they reached the minimum retirement age. Moreover, 66 percent reported that they would choose the same career again if the choice were theirs to make. Seventy-seven percent of superintendents of large districts with enrollments over 29,000 reported such satisfaction with their career choice.

Retirement systems tied to states and even districts may limit the mobility of administrators. SASS results from 1993–1994 indicate that labor mobility across state lines is limited for public school principals but is reasonably high for private school principals. Only 7 percent of those public school principals who had held a prior principalship had transferred from a public school in another state. In contrast, 38 percent of private school principals had most recently moved from a private school in another state (see Appendix A, Figure A.8).[18]

A similar lack of state-to-state mobility was evident among superintendents. While superintendents quite commonly moved among districts in one state, only 11 percent left the state where they had first become an administrator at any point in their career (Glass, Bjork, and Brunner, 2000). This, and the information presented earlier on the tendency of public school principals to stay within state lines, suggests that states are relatively closed systems in terms of the careers of public school administrators. This may be heavily influenced by the fact that most state pensions for public school administrators cannot be transported from one state to another.

---

[16]There is a rich body of literature examining the effects of different policies on retirement behavior that organizations can use to manage employee retirement behavior when facing a possible human resource crisis (Parsons, 1996).

[17]The 1999–2000 SASS dropped questions about retirement plans.

[18]Our analysis used data from the 1993–1994 SASS. The 1999–2000 survey omitted the question on the moves principals make.

SUMMARY

Our analyses of movement into and out of the administrative career field and the factors influencing that movement provide little support for the view that people are being lured from school administration into other careers. The rates at which people enter into school administration from other career fields and leave school administration for other fields have remained stable over time. In addition, we could find no major shift in the factors that would be expected to influence entry and exit. In particular, we found that the real salary of school administrators grew modestly over time and closely tracked the salary changes of jobs in other managerial professions.

There appear to be moderate financial incentives for individuals to move from teaching to administration. We found that school administrators earned on average 24 percent more than teachers did, public school principals earned 33 percent more than experienced teachers in the same school did, and private school principals earned 44 percent more than experienced teachers in the same school did.

Although our analysis uncovered no *systematic* differences across schools in the salary differential between principals and experienced teachers, we did find a substantial amount of *unexplained* variation.[19] There were, of course, principals who earned less than or not much more than experienced teachers in the same school did, but this phenomenon was found in schools of all types and was not peculiar to schools with certain characteristics (for example, urban or low-income schools).

Our analysis did reveal differences across states in the salary differential between principals and teachers. It is possible that states whose salary differential is low could have a harder time inducing teachers to become principals. However, it is also possible that these states' salary differential is lower precisely *because* it is easy to attract teachers into school administration. State policymakers may find it useful to evaluate their labor market conditions in view of the results on this subject (see Appendix B).

Private school administrators—principals, in particular—have traditionally earned less than their public school counterparts. However, our analysis indicates that the pay gap between the two sectors has been narrowing. Because there are no adequate measures of school administrator quality in the data, it is impossible to say whether the diminishing pay gap may be causing better candidates to move from the public to the private sector. We do know that the average experience of private school principals increased by over two years from 1988 to 2000, whereas the average experience of public school principals declined.[20] In view of these shifts, it would be worthwhile to continue to monitor the movement of administrators between the public and private sectors.

Certification requirements and human resource practices seem to pose substantial barriers (both formal and informal) to entry into school administration, particularly

---

[19]In the private sector, there is a systematic difference in that the pay differential for principals of Catholic and other religiously affiliated schools is less than that for principals of nonsectarian schools.

[20]Experience as an administrator can be viewed as one measure of quality.

for those who are not teachers. According to our literature review, there are also other barriers inhibiting movement between teaching and administration. The evidence suggests that even though there are more than enough certified people to fill existing administrative positions, the expense and effort that go into acquiring certification may still pose a barrier to potentially interested teachers. In addition, it is likely that there are cultural and structural barriers inhibiting career transitions.

As discussed in Chapter Three, the average age of all principals is increasing, as is the average age of new principals. Also, public school principals are increasingly likely to be between the ages of 45 and 55. These trends suggest that, particularly in public schools, people are entering the principalship at older ages and leaving at younger ages, resulting overall in a shorter tenure in administrative positions. Much work could be done to fully understand the incentives facing school administrators as they approach retirement and the policy changes that could influence their decisions to leave the labor force.

As we noted at the start of this chapter, other ways of defining the career field might be useful for examining policy-relevant questions. Although national data do not allow movement into and out of a state to be examined, district or school state-level administrative data offer the possibility of longitudinal analyses that track movements across such boundaries.[21]

---

[21]RAND reviewed data availability at the state level and found that 29 states retain administrative personnel records at that level in a way that makes it possible to link records across years and examine career moves within the state public education system. Many of these states have data only from the mid-1990s, which limits the ability to do longitudinal analyses. However, 13 of them have data going back 10 years or more.

Chapter Five

MOVEMENT WITHIN THE SCHOOL ADMINISTRATIVE CAREER FIELD

Movement between the different school administrative positions—from assistant principal to principal, from principal to superintendent, from superintendent to district administrator, etc.—can be a natural part of a career in education. Such within-field movement exposes people to a wide variety of the activities in which school systems engage and provides insight into the complexity of the different jobs.

This chapter examines these types of moves within the career field, as depicted in Figure 5.1. We first look at turnover, then proceeding to the moves that are made and the factors that influence them.

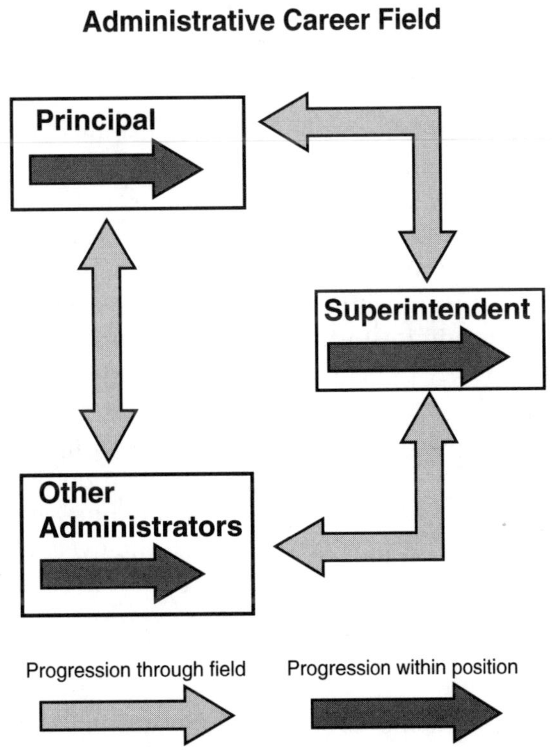

Figure 5.1—Movement of School Administrators Within Administrative Career Field

TURNOVER

Cross-sectional data on the experience of principals (discussed in Chapter Four) suggest that there may be a high exit rate among new principals who decide that the job is not a "good fit" for them, followed by a long period of commitment to the position for those who stay. In 1999–2000, public school principals had an average of nine years of experience as a principal, and private school principals had an average of 10.2 years (see Chapter Three, Table 3.1). However, the experience levels were not evenly distributed around these averages. Thirty percent of both public school principals and private school principals had 12 or more years of experience. Just under 30 percent of both (and nearly half of charter school principals) had three or fewer years of experience (see Appendix A). If this were solely a recent phenomenon, we might attribute a high proportion of new principals to a recent increase in the number of retirements. However, the same patterns are evident in previous survey waves as well. The high fraction of principals with three or fewer years of experience suggests that many individuals entering the principalship do not stay very long. Conversely, the data also indicate that a substantial fraction of people stay in the principalship—even a single principalship—for a very long time. Moreover, we observed no systematic patterns indicating that urbanicity or student demographic characteristics influence the likelihood that a principal stays in place.

Similarly, data from the state of Illinois show high attrition (18.8 percent) among principals with one year of experience or less, and low attrition (typically between 1 and 5 percent) among principals with two to 31 years of experience (Illinois State Board of Education, 2000). Joy (1998) suggests that "poor fit" is a particular problem for female principals, who often leave after a short tenure.

Papa, Lankford, and Wyckoff (2002) examined the positions held in the subsequent six years by individuals who had assumed their first principalship in the New York state education system in 1992. Their analysis suggests that turnover is high and that only a small proportion of it stems from people leaving the principalship to return to teaching. They found that fewer than 2 percent of the exiting principals returned to teaching in the next year (for their study, 1993). More commonly, the individuals moved into some other administrative position or left the public school sector entirely. The fact that many principals moved to another administrative position emphasizes the dynamic nature of the administrative career path and cautions policymakers against considering departures from the principalship as a "loss" to public schools. The study found that although a small proportion, 2.3 percent, of the exiting principals had left the career field within one year of assuming the principalship, 15 percent had left it after four years, and over 22 percent had left the New York state education system entirely by 1998.

MOVEMENT WITHIN FIELD

Very little is known about the moves school administrators make within their field. We do know that individuals are likely to hold another administrative position before assuming a principalship. According to the 1999–2000 SASS, 66.8 percent of public school principals and 44.2 percent of private school principals had held an assistant principalship or program director position before becoming principals. Thirty-six percent of both public and private school principals had served as department heads, and 25 percent of public and 29 percent of private school principals had served as curriculum specialists (Gruber et al., 2002).

For both private and public schools, these percentages varied substantially by state, community type, and student enrollment, with principals in rural areas, midwestern states, and small schools being less likely to have served in such positions prior to becoming principals.

In tracking the subsequent six years of the group of first-time principals in 1992 in the state of New York, Papa, Lankford, and Wyckoff (2002) found that a majority of the principals had spent time as assistant principals. Surprisingly, 36 percent of them were no longer principals in the same school by the next school year. Twenty-two percent had moved into another administrative position in the same district, many becoming assistant principals, which suggests they may have been serving as principal on an interim or temporary basis. After six years, only 34 percent of the original group were still serving as principal in the same school. Over 12 percent had left for another school in the same district, over 8 percent had moved to another district, and over 20 percent were in another administrative position in either their original or another district.

The 2000 American Association of School Administrators (AASA) survey provides clues about the paths taken to the superintendency (Glass, Bjork, and Brunner, 2000). The vast majority (80 percent) of superintendents who responded to the survey had taken one of two common paths after first being a teacher. Forty-nine percent had taken the first path—i.e., had held both a principalship and another administrative position in a district central office before assuming a superintendency. This path was very common in the largest districts (those with over 25,000 students), where 68 percent of superintendents had taken it. Thirty-one percent had taken the second common path—i.e., had held a principalship and then gone directly into a superintendency with no district central office experience. This path was more common among superintendents in the smallest districts (those with fewer than 300 students), where 48 percent had taken it. The difference between the two paths likely reflects the fact that small districts lack the central office positions that exist in large districts.

Thirty-five percent of the responding superintendents reported that their first administrative position was that of assistant principal; 41 percent reported principal. Not surprisingly, only 18 percent of those in the smaller districts reported assistant principal as their first position. The smaller districts are likely to have smaller schools, and smaller schools are less likely to have assistant principals.

In spite of the conventional wisdom that the superintendency has a revolving door (there is high turnover in the position) (Gewertz, 2002), the average tenure in current positions among respondents to a national survey of school superintendents was 7.25 years (Cooper, Fusarelli, and Carella, 2000). This had not changed much since previous surveys. However, another survey conducted in summer 2001 indicates that the average tenure of superintendents of major urban school districts is under three years (Council of the Great City Schools, 2001).

OTHER INFLUENCING FACTORS

The 2001–2002 salary survey for public school personnel (Educational Research Service, 2002) indicates that public school superintendents were the most highly paid administrators, earning $121,794 on average, in the year of the survey. Average salaries for associate and assistant superintendents were slightly lower, at $107,458 and $96,627, respectively. Average salaries for other district-level administrators (such as director of instructional services and director of public affairs) ranged from $66,351 to $83,035 depending on the position. The average salary for school principals ranged from $73,114 for elementary principals to $83,944 for high school principals. Assistant principals earned about 20 percent less; their average salaries ranged from $60,672 to $67,822 depending on school grade level.

Pounder and Merrill (2001) surveyed assistant principals in high schools and principals in junior high schools in one western state on their attitudes toward the desirability of being a high school principal and their perspectives on a variety of other factors. The researchers then analyzed the relationship between the attitudes and perspectives.

The strongest positive relationship they found was between the desire to achieve and to improve education and the view that being a high school principal is desirable. The second strongest relationship had to do with the position's time demands, with higher perceived time demands reducing desirability. Salary and benefits "had the third strongest significant relationship to job desirability, reflecting the perceived pecuniary advantages of the high school principalship over many other educator positions" (Pounder and Merrill, 2001, p. 47). The authors suggest that potential high school principals see the primary tradeoff associated with the position as one of more-rewarding work and higher pay in exchange for less free time.

SUMMARY

Despite recent attention to non-traditional principals and superintendents (e.g., those hired from outside the education career field), it is still the case that most public school principals have served as assistant principals and that most superintendents have held other school- and district-level administrative positions.

In general, there appear to be moderate financial incentives for individuals to move "up the career ladder" within school administration. The average salary of assistant principals falls between the average salary of teachers and that of principals; central office administrators earn more than principals do but less than superintendents.

Chapter Six

MOBILITY WITHIN THE PRINCIPALSHIP

Principals, superintendents, and other administrators can and do move between jobs that carry the same official title. Such movement is reflected in position turnover (for example, as a principal or a superintendent moves from one school to another) but need not generate overall job vacancies. Our analysis generated little empirical support for the idea that there is a nationwide crisis in the labor market for school administrators. However, that does not rule out the possibility that certain types of schools are systematically having difficulty attracting and retaining school administrators. For example, urban schools serving low-income populations might systematically be losing principals to suburban schools serving high-income populations. This chapter focuses specifically on one type of school administrator, the principal, exploring whether the market for principals varies in systematic ways by school characteristics and the factors driving any relationships that exist.

We begin by discussing research that suggests experienced teachers make active choices to move out of—i.e., sort out of—urban schools serving low-income and minority populations. Evidence of such sorting is consistent with the notion that teachers move out of urban, low-income schools as they gain more experience and become more desirable in the teacher labor market. Such evidence has been used to support the idea that because a teacher's job is more difficult in urban, low-income schools serving high-minority populations, teachers need to be more highly compensated to remain in such environments.

We then examine whether similar relationships hold true for principals. We take advantage of the richness of the Schools and Staffing Survey (SASS), which contains information on school characteristics, principals' salary and experience, and principals' perceptions of problems in their schools, to examine the interrelationships among school characteristics, principal sorting, and some measure of "job difficulty" in a more comprehensive way. Specifically, we use these data to examine three important questions:

1. Is there an empirical relationship between school characteristics and principals' perceptions of problems in their school? The observable characteristics of schools are widely assumed to be good proxies for problems existent in schools. In particular, schools with a higher proportion of minority and low-income students are often assumed to have more problems. In this chapter, we examine these relationships empirically. Policymakers generally do not have access to in-

formation on principals' perceptions of problems in specific schools, but the discovery of clear relationships between school characteristics and problems would make it possible to use school characteristics as a proxy for school problems.

2. Are there systematic relationships between school characteristics and principals' salaries, and, if so, do these relationships appear to compensate principals who work in schools whose characteristics are associated with more problems?
3. Is there evidence that more-experienced principals are sorting into schools with certain observable characteristics and/or fewer problems?

SCHOOL CHARACTERISTICS AND EMPLOYMENT DECISIONS: FINDINGS FROM STUDIES OF TEACHERS

Recent studies of teacher mobility suggest that a substantial amount of teacher mobility can be explained by observable school characteristics. Specifically, teachers sort out of schools serving disadvantaged students. If experience is valued in the teacher market (i.e., if experience is viewed as a measure of teacher quality), sorting based on experience level is consistent with the theory of compensating differentials (discussed in Chapter Two) and suggests that the observable characteristics of schools may be a proxy for teachers' working conditions.

A study of Texas teachers found that teachers in academically low-performing schools were much more likely than teachers in high-performing schools to leave teaching (Hanushek, Kain, and Rivkin, 2001). The study also found that teachers who moved from one school to another went to schools with higher student achievement measures, a lower proportion of low-income students, and a lower proportion of minority students. This was particularly true for teachers who switched schools within an urban district. Similar results were found by Carroll, Reichardt, and Guarino (2000) in a study of California teachers. They found that teachers who transferred were more likely to transfer out of high-minority schools and districts and into low-minority schools and districts, and that high-minority schools thus tended to have higher vacancy rates than other schools did. In addition, the high-minority schools were found to be less successful in attracting credentialed teachers to fill their vacancies. Taken together, these disparities in recruitment and retention reinforced an inequitable distribution of uncredentialed teachers across schools with different levels of minority student enrollment.

These inequities can become particularly severe when demographic trends or policy initiatives create a strong overall market demand for teachers. For example, a study of the California class size reduction initiative (Stecher and Bohrnstedt, 2002) found that the percentage of K–3 teachers lacking full credentials increased from 1.8 percent in 1995–1996 to 13.9 percent in 1999–2000 statewide. That increase was not spread evenly across schools, however: in 1999–2000, schools with less than 7.5 percent low-income students had less than 5 percent of such teachers, whereas schools with 30 percent or more low-income students had over 20 percent. Prince (2002) reports several examples of district- and school-level variation in teacher experience that reflect a tendency for experienced teachers to concentrate in schools serving students from non-minority, high-income families, leaving schools serving minority, low-income populations to be served by less experienced teachers.

This chapter examines whether similar patterns hold for principals. We begin by considering whether observable school characteristics are related to how difficult principals perceive their job to be. We then examine the relationship between principals' pay and school characteristics to consider whether principals in more-problematic schools earn more. Finally, we examine evidence of principal sorting.

PRINCIPALS' PERCEPTIONS OF SCHOOL PROBLEMS

The SASS presents some specific issues and asks principals to rate the degree to which each is a problem in their school. We conducted a factor analysis and used the results to group the school-problem questions into three broad categories:

1. *Individual student problems*—questions on student drug and/or alcohol abuse, pregnancy, dropping out, cutting class, and student apathy.
2. *Poverty and family-related problems*—questions on students coming to school unprepared to learn, student absenteeism, student tardiness, poverty, lack of parental involvement, and poor student health.
3. *School conflict*—questions on vandalism of school property, physical conflict among students, robbery or theft, student disrespect of teachers, and possession of weapons.

These groupings were then used to examine whether there is a statistical relationship between observable school characteristics and principals' perceptions of school problems. We assumed that principals who reported more problems in their school found their job to be more challenging, and we used the reports of school problems as a proxy measure of how difficult the job of principal is. This analysis helped us begin to get at the working conditions faced by principals and whether we can associate certain types of schools with more-challenging working conditions for principals.

We found the observable characteristics of a school to be significantly related to principals' perceptions of school problems (details of the analysis are in Appendix C). We grouped the problems into the three categories described above. The dependent variables for our regression analyses were the averages of the problem scores for each category; the independent variables were as follows:

- *Principal characteristics*: race/ethnicity, gender, teaching experience, and experience as a principal.
- *School characteristics*: grade level, enrollment, percentage of minority students, percentage of limited English proficient (LEP) students, percentage of students enrolled in free and reduced-price lunch programs (i.e., low-income students), student diversity (i.e., degree to which the student body is balanced across racial

and ethnic groups),[1] and school type (charter, Bureau of Indian Affairs [BIA], religious affiliation).

- *Community characteristics*: urbanicity and state indicators.

Compared with private school principals, public school principals perceived their schools as having significantly more severe problems of all types. In general, the influence of specific student and school characteristics on principals' perceptions of school problems was similar in both public and private schools, but the magnitude of the effect was generally larger for public schools. The tables presented below show the results of the regression analysis in which the individual student problem category (category 1) score (MSCORE1) was used as the dependent variable. The relationships were generally similar in direction for the other two categories of problems (differences are discussed in detail in Appendix C).

The statistically significant relationships we found between school characteristics and the individual student problems reported by principals are summarized in Tables 6.1 (for public school) and 6.2 (for private school). The magnitude of each relationship is expressed in terms of standard deviations of the problem score estimate. For public schools, the mean value of MSCORE1 is 0.52, with a standard deviation of 0.47; for private schools, the mean value is 0.25, with a standard deviation of 0.38. An impact of one standard deviation suggests that the characteristic has an important effect on perceptions of school problems.

Table 6.1

Summary of School Characteristics with a Relationship to Principals' Reports of Individual Student Problems, Public Sector

	Impact of Characteristic (standard deviations of MSCORE1)	
School Characteristic	Fixed or at Sample Mean	Maximum
Elementary school (vs. high school)	–2.3	
Combined school (vs. high school)	–1.7	
Middle school (vs. high school)	–1.7	
Rural (vs. urban)	–0.12	
Charter (vs. traditional public)	–0.17	
BIA (vs. traditional public)	0.26	
Larger student enrollment	0.1	1.21
Larger fraction of students on free and reduced-price lunch	0.15	0.4
Higher percentage of minority students	0.19	0.25

SOURCE: 1999–2000 SASS.

NOTE: The numbers in the table reflect the size of the effect in terms of standard deviations in the MSCORE1 variable. Relative to a comparable high school, an elementary school has an average MSCORE1 value that is 2.3 standard deviations lower.

[1]See Appendix A for a detailed description of this measure.

Table 6.2

Summary of School Characteristics with a Relationship to Principals' Reports of Individual Student Problems, Private Sector

	Impact of the Characteristic (standard deviations of MSCORE1)	
School Characteristic	Fixed or at Sample Mean	Maximum
Elementary school (vs. high school)	–1.34	
Combined school (vs. high school)	–1.13	
Middle school (vs. high school)	–0.92	
Catholic (vs. nonsectarian)	–0.34	
Other religious (vs. nonsectarian)	–0.47	
Larger student enrollment	0.05	0.74
Larger fraction of students on free and reduced-price lunch	0.04	1.42

SOURCE: 1999–2000 SASS.

NOTE: The numbers in the table reflect the size of the effect in terms of standard deviations in the MSCORE1 variable.

The strongest relationship we found was between principals' perceptions of individual student problems and the grade level of the school.[2] High school principals reported more severe problems than middle school principals did, who in turn reported more severe problems than elementary school principals did. The magnitude is over one standard deviation in both sectors. This relationship between problem and school grade level holds, albeit with smaller magnitude, for the other two problem categories (poverty and family-related problems and school conflict problems) as well. The second strongest relationship we found was with school size. Problems generally increased with school size; principals of larger schools reported greater problem severity than did principals of smaller schools.[3] School size appears to have the strongest relationship with individual student problems and school conflict problems, suggesting that larger schools pose serious challenges for school principals.

Principals in schools with a larger proportion of students in free and reduced-price lunch programs and a higher percentage of minority students perceived more school problems, but the relationship here was much weaker than that between grade level and school problems.[4] For public schools, a higher degree of student diversity increased principals' reports of poverty and family-related problems but did not affect the other two categories.

[2]The magnitude of the grade-level relationships was smaller for categories 2 and 3—poverty and family-related problems and school conflict problems.

[3]The relationships are nonlinear for category 2 and 3 problems. The critical enrollment level for both of these categories was 1,500 students. As schools grew in size beyond this level, the poverty and family-related problems and school conflict problems tended to decline.

[4]The magnitude of the relationship between these characteristics and the category 2 and 3 problems was larger.

We found urbanicity to be related to principals' ratings of the various problems—urban principals reported more problems than did rural principals—but the effect was very small. There was no statistically significant difference. We found little difference in the perceptions of principals by urbanicity when we controlled for other characteristics associated with urbanicity (such as school size, percentage of LEP students, percentage of minority students, and student diversity).

The student body's racial/ethnic characteristics were found to have a statistically significant nonlinear relationship to principals' reports of individual student problems in the public sector only. These characteristics were not found to be related to poverty and family-related problems or school conflict problems. Problems increased as the percentage of minority students increased to about 65 percent; beyond that level, however, problems decreased. The maximum effect of minority enrollment on individual student problems (e.g., the difference between two schools, one with 0 percent and one with 65 percent minority enrollment) was rather small—only one-quarter of a standard deviation. Student diversity had a similar nonlinear relationship with principals' reports of poverty and family-related problems in public schools.

The results for private schools were quite different. The coefficients on the diversity index were significant in the case of the poverty and family-related problems and the school conflict problems. Poverty and family-related problems were higher in more-diverse schools. The difference in problem ratings between a homogeneous and a totally diverse private school would be 0.45 points on the rating scale, or close to three-quarters of a standard deviation. As for school conflict problems, they decreased as diversity increased to moderate levels (DIVINDEX = 0.22); diversity increases beyond that point, however, were associated with more problems. Given these coefficients, principals in completely diverse private schools would worsen their conflict ratings by 0.31 points, or over three-quarters of a standard deviation.

School type also proved to have some relationship to principals' reports of school problems. Charter school principals reported problems as less severe than did principals of comparable, traditional public schools. Principals at BIA schools reported slightly more problems. Private schools with a religious affiliation tended to have fewer problems than did nonsectarian schools.

Most of the principals' characteristics had minor or insignificant effects on principals' perceptions of school problems, all other things being equal. A principal's race/ethnicity did have a significant effect, however, except in the case of Native American principals. Holding all else equal (in particular, school characteristics), black, Asian, and Hispanic principals saw fewer problems in their schools than white principals did. To shed some light on this finding, we examined additional school-level data on documented reports of student threats and attacks on teachers. We concluded that minority and white principals did not have different perceptions of what constitutes a problem. Minority principals, particularly black principals, tended to give higher ratings on questions such as, "To what extent is student disrespect of teachers a problem?" than did white principals in schools having similar numbers of documented student threats and attacks on teachers. This suggests that the reason for minority principals reporting fewer problems is not that they have a higher threshold than white principals for what constitutes a problem.

In summary, we found substantial evidence relating principals' perceptions of the severity of problems in their school with observable characteristics of their school. Private school principals reported fewer problems than public school principals did, suggesting that the working conditions in the private sector are better. Although the racial/ethnic composition of the student body does appear to have affected principals' reports of school problems, the relationships were neither strong nor consistent for the three categories of problems. We did not find that schools with more minority students necessarily had more reported problems than schools with fewer minority students had. For both the public and the private sector, we found that larger schools, high schools, and schools with a higher percentage of students enrolled in free and reduced-price lunch programs were associated with more problems. Charter school principals reported fewer problems, as did principals of religious (versus nonsectarian) private schools.

PRINCIPALS' PAY AND SCHOOL CHARACTERISTICS

The analysis described above suggests that some schools present principals with greater challenges than others do and that the observable characteristics of a school can explain some of the variation. As a result, it is useful to examine whether compensation varies in systematic ways with school characteristics. To consider this question, we conducted a regression analysis that looked at the relationship of principals' salaries to school and individual principals' characteristics (see Appendix B). This regression analysis used the same independent variables used in our analysis of principals' perceptions of school problems. Our hypothesis was that schools might not have the flexibility to financially compensate principals in schools whose observable characteristics are associated with a higher level of problems. We found, however, that principals' salaries do indeed vary with school characteristics, and that the manner in which they vary provides higher compensation to principals in schools whose characteristics are associated with more reported challenges.

Tables 6.3 and 6.4 summarize the relationships between school characteristics and principals' salaries in the public and private sectors, respectively.[5] For characteristics that are categorical variables (such as school grade level, where a school can fall into one of four categories), we report (first column of the table) the difference in salary, relative to the reference group noted in parentheses, that is attributed to that characteristic. For characteristics that are continuous variables (such as student enrollment), the relationship varies with the characteristic's value. We report the fixed impact, or the impact evaluated at the sample mean for that characteristic, as well as

---

[5]We include only those relationships that are significant at the 10 percent level. State dummy variables are also significant in the public sector regression but are not included in Table 6.3.

Table 6.3

Summary of School Characteristics with a Relationship to Principals' Salaries, Public Sector

School Characteristic	Impact of Characteristic ($ per year)	
	Fixed or at Sample Mean	Maximum
Elementary school (vs. high school)	–1,190	
Combined school (vs. high school)	–1,249	
Middle school (vs. high school)	–730	
Rural (vs. urban)	–7,306	
Charter (vs. traditional public)	–12,540	
BIA (vs. traditional public)	6,486	
Larger student enrollment[a]	4,645	23,210
More diverse student body[a]	2,973	3,401
Larger fraction of LEP students	222	4,387
Larger fraction of students on free and reduced-price lunch	–2,269	–6,034
Higher percentage of minority students	2,908	6,448

SOURCE: 1999–2000 SASS.

[a]The relationships between principals' salaries and enrollment and diversity are nonlinear: salary increases with these characteristics up to a point but then begins to decline.

Table 6.4

Summary of School Characteristics with a Relationship to Principals' Salaries, Private Sector

School Characteristic	Impact of Characteristic ($ per year)	
	Fixed or at Sample Mean	Maximum
Elementary school (vs. high school)	–5,612	
Combined school (vs. high school)	–6,451	
Suburban (vs. urban)	–2,987	
Rural (vs. urban)	–6,376	
Catholic (vs. nonsectarian)	–19,952	
Other religious (vs. nonsectarian)	–19,176	
Larger student enrollment[a]	11,920	40,048
Larger fraction of LEP students	105	15,358

SOURCE: 1999–2000 SASS.

[a]The relationship between principals' salaries and enrollment is nonlinear: salary increases with enrollment up to a point but then begins to decline as schools get very large.

the maximum impact a characteristic can have for those characteristics that are continuous variables.[6]

Our analysis of school principals' salaries using 1999–2000 SASS data showed that high school principals earned more, all things being equal, than principals of all

[6]For characteristics that enter the regression equation in a linear way, that maximum impact occurs at either the largest or the smallest value of the characteristic. For those that enter the model in a quadratic fashion, the maximum impact can occur at midrange values of the characteristic.

other types of schools did. In public schools, they earned about $1,200 per year more than principals of both elementary and combined schools did, and over $700 per year more than middle school principals did. In private schools, the difference was greater: High school principals earned about $6,000 per year more than principals of both elementary and combined schools did.

The data reveal a nonlinear relationship between principals' salaries and student enrollment, with salary increasing up to enrollment levels of about 5,000 in public schools and 1,200 in private schools, and declining thereafter. An evaluation at the average school size in the sample revealed that the effect of enrollment level on salary was about $4,600 per year in the public sector and $12,000 per year in the private sector using the respective sample means.[7] The relationship between salary and enrollment was a substantial one: principals of public schools with enrollments of about 5,000 earned over $23,000 per year more than principals of very small schools did, and principals of private schools with enrollments of 1,350 earned about $40,000 per year more than principals of very small schools did.[8]

Among public schools, nonlinear relationships were also evident between salary and student diversity. The effect of diversity evaluated at the sample mean was about $3,000 per year. The diversity factor could add up to $3,400 per year to a principal's salary at moderate levels of diversity (DIVINDEX = 0.53). Beyond this point, however, salary declined as diversity increased, but principals of the most diverse schools still earned more than principals of completely homogeneous schools did. In public schools, principals' salaries also increased as the percentage of minority students increased, such that principals of schools with 100 percent minority enrollment earned about $6,500 per year more than principals of comparable all-white schools did.[9] Although the relationship is nonlinear, it is an increase over the entire range of the data.

We found the percentage of students enrolled in free and reduced-price lunch programs to be negatively related to principals' salaries in the public sector. An evaluation at the sample mean showed the effect to be about $2,200 per year, and principals at schools with 100 percent of students in the programs earned $6,000 per year less than did principals in schools with no students in the programs.[10] The percentage of LEP students had an opposite relationship. Because the average percentage of LEP students was so low (5 percent), the effect on salary evaluated at the average was only $222 per year. However, the effect of this characteristic can be substantial. Principals in schools with 100 percent LEP students earned about $4,400 per year more than did their counterparts in schools with no LEP students.[11] The percentage of LEP students is also positively related to principals' salaries in the private sector. Again, the effect evaluated at the sample mean was quite small—just over $100 per

---

[7]Average school size was 532 in the public sector and 221 in the private sector.

[8]These relationships with grade level and enrollment are similar to what was observed in 1994.

[9]These relationships between principals' salaries and school characteristics appear to be stronger than they were in 1994.

[10]This relationship was not significant in 1994.

[11]This relationship is similar to what was observed in 1994.

year—but principals at schools with 100 percent LEP students earned about $15,000 per year more than did principals at comparable private schools with no LEP students.

The analysis revealed no statistically significant difference between salaries earned by suburban versus urban public school principals after we controlled for other factors. In the private sector, suburban principals earned slightly less than their urban counterparts did. Rural principals earned $6,000 to $7,000 per year less than their urban counterparts did in both the private and the public sector. Urban public school principals appear to have made gains relative to their suburban and rural counterparts after 1993–1994, when urban principals earned only slightly more than rural principals did and less than suburban principals.

Charter school principals earned substantially less per year—about $12,500 less—than principals in comparable traditional public schools did. This is interesting, given the conventional wisdom that charter school principals assume a broader range of administrative responsibilities in their schools. In contrast, principals at BIA schools earned nearly $6,500 per year more than their counterparts at traditional public schools did. (This reflects an increase over 1993–1994.) In the private sector, we found that principals of Catholic and other religiously affiliated schools earned substantially less per year—just under $20,000 less—than their counterparts in nonsectarian schools did.

The data analysis revealed substantial differences across states in terms of salary paid to public school principals. All other things being equal, a principal in New Jersey (the state where principals fared best) earned over $13,000 per year more than a principal in a comparable school in California did, whereas a principal in Louisiana (the state where principals fared worst) earned about $19,000 less than a principal in California did. The parameter estimates thus helped us identify states where principals were relatively well paid (Alaska, Connecticut, New Jersey, New York, and Michigan), as well as states where principals were relatively less well paid (Alabama, Arkansas, Arizona, Florida, Louisiana, Mississippi, the Carolinas, the Dakotas, New Mexico, Oklahoma, Utah, and Tennessee).

Overall, our analysis of principals' salaries suggests that the compensation of school principals does in fact vary according to school characteristics. This provides some support for the hypothesis that principals may be compensated differently for different working conditions.

EVIDENCE OF PRINCIPAL SORTING BY SCHOOL CHARACTERISTICS AND REPORTS OF SCHOOL PROBLEMS

Although the evidence suggests that compensation varies such that principals who work in schools with less desirable working conditions are paid more than others are, it is certainly possible that they are not paid enough more to encourage them to work in certain types of schools. That is, when given the choice, principals in "less desirable" schools may leave for "more desirable" schools.

One indicator of the inadequacy of compensation differences would be evidence that "better" principals are concentrated in schools with "more desirable" characteristics. If such sorting does occur, some of it may be explained by unobserved differences (principals' perceptions of school problems) across schools, and some by observable differences across schools. As is the case with teachers, experience is typically viewed as a desirable characteristic, and schools do seek out experienced principals (Roza et al., 2002). In our analysis of this issue, we used principals' experience as a proxy for quality and examined whether such sorting occurred. That is, we examined whether principals with more experience are more likely to be found in schools with certain characteristics.

We performed a regression analysis using years of experience as a principal as the dependent variable. The independent variables included

- *School characteristics*: grade level, enrollment, percentage of minority students, percentage of LEP students, percentage of students enrolled in free and reduced-price lunch programs, student diversity, and school type.
- *Community characteristics*: urbanicity and state indicators.
- *Principals' reports of school problems*: mean scores of reported problems in each of the three problem categories—individual student problems, poverty and family-related problems, and school conflict problems (as described above, in section on principals' perceptions of school problems).

Although we included a principal's personal characteristics in the salary and salary ratio regression, we did not do so in this regression, because our focus was on the relationship between a principal's experience and school characteristics.

Tables 6.5 and 6.6 summarize the relationships between school characteristics and principals' experience in the public and private sectors, respectively.[12] For characteristics that are categorical variables, we report the difference in experience relative to the reference group noted in parentheses; for characteristics that are continuous variables, we report the impact evaluated at the sample mean for that characteristic, as well as the maximum impact that characteristic had.

Our analysis yielded limited evidence of a relationship between principals' experience and observable school characteristics (see Appendix B for details). The explanatory power of the regression models was very low (R^2 = 0.05 for public schools, 0.03 for private schools), with half of the variation for public schools explained by state-fixed effects. However, the parameter estimates do reveal some statistically significant relationships between school characteristics and principals' experience. In both public and private schools, enrollment was found to be related to principals' experience in a nonlinear way. The experience of principals tended to increase as schools grew to enrollment levels of about 2,200 in public schools and 1,700 in private

[12]We included only those relationships that are significant at the 10 percent level. State dummy variables are also significant in the public sector regression but are not included in Table 6.5.

Table 6.5

School Characteristics with a Relationship to Principals' Experience, Public Sector

School Characteristic	Impact of the Characteristic (years)	
	Compared to Omitted Category or at Sample Mean	Maximum Impact
Elementary school (vs. high school)	0.8	
Charter (vs. traditional public)	−1.5	
BIA (vs. traditional public)	1.1	
Larger student enrollment[a]	0.7	1.5
Principals' perceptions of conflict	−0.4	−2.0

SOURCE: 1999–2000 SASS.

[a]The relationship between experience and enrollment is nonlinear: experience increases with enrollment up to a point but then begins to decline as schools get very large.

Table 6.6

School Characteristics with a Relationship to Principals' Experience, Private Sector

School Characteristic	Impact of the Characteristic (years)	
	Compared to Omitted Category or at Sample Mean	Maximum Impact
Combined school (vs. high school)	1.1	
Catholic (vs. nonsectarian)	−1.5	
Larger student enrollment[a]	1.4	5.5
Larger fraction of students on free and reduced-price lunch	−0.1	2.8

SOURCE: 1999–2000 SASS.

[a]The relationship between experience and enrollment is nonlinear: experience increases with enrollment up to a point but then begins to decline as schools get very large.

schools. Compared with principals of very small schools, principals of public schools with 2,200 students had approximately 1.5 more years of experience, and principals of private schools with 1,700 students had about 5.5 more years of experience. Beyond this point, however, principals' experience began to decline with school size. Our analysis also suggests that, all other things being equal, elementary (public only) and combined school principals had about one more year of experience than high school principals did. Compared with principals of traditional public schools, charter school principals had one less year of experience, and BIA school principals had one more. In the private sector, we found that Catholic school principals were less experienced than principals of nonsectarian schools were.

Such observable characteristics as the demographic characteristics of the student population and school urbanicity had no statistically significant relationship with principals' experience in the public sector. In contrast, private schools with a higher proportion of students enrolled in free and reduced-price lunch programs had principals with fewer years of experience.

Our analysis suggests that principals' reports of school conflict problems explain some of the variation in public school principals' experience that is not explained by observable school characteristics. After controlling for observable school characteristics, we found that principals who reported more school conflict problems tended to have less experience. The difference in principals' experience was about two years for schools with low levels of school conflict problems versus schools with high levels. This relationship was found only for school conflict problems and only in public schools. We found no relationship between principals' experience and either individual student problems or poverty and family-related problems in public schools. And in the private sector, principals' reports of all three categories of problems were not related to experience.

Our analysis also revealed substantial differences across states in the experience of public school principals. Some states (such as Nebraska, Iowa, Pennsylvania, and West Virginia) had much more experienced principals than did other states (such as Alaska, Georgia, and Rhode Island). It is also interesting to note that many of the southeastern states saw a decline in the experience of their principals relative to the experience of principals in other states between 1994 and 2000.

SUMMARY

Our analysis suggests that principals' perceptions of school problems vary in systematic ways according to observable school characteristics, and that principals in schools with characteristics associated with more severe problems tend to earn more. We found little evidence that experienced principals were sorting or had been sorted based on observable school characteristics. Principals' reports of school problems seem to have been higher in public schools, in schools with higher proportions of students enrolled in free and reduced-price lunch programs, in high schools, and in schools with larger enrollments. At the same time, public school principals earned substantially more than private school principals did, high school principals earned more than elementary school principals did, and principals of larger schools tended to earn more (to a point).

There is one key exception to these problem-characteristic-salary relationships. Principals in public schools with a larger fraction of students enrolled in the free and reduced-price lunch programs earned *less* than did their counterparts in schools with a smaller proportion of such students, even though principals perceived these schools as "more problematic." In spite of this disconnect between problems and salary in schools with more students in these programs, however, we found no evidence that the principals in these schools had less experience. In other words, there is no evidence that experienced principals are fleeing schools that have more students enrolled in free and reduced-price lunch programs (i.e., more low-income students) for those that have fewer such students.

We found limited evidence of principal sorting. Elementary school principals in the public sector and combined school principals in the private sector had on average about one more year of experience as a principal than high school principals had. In view of the fact that principals' perceptions of problems were substantially worse in high schools, this raises the possibility that the higher salaries paid to high school principals are not high enough to compensate for the differences in working conditions relative to those in elementary or combined schools. Alternatively, the extra year of experience could simply reflect the fact that elementary school principals are more likely to move from teaching to the principalship without serving as assistant principals and thus have longer careers as principals.

We also found that when we controlled for observable school characteristics, principals who reported higher levels of school conflict problems tended to have less experience. This is consistent with a situation in which principals move from schools with more conflict to those with less as they gain more experience, or with a situation in which turnover is higher in schools with more conflict.[13]

Our analysis revealed a substantial amount of variation across states in terms of principals' salaries and experience. Simplistically, one might think that states where principals receive higher salaries than teachers do will have an easier time attracting teachers into the principalship. Similarly, one might think that states offering higher nominal salaries will have an easier time attracting school administrators from other states or from other career fields. It may be that a combination of factors—salary, salary ratio, labor market conditions, growth in the number of schools in the state, etc.—is influencing the relative experience level of principals in a particular state. We found no evidence that low-paying states have the least-experienced principals. Indeed, Nebraska and West Virginia, which offer some of the lowest principal salaries, had the most-experienced principals.

---

[13]Of course, since the problem measure reflects principals' perceptions, it is also possible that inexperienced principals simply perceive conflict problems as more severe.

Chapter Seven

CONCLUSIONS

Earlier chapters of this report covered our review of existing research and our analyses of data on school administrators, all of which were aimed at understanding the careers of administrators in K–12 schools. We presented an overview of the existing information on school administrators' characteristics; the moves into, through, and out of the school administrative field that people make; and the factors influencing those moves. We found little evidence of a nationwide crisis in the school administrator market. We did, however, find issues that may be of concern to policymakers.

AGING TRENDS MAY IMPLY SHORTER CAREERS IN SCHOOL ADMINISTRATION

Overall, it appears that school administration is a stable professional area experiencing neither tremendous growth nor tremendous decline. The national trends obscure some important regional variations, however, and high rates of growth in the number of school administrators suggest that strong demand may be putting pressure on labor markets in some western states.

Many policymakers are concerned about the impending retirement of a large proportion of current school administrators. Our analyses suggest that principals are indeed an aging group, but that school and district choices in hiring principals and the existing retirement programs may be contributing to this trend. Not only is the average age of principals increasing, but so is the average age of new principals (i.e., those who have three or fewer years of experience as a principal). At the same time, the prevalence of principals over age 55 has not changed. Taken together, these findings imply that new principals will spend fewer years in the principalship than previous new principals did before reaching retirement age. This is more of an issue in the public sector, where principals appear to be much less likely to remain on the job after 55.

Although the trends suggest that new principals will now have shorter careers, recent studies emphasize that schools and districts view administrative experience as a desirable quality and seek out experienced individuals to fill vacant school administrative positions.

ALTERNATIVE CAREER OPPORTUNITIES FOR SCHOOL ADMINISTRATORS ARE NEITHER MORE NOR LESS ATTRACTIVE THAN BEFORE

We found little evidence that labor market forces are having a negative impact on the attractiveness of school administration as a career option. In other words, we found no evidence of high or increased rates of exit to suggest that people are being lured away from school administrative positions by jobs in other sectors of the economy. We also found little evidence to support the idea that the incentives for school administrators to leave the education career field have changed in recent years. When we compared school administration to professional management options outside of education, we found no evidence that the real hourly wage of school administrators has changed relative to that of other professional managers over the years 1983 to 1999. In addition, we saw little evidence that school administrators are in fact leaving to take jobs in other sectors of the economy. Those who exited school administration typically left the labor force entirely or returned to teaching. On average, those leaving experienced a decrease in the average number of hours they worked per week and in their average wage. Thus, it does not appear that school administrators are being lured away from their positions by high-paying private-sector jobs.

PAY GAP BETWEEN ADMINISTRATIVE POSITIONS IN THE PUBLIC AND PRIVATE SECTORS IS SHRINKING

Although our analyses do not raise general concerns about the labor market conditions for school administrators, they do indicate that administrative salaries have increased more rapidly in private schools than in public schools over the past decade. As a result, public schools may be facing greater competition from private schools when trying to fill school administrative positions.

A key question for policymakers is whether this change in relative compensation has led more public school principals to move into the private sector. It is still true that public school principals earn substantially more than private school principals do. However, we also know that compared with public school principals, private school principals reported fewer problems in their schools. Our analyses suggest that movement of principals and other administrators between the public and private sectors is uncommon but does occur. As of 1994, transfers of principals and other administrators between the private and public sectors appeared to be roughly equal, rather than a mass exodus from the public to the private sector. However, private school principals were slightly more likely to move to the public sector than vice versa. We know that between 1988 and 2000, the average years of experience as a principal for current principals declined in public schools but increased in private schools. Unfortunately, the existing data did not allow us to examine trends in movement between the two sectors over time, or to specifically address the question of whether public school principals became more likely to leave for the private sector in the past decade. Thus, although the evidence raises concerns, we cannot, at a national level, address the question of whether the narrowing in the salary gap between public and private school principals has made administrative positions more attractive in the private sector than in the public sector.

TEACHING IS A GATEWAY TO SCHOOL ADMINISTRATION

Although there are many potential pathways to school administration, a vast majority of principals and superintendents begin their career as a teacher. Certainly, certification requirements play some role in the pervasiveness of this pattern. However, the fact that nearly 90 percent of private school principals—who are not subject to state certification requirements—have served as teachers suggests that such requirements are not the only reason schools tend to draw school administrators from the pool of teachers. Additional, informal barriers that discourage non-teachers may be embedded in the hiring process and the expectations of those reviewing résumés.

Because teaching is the main gateway to school administration, an understanding of the factors that encourage teachers to move into administrative positions and deter them from doing so is crucial. Certification requirements for administrators, which typically require certified teachers to obtain additional credits or degrees from an approved program, may pose a barrier to teachers and to people outside the education field.

Other professions may provide insight for the education sector as to how to manage career transitions from teaching to administration. Cultural barriers between managers and practitioners are common in organizations that rely on skilled technical professionals. Such organizations typically create a dual career track consisting of career advancement opportunities for those who move into management and for those who instead develop into highly experienced practitioners. Other structural barriers may exist as well, in the form of tenure and retirement systems.

A key issue is whether teachers have a financial incentive to move from teaching to school administration. Our analysis revealed that financial incentives generally do exist but are weak or nonexistent at certain individual schools. We found that on an adjusted annual basis, public school principals earned 33 percent more and private school principals earned 44 percent more than experienced teachers in the same school did. In the public sector, we found no evidence to suggest that the magnitude of the pay differential was related to observable school characteristics; in the private sector, we found that the pay differential for principals of Catholic and other religiously affiliated schools was less than that for principals of nonsectarian schools. When we compared the hourly wage of school administrators with that of teachers, we also found that administrators earned more.

Despite concerns to the contrary, there appears to be no shortage of people who are officially qualified to assume (i.e., are *certified* for) school administrative positions. Certainly, certification requirements may pose a barrier to people—particularly those with non-teaching backgrounds—who might be interested in becoming a principal. If this were a significant problem, the barrier could be removed or relaxed to ease the way for such people to join the pool of potential principals. So far, however, the certification data suggest that the number of people expending the extra effort needed to meet the certification requirements remains ample.

Finally, it is worth pointing out that while teaching is the gateway to school administration, only a small fraction of teachers need to move into school administration to ensure an adequate supply. The number of school administrators is less than 10 percent of the number of teachers.

THERE IS LITTLE EVIDENCE OF PRINCIPAL SORTING BASED ON OBSERVABLE SCHOOL CHARACTERISTICS

Our analysis suggests that a school's observable characteristics can serve as a useful proxy for the degree of problems in the school. It also revealed that principals at the types of schools that tend to have more problems (e.g., larger, more diverse high schools) tend to earn more money than do those at schools with fewer problems.

There is one important exception to the consistent relationships among school problems, school characteristics, and principals' salaries. In public schools, principals whose schools had a larger fraction of students enrolled in the free and reduced-price lunch programs (i.e., low-income students) earned *less* than did principals whose schools had a smaller proportion of such students, even though the schools with the larger fraction were perceived as "more problematic" by principals.

In spite of this disconnect between school problems and principals' salaries in schools with more low-income students, we found no evidence that the principals in these schools had less experience compared to other principals. In other words, there is no evidence that principals are fleeing low-income schools to go to high-income schools.

Our analysis of principals' experience revealed no evidence to support the idea that principals tend to move away from schools with certain observable characteristics as they gain more experience. In particular, we found no evidence that more-experienced principals were systematically choosing to work in suburban schools, schools with smaller enrollments, and schools with a smaller proportion of minority, low-income, or LEP students.

We did find (after controlling for observable school characteristics) that principals in schools with more reports of one type of problem—school conflict problems—did have less experience. We concluded that there is some relationship between principals' reports of school problems and observable school characteristics, but that there is also some variation in principals' perceptions of school conflict problems that is unexplained by the observable school characteristics.

There are at least two possible explanations for the relationship among principals' experience, school characteristics, and school problems. First, the market for school principals may be following the logic of the theory of compensating differentials, and the observed differences in the salaries offered by schools with different characteristics are adequately compensating principals for the added difficulty of the job that can be explained by the observable school characteristics. The fact that experienced principals are sorting out of schools with a high level of reported school conflict problems could reflect the fact that observable school characteristics do a poor job of predicting which schools have conflict problems, and hence compensation variation that is tied to observable school characteristics does not reward principals at conflict-ridden schools. Second, it may be that principals are assigned to positions and do not gain more leverage to choose where they work as they gain more experience. Both explanations are inconsistent with the notion that there is a crisis in the ability of schools to attract and retain principals.

FINANCIAL INCENTIVES TO ENTER AND LEAVE SCHOOL ADMINISTRATION DIFFER BY STATE

Overall, our analysis provided little evidence of a national crisis in terms of the characteristics of school administrators, moves into and out of administrative positions, and the incentives driving these moves. However, our results did reveal some important differences in financial incentives for principals across states.

Principals in some states fared differently than principals in other states did. In some states (such as Connecticut and New Jersey), principals were highly paid relative to both principals in other states and teachers in their own state. In other states (such as Hawaii, North Carolina, the Dakotas, and Wyoming), principals were poorly paid relative to principals in other states but well paid relative to teachers in their own state. Another type of difference (evident in Michigan) was that principals were well paid relative to principals in other states but poorly paid relative to teachers in their own state. Finally, in some states (West Virginia and Utah, for instance), principals were poorly paid relative to both principals in other states and teachers in their own state. These findings may be of interest to state policymakers when they are considering the results of this analysis vis-à-vis their own market conditions.

IN SPITE OF A STABLE NATIONAL PICTURE, INDIVIDUAL SCHOOLS AND DISTRICTS FACE CHALLENGES IN RECRUITING AND RETAINING SCHOOL ADMINISTRATORS

Our analysis focused on national and state averages and on systematic variation by school characteristic. Based on our results, we conclude that there is no national crisis and, indeed, no crisis generally facing certain types of schools (urban, low-income, etc.). However, it is important to keep in mind that the data revealed a significant amount of local variation. There are over 14,000 school districts and over 100,000 schools in the United States. In some of these, principals earned less than experienced teachers in the same school did. And in some of the schools, principals were in their first year on the job. Although we have no data on turnover at the school level, some schools are likely to be experiencing frequent turnover. However, our analysis suggests that such problems are decidedly local in nature. For example, we found that some urban, low-income schools were having trouble keeping experienced principals, whereas other such schools succeeded in retaining principals over long periods of time.

RECOMMENDATIONS AND AREAS FOR FUTURE STUDY

Our analysis provides no evidence to support the notion of a nationwide crisis in the ability of K–12 schools to attract and retain school administrators. It does, however, raise issues for policymakers and education administrators to consider.

Trends in the age and experience distribution of school principals suggest that public schools are hiring increasingly older people into the principalship and that relatively few principals remain in their positions beyond age 55. If experience is a desired characteristic for school principals, then policymakers should consider policies and programs to promote the entry of people into the principalship earlier in their career and/or to keep them in the job beyond age 55.

In view of recent increases in the compensation offered to private school administrators, as well as the decline in the experience of public school principals and the increase in the experience of private school principals, public policymakers should pay close attention to possible competition from the private sector. District administrators or state policymakers might try to identify a way to monitor, at a local and a regional level, movement of administrators between the public and private sectors and the relative salaries between the two sectors. One issue worth exploring in greater detail is the extent to which principals retire from the public sector at relatively early ages and then take jobs in the private sector. A more in-depth exploration of the relative working conditions in the private versus the public sector may be worthwhile as well, especially given the argument that private school principals accept lower pay because they value the greater job flexibility they have relative to public school principals.

A richer understanding of charter school principals might help policymakers appreciate the importance of such flexibility in attracting people into administrative positions. Charter school principals earn substantially less than their counterparts in other public schools do. We found that 49 percent of charter school principals had been principals at another school. Why are such people willing to accept the lower salaries offered by charter schools? Working conditions that relate to flexibility and control may be important to these individuals.

A key point of our analysis is that teaching is the main gateway to school administration. For the most part, tomorrow's administrators are today's teachers, a fact that has several important implications for policymakers to consider.

First, to attract high-quality administrators, one must attract high-quality potential administrators into the teaching pool. Second, changes in teachers' wages and working conditions can affect the incentives teachers have to move into administration. The spillover effect of teacher pay increases or class size reductions should be kept in mind. Third, teaching is the fundamental activity going on in schools, so while some teachers do need to be developed into administrators, most teachers will remain in the classroom for their entire career. A focus on school administration thus should not overlook the need to cultivate and reward experienced, expert teachers who remain in the classroom. Finally, seeing teaching as the main gateway to school administration may simply be a self-fulfilling prophecy. Formal barriers (such as certification requirements) and informal barriers (such as district hiring practices) all but exclude people with no teaching experience from consideration for administrative positions. If policymakers are serious about drawing people from outside of education into school administration, these barriers must be addressed.

To the extent that there are problems in the market for school administrators, they are local and idiosyncratic. This presents a challenge to policymakers because there is no easy target toward which to aim solutions. It does not appear that urban schools, low-income schools, and schools with a large number of LEP students are systematically having more trouble than suburban, high-income schools in this labor market. If we had observed such systematic trends, policy recommendations would be easier to craft. Instead, our analysis suggests that one must closely monitor local market conditions and personnel management practices in order to craft targeted solutions. While the primary monitoring burden will fall on district administrators, solutions to identified problems may require state-level intervention wherever an entire district cannot summon the resources to compete with neighboring districts or fails to adequately monitor or respond to local labor market conditions.

Finally, although our analysis revealed no evidence that schools with a high proportion of low-income students were having trouble attracting and retaining experienced principals, our findings on incentives suggest that this is an area for policymakers to monitor closely. Working conditions in such schools are harder, as measured by principals' reports of school problems, and salaries are lower. It may be that some schools and districts with a large proportion of low-income students do not have the resources to attract principals by compensating them financially for the more difficult working conditions. This issue may need to be addressed at the state level.

THERE IS STILL MUCH MORE TO BE LEARNED

Our review of the literature on the careers of school administrators indicated that there is still much to be learned. We were able to generate a useful set of information about administrative careers using the existing national data, but a greater understanding of these careers requires richer data.

One major item that limited our analysis was the lack of information on principal quality. Most companies and government organizations have performance review processes in which individuals are given a performance rating. Although such procedures may exist for school administrators in some schools and districts, the data are not available in any systematic way that makes them usable for research or comparison purposes. Other approaches to measuring principal quality are possible, but they pose important challenges. This area is worthy of future attention.

The existing literature and cross-sectional data focus on describing the current stock of school administrators and ignore career moves and the factors influencing those moves. A more thorough understanding of the flows and how they could be influenced by policy would be useful to policymakers and educational administrators.

We think that an analysis of state-level administrative data will provide the most useful insights on the career flow issues of school administrators. Such data allow one to examine the career choices that individuals make over time and the benefits they receive from those choices. As discussed earlier, SASS data suggest that administrative careers typically are constrained by state but not district boundaries. Moreover, states differ on important dimensions that restrict career flow and influence the demand for administrators.

Several states have longitudinal data on teachers and administrators that allow individuals to be tracked as they move from teaching through administrative positions in the state. Using individual-level data from a single state, one can track careers as people move across schools and districts. Note that a focus on states does not imply that school or district issues are irrelevant. Indeed, some important empirical observations related to these levels may emerge from such an analysis. For example, some districts or schools may be losing principals to other districts. Because state data include district and often school identifiers, career flows can also be considered from these perspectives within the context of a state-level analysis. An identification of districts to examine in greater depth would follow a preliminary state-level analysis. Such an analysis would begin to answer the flow questions posed earlier—the questions most relevant to policymakers. Finally, with a state-level analysis, the relationship between issues of compensation, working conditions, and turnover could be explored in greater detail.

GENERAL ANALYSIS OF SCHOOLS AND STAFFING SURVEY

The Schools and Staffing Survey (SASS) is a large-scale survey of a nationally representative sample of public and private school teachers and principals conducted by the National Center for Education Statistics (NCES) in the U.S. Department of Education. The survey asks questions ranging from basic demographic and salary information to career history information to attitudes toward job, school, and career. Table A.1 summarizes the types of information available from each survey that relate to career paths. There have been four surveys, each covering a specific school year: 1987–1988, 1990–1991, 1993–1994, and 1999–2000.

Table A.1

Schools and Staffing Survey (SASS) Data Availability on School Principals

✓ Public
✣ Private

	1987–88	1990–91	1993–94	1999–00
I. Demographics				
Age/year of birth, gender, race, Hispanic origin	✓✣	✓✣	✓✣	✓✣
II. Education				
Which of the following college degrees have you earned?	✓✣	✓✣	✓✣	
• Associate degree/vocational certificate				
• Bachelor's degree				
• 2nd bachelor's degree				
• Master's degree				
• 2nd master's degree				
• Professional diploma/ed specialist				
• Doctorate				
• First professional degree (JD, MD)				
Major field code				
Year received				
2nd major (minor) field of study			✓✣	
College or university of first bachelor's degree			✓✣	
Highest degree earned		✓✣	✓✣	✓✣
1. No degree				
2. Bachelor's				
3. Master's				
4. Professional/Ph.D.				
III. Teaching Experience				
Currently teaching in school in which you are currently serving as principal?			✓✣	✓✣

Table A.1 (continued)

	1987–88	1990–91	1993–94	1999–00
Years of elementary/secondary teaching	✓✛			
Years of elementary/secondary teaching PRIOR to becoming a principal		✓✛	✓✛	✓✛
Years of elementary/secondary teaching SINCE becoming a principal		✓✛	✓✛	✓✛
Total years of teaching experience	✓✛		✓	
Primary teaching assignment	✓✛	✓✛	✓✛	
Secondary teaching assignment	✓✛			
Teaching experience out of field				
IV. Non-Teaching Experience				
Before becoming a principal, what other positions did you hold? 1. Department head 2. Assistant principal/program director 3. Guidance counselor 4. Athletic coach 5. Sponsor for student club/debate team 6. Librarian/media specialist (93–94; 99–00) 7. Other (90–91; 93–94) 8. None of the above	✓✛	✓✛	✓✛	✓✛
Years as principal in this school	✓✛	✓✛	✓✛	✓✛
Years as principal in other schools	✓✛	✓✛	✓✛	✓✛
If you have served as a principal in other schools, which best describes the location in which you last served? • Served in same public school district • Served in different public school district in this state • Served in public school district in another state • Served in a private school • Other—specify			✓✛	
Which grade levels were served in the school in which you last served as principal?			✓✛	
Years of experience in: • Other school district/administration • Non-teaching, non-administrative position (in education) • Professional position outside of education	✓✛	✓✛		
Aside from college coursework for a degree, have you had any of the following types of training for your current position? • In-service training in evaluation and supervision • Training in management techniques • An administrative internship • None of the above	✓✛	✓✛	✓✛	
Prior to becoming an administrator, did you participate in any district or school training or development program for ASPIRING school administrators?		✓✛	✓✛	✓✛
How long do you plan to remain a principal? • As long as I am able • Until I am eligible to retire • Will probably continue unless something better comes along • Definitely plan to leave as soon as possible • Undecided at this time		✓✛	✓✛	
In how many years do you plan to retire from your position as a principal?		✓✛		

Table A.1 (continued)

	1987–88	1990–91	1993–94	1999–00
In which year will you be eligible to retire from your position as a principal?			✓✣	
In what year do you plan to retire?			✓✣	
How many breaks in service of more than one year have you had?			✓✣	
• Were any of these due to a reduction-in-force or layoff?				
• How long was your most recent?				
• How many consecutive years served as principal since most recent break?				
V. Salary and Benefits				
Annual salary (before taxes)	✓✣	✓✣	✓✣	✓✣
# months employed per year in this school	✓✣	✓✣	✓✣	
Benefits received in addition to salary	✓✣	✓✣	✓✣	
• Housing/housing expenses				
• Meals				
• Tuition for children				
• College tuition for yourself				
• Medical insurance				
• Dental insurance				
• Group life insurance				
• Transportation expenses				
• Pension contributions				
• Child care (93–94)				
• None of the above				
VI. Time Allocation				
For your most recent full week, what is your best estimate of the number of hours you spent on school-related activities during and after school hours?	✓✣			
• Administration				
• Curriculum matters				
• Teacher supervision/evaluation				
• Working w/teachers				
• Student discipline				
• Working w/students/teachers				
• Parent/community relations				
• Teaching classes				
• Preparing for classes				
• Fundraising/obtaining resources				
Total hrs/week spent on school-related activities	✓✣			
In the last month, how often did you engage in the following activities in your role as principal?				✓✣
• Facilitate achievement of school mission through activities such as consensus building, planning, obtaining resources, monitoring progress				
• Supervise/evaluate faculty				
• Guide development/evaluation of curriculum and instruction				
• Facilitate student learning (e.g., establish high expectations)				
• Provide and engage staff in PD activities				
• Build professional community				
• Develop public relations (parents, community members)				
• Maintain physical security of students/staff				

Table A.1 (continued)

	1987–88	1990–91	1993–94	1999–00
• Manage school facilities, resources, procedures • Attend district-level meetings, carry out district-level responsibilities [Excluded for private schools]				
VII. Professional Development for Principals In the last 12 months, have you participated in the following kinds of professional development? • University courses related to your role as principal • Visits to other schools designed to improve your own work as principal • Individual or collaborative research on a topic of interest to you professionally • Mentoring and/or peer observation and coaching of principals, as part of a formal arrangement recognized/supported by school or district • Participating in a principal network • Workshops or conferences related to your role as principal • Workshops or training in which you were the presenter • Attending professional association meetings				✓✣
VIII. Principal's Goals for School Which do you consider the most important; second most important; third most important? • Building basic literacy skills (reading, math, writing, speaking) • Encouraging academic excellence • Promoting occupational or vocational skills • Promoting good work habits and self-discipline • Promoting personal growth (self-esteem, self-knowledge, etc.) [For private schools this becomes: Fostering religious or spiritual development] • Promoting human relations skills • Promoting specific moral values • Promoting multicultural awareness or understanding		✓✣	✓✣	✓✣
IX. School Characteristics				
Percent minority students, percent minority teachers, enrollment (total and by grade level)	✓✣	✓✣	✓✣	✓✣
School program type 1. Regular 2. Montessori 3. Special program emphasis 4. Special education 5. Alternative 6. Vocational/technical 7. Other	✓✣	✓✣	✓✣	✓✣
Sector (public/private)	✓✣	✓✣	✓✣	✓✣
Religious affiliation [Private schools only] • Catholic—parochial • Catholic—Diocesan • Catholic—private • Other religious—Christian conservative • Other religious—affiliated • Other religious—unaffiliated • Nonsectarian—regular • Nonsectarian—special emphasis • Nonsectarian—special education	✣	✣	✣	✣

Table A.1 (continued)

	1987–88	1990–91	1993–94	1999–00
Highest annual tuition charged	✣	✣	✣	✣
Census region	✓✣	✓	✓✣	✓✣
• Northwest				
• Midwest				
• South				
• West				
Locale (community type)	✓✣	✓✣	✓✣	✓✣
• Large central city				
• Mid-sized central city				
• Urban fringe or large city				
• Urban fringe or mid-sized city				
• Large town				
• Small town				
• Rural				
X. School Site Councils/Governance				
Does this school have a decisionmaking body such as a school site council? [Public]				
Does this school have a decisionmaking body such as a school board? [Private]				✓✣
Are the following persons part of this decisionmaking body?				✓✣
• School principal				
• School vice principal/assistant principal				
• Teachers				
• Department heads				
• Students				
• Parents				
• Community representatives				
• Superintendent or other district representatives [For private schools this is: Diocesan or other governing institution representative]				
XI. School Performance Goals				
Has your district or state established school performance goals?				✓
Is your school required to meet district or state performance goals?				✓
Did your school meet the minimum goals?				✓
As a result of meeting goals, did your school:				✓
• Receive cash bonuses or additional resources that support schoolwide activities				
• Receive cash bonuses or additional resources to distribute to teachers				
• Receive non-monetary forms of recognition				
If it did not meet goals, was your school:				✓
• Required to write a school or program improvement plan				
• Put on an evaluation cycle with required targeted improvement dates				
• Provided with technical assistance from outside experts on how to improve				
• Provided with additional resources to support instructional improvement				
• Required to replace the principal with a new principal, an administrative director, or a manager				
• Subject to reconstitution or takeover regulations				
• Penalized by a reduction in state or district funding				
Does your school have a formal school improvement plan?				✓

Table A.1 (continued)

	1987–88	1990–91	1993–94	1999–00
Do you use any of the following to assess your school's progress on this plan? • State or national tests • Parent or student surveys • Portfolio products				✓
XII. School Problems For each of the following matters, indicate whether it is a serious problem, a moderate problem, a minor problem, or not a problem in your school: • Student tardiness • Student absenteeism • Teacher absenteeism • Students cutting class • Physical conflicts • Robbery/theft • Vandalism of school property • Student pregnancy • Student use of alcohol • Student drug abuse • Student possession of weapons • Physical abuse of teachers • Verbal abuse of teachers	✓✢	✓✢	✓✢	✓✢
For each of the following matters, indicate whether it is a serious problem, a moderate problem, a minor problem, or not a problem in your school: • Students dropping out • Student apathy • Student disrespect of teachers • Lack of academic challenge • Lack of parent involvement • Parent alcohol/drug abuse • Poverty • Racial tension • Cultural conflict In 93–94 and 99–00: • Students come to school unprepared to learn • Poor nutrition • Poor student health • Student problems with English language [Not in 99–00]		✓✢	✓✢	✓✢
XIII. School Progress On a scale from 1 to 5, where 1 is "Poor" and 5 is "Excellent," how would you rate the quality of the following? 1. All teachers in this school 2. Experienced teachers (3+ years of experience) 3. New teachers (<3 years)		✓✢		
How far along is your school in: • Implementing educational goals • Implementing organizational/governance goals • Establishing a secure financial base • Attracting and retaining students • Developing a student assessment system • Involving parents in the school				✓✢
XIV. School Staff Programs/Issues Does this school have a formal teacher evaluation program; program to help beginning teachers?	✓✢			

Table A.1 (continued)

	1987–88	1990–91	1993–94	1999–00
Indicate how much ACTUAL influence you think different groups or individuals have on decisions concerning the following activities [Note: groups and activities vary across survey waves]: Activities: I. Establishing curriculum II. Hiring new full-time teachers III. Setting discipline policy IV. Deciding how the budget will be spent V. Determining content of in-service programs VI. Evaluating teachers VII. Setting performance standards for students of this school Groups/individuals: • School district • Principal/head • Teachers • State department of education • School board or governing/diocesan board • Librarians/media specialists • Parent association • School district staff • Curriculum specialists • School site council • College/university partners	✓✣	✓✣	✓✣	✓✣
In general, how difficult was it to find qualified applicants to fill teaching vacancies for the 1987–88 school year?	✓✣			
Actions taken if unable to fill a vacancy with a full-time teacher	✓✣			
XV. Teacher Performance				
What percentage of faculty are presently teaching to high academic standards?				✓✣
Are the following barriers to dismissal of poor or incompetent teachers in this school? • Personnel policies • Termination decisions not upheld by 3rd party adjudicators • Inadequate teacher assessment documentation • Tenure • Teacher associations and organizations • Dismissal too stressful and uncomfortable for those involved				✓✣
XVI. Professional Development for Teachers				
How important are each of the following in determining the in-service professional development activities of teachers in this school? • Special state initiatives • District-level initiatives or improvement plans • School improvement plans • Implementation of state or local academic standards • Implementation of state or local skills standards • Teacher preferences				✓✣

Table A.1 (continued)

	1987–88	1990–91	1993–94	1999–00
For private schools: • Initiatives of your private school association or organization • School improvement plan • Implementation of academic standards • Teacher preferences				
How often is professional development for teachers at this school (always, frequently, sometimes, rarely, never): • Designed or chosen to support school improvement goals • Designed or chosen to support district improvement goals (not included for private schools) • Designed or chosen to support the implementation of state or local standards [For private schools this is: Designed or chosen to support the implementation of academic standards] • Evaluated for evidence of improvement in teacher classroom practice • Evaluated for evidence of effects on student achievement • Considered part of teachers' regular work • Planned by teachers in this school or district • Presented by teachers in this school or district • Accompanied by the resources that teachers need to make changes in the classroom (time and materials)				✓✣
In the last year, have you participated in professional development activities with teachers from your school?				✓✣
Does school provide professional development time for teachers during regular contract hours?				✓✣
Are the following used to provide teachers with time for professional development during regular contract hours? • Substitute teachers • Early dismissal or start for students • Professional days built in before beginning of school year • Professional days built in during school year • Common planning time for teachers • Reduced teacher workloads				✓✣
Does your school have its own budget for PD (amount of money that you control)?				✓

Fiore and Curtin (1997) provide an extensive descriptive overview of current principals based on their analysis of the 1987–1988, 1990–1991, and 1993–1994 surveys. They present detailed summary tables on principals' characteristics and attitudes, and a wide variety of cross-tabulations on the survey information. We report selected summary data here and refer the reader to Fiore and Curtin, 1997, for further details.

Gruber et al. (2002) provide a descriptive overview of the results of the 1999–2000 SASS, although their information on principals is limited. Here, in this appendix, we present the additional means and cross-tabulations that we find relevant to career issues. We analyzed the restricted-use data from each wave of the SASS. Unless noted otherwise, our analysis was conducted using SAS, and corrected standard errors were generated using SUDAAN.

CONSTRUCTED VARIABLES

In general, our summary and analyses rely on variables that either are included in the SASS or are straightforward manipulations of SASS variables (e.g., the square of enrollment). However, two variables that we constructed using the data deserve further attention.

First, we constructed a grade-level variable for each school based on its response to a question about which grade levels are served by the school. Each school in the sample is categorized into one of the following four school types: elementary, middle, high, and combined (schools that serve children of both elementary and middle school age or that serve children whose ages span the range from traditional elementary to traditional high school).

We also constructed a variable called the diversity index, which is a normalized index of integration for n groups, following White (1986). This index allows us to measure diversity in terms of the racial/ethnic balance of all subgroups, rather than just in terms of non-whites. For example, a school with 90 percent black students has a magnitude of 0.90 with the percent minority measure, a measure that reflects not diversity, but the proportion of minority students in the school. With the index of integration, however, this school gets a coefficient close to 0, meaning it is a very homogeneous, or low-diversity, school. In addition, whereas the percent minority variable does not distinguish between schools with different racial/ethnic mixes (e.g., a school that is 90 percent black and a school that is 40 percent black and 50 percent Hispanic are both 90 percent minority), the normalized integration index indicates just how balanced a school's racial subgroups are.

Research with management teams has empirically shown that highly homogeneous teams (almost all of one group) and highly heterogeneous, or diverse, teams (loosely defined as having no group much larger than any other) actually promote team cooperation and communication. Moderately heterogeneous, or unbalanced, teams (e.g., one-third from one country and two-thirds from another) are frequently hindered by conflict and non-cooperation (Earley and Mosakowski, 2000).

The normalized integration index is calculated as

$$I = n / (n - 1) \sum_{r=1}^{n} Q_r (1 - Q_r)$$

where Q_r is the fraction of the population of group r, and n is the number of groups.[1] The index I can thus be interpreted as "the probability that two members of the population chosen at random will be of different subpopulations" (White, 1986, p. 201). It is normalized by n so that it ranges from 0 to 1. The lowest value, 0, indicates that all members of the group are from the same racial/ethnic group—complete homogeneity. The highest value, 1, indicates that all groups are equally

---

[1]For example, if we have five racial/ethnic categories (say, white, black, Hispanic, Asian, and Native American), n will equal 5.

represented—complete heterogeneity. Mid-values indicate unevenness in the proportions of two or more racial/ethnic groups.

In Tables A.2 through A.6 and in the regression analysis in Appendix B, we make use of a concept called the "salary ratio," which reflects the pay gap between a principal and the experienced teachers in the same school. This can be loosely thought of as the pay premium principals receive relative to teachers in their school. To construct this ratio, we first calculate the average salary of teachers with 10 or more years of experience in the school. The ratio is then simply:

$$\text{Salary ratio} = (\text{principal salary} - \text{average experienced teacher salary}) / \text{average experienced teacher salary}$$

Higher values of the salary ratio imply a larger gap between the principal's and the average experienced teacher's salaries. A ratio of 0 suggests that the principal receives the same pay as the average experienced teacher; a ratio of 1 suggests that the principal receives twice the salary of the average experienced teacher. Negative values indicate that the principal earns less than the average experienced teacher at the same school.

It is important to emphasize that our definition averages the salaries of all teachers with 10 *or more* years of experience at a particular school. In other words, we are not comparing principals' salaries with those of teachers with exactly 10 years of experience. Indeed, the average number of years of experience among "experienced teachers" so defined is 21.5 for public schools and 21.0 for private schools. We considered many possible definitions of *experience*. In particular, we tried increasing the years of experience for teachers and including only teachers with a master's degree or higher in the comparison pool. However, as our definition grew more restrictive, we started losing a substantial number of observations, because many schools had no teachers who fit the more restrictive definitions.

The teacher salary information from the SASS does not include additional pay teachers may receive for supplemental activities, such as coaching, tutoring, or moonlighting. In addition, we know that principals typically work more hours per day and more days per year than teachers do. Although we have no basis for adjusting salary based on hours worked per day, previous waves of the SASS did ask principals for information on the length (in months per year) of their contract. However, this question was dropped from the 1999–2000 SASS. We discuss the issue of contract length in greater detail in Appendix B, but note here that the salary ratio information we present in this report is not adjusted for differences in contract length. We were able to make this adjustment using 1993–1994 SASS data for public school principals and teachers only. What we found was that it reduced the average salary ratio from 0.50 to 0.35.

Overview Tables

Tables A.2 through A.6 summarize information on principals that is discussed in the main body of the report. Sample means are given in all tables, with corrected standard errors (generated using SUDAAN) in parentheses. "New" principals are defined as those with three or fewer years of experience as a principal. School grade level categories are defined as follows: elementary schools are those whose highest grade is less than or equal to grade 6; middle schools are those whose lowest grade is 5, 6, or 7 and whose highest grade is 7 through 10; high schools are those whose lowest grade is greater than 5 and whose highest grade is 11 or 12; and combined schools are those whose lowest grade is less than 5 and whose highest grade is 7 or above.

AGE OF PRINCIPALS

The main body of the report presents age distribution charts in which the percentage of principals who are a certain age is on the y axis and age is on the x axis. Here, we present cumulative age distribution charts, which are slightly more complicated to read than the others but convey more information. These charts, shown as Figures A.1 through A.4, plot the percentage of all principals who are a given age or younger. The difference between the cumulative distributions at any two age points tells the percentage of all principals who fall in that age range. So, for example, Figure A.1 reflects the fact that 63 percent of all public school principals are 50 or younger, 85 percent are 55 or younger, and therefore 22 percent (85 minus 63) are between 51 and 55. Places where the curve is steep reflect age ranges in which principals are concentrated. Places where the curve is flat reflect age ranges in which there are relatively few principals.

Table A.2

Description of All School Principals, 1987–1988 Through 1999–2000

	Public School				Private School			
	87–88	90–91	93–94	99–00	87–88	90–91	93–94	99–00
Number of principals	77,890	78,890	79,618	83,909	25,401	23,881	25,015	26,231
Average age	47.8	48.3	48.7	49.3	46	47.4	48.1	49.9
	(0.1)	(0.1)	(0.1)	(0.1)	(0.2)	(0.2)	(0.3)	(0.2)
Average annual salary ($)[a]	61,100	62,714	63,742	66,487	29,951	32,318	34,526	41,656
	(151)	(157)	(148)	(158)	(630)	(558)	(458)	(564)
Average contract length (months)[b]	11.1	11.2	11.2	n/a	11.3	11.4	11.4	n/a
	(0.1)	(0.1)	(0.1)		(0.3)	(0.4)	(0.2)	
Average years of experience as principal	10.0	9.3	8.7	9.0	8.0	8.7	7.8	10.2
	(0.1)	(0.1)	(0.1)	(0.1)	(0.2)	(0.2)	(0.2)	(0.2)
Percent women	24.6	30.0	34.5	43.7	52.0	51.3	53.6	54.6
	(0.5)	(0.7)	(0.7)	(0.7)	(1.4)	(1.2)	(1.1)	(1.1)
Percent minority	13.4	14.1	15.7	17.8	7.0	6.3	7.5	11.1
	(0.4)	(0.5)	(0.5)	(0.6)	(0.9)	(0.7)	(0.7)	(0.8)

SOURCE: SASS.

[a]In real 2000 dollars.

[b]The 1999–2000 SASS did not ask principals to report.

Table A.3

Description of All School Principals, 1999–2000

	Public Schools	Charter Schools	Private Schools
Number of principals	83,909	988	26,231
Average age	49.3	48.3	49.9
	(0.1)	(0.1)	(0.2)
Average annual salary ($)[a]	66,487	53,920	41,656
	(158)	(281)	(564)
Average years of experience as principal	9.0	6.9	10.2
	(0.1)	(0.1)	(0.2)
Average years of teaching experience	14.0	12.1	14.5
	(0.1)	(0.1)	(0.2)
Average unadjusted salary ratio	0.52	0.49	0.63
	(0.01)	(0.02)	(0.03)
Percent new principals	29.9	48.4	28.8
	(0.6)	(0.7)	(1.2)
Percent first-time principals	48.2	51.0	61.6
	(0.7)	(0.8)	(1.1)
Percent women	43.7	54.0	54.6
	(0.7)	(0.8)	(1.1)
Percent minority	17.8	29.4	11.1
	(0.6)	(0.5)	(0.8)

SOURCE: SASS.
[a]In real 2000 dollars.

Table A.4

Description of Public School Principals, by Grade Level, 1999–2000

	Elementary	Middle	High	Combined
Number of principals	48,901	11,460	16,868	6,446
Average age	49.5	48.6	49.1	49.3
	(0.1)	(0.2)	(0.1)	(0.4)
Average annual salary ($)[a]	66,235	67,208	68,319	62,179
	(228)	(467.4)	(289)	(906)
Average years of experience as principal	9.3	8.2	8.5	9.1
	(0.2)	(0.3)	(0.1)	(0.4)
Average years of teaching experience	14.2	13.6	13.9	13.7
	(0.1)	(0.2)	(0.2)	(0.3)
Average unadjusted salary ratio	0.48	0.54	0.61	0.52
	(0.01)	(0.01)	(0.01)	(0.02)
Percent new principals	28.5	34.5	30.7	30.9
	(0.9)	(1.6)	(0.8)	(2.1)
Percent women	55.0	31.4	21.3	40.0
	(1.0)	(1.5)	(0.9)	(2.1)
Percent minority	18.7	16.4	14.2	22.5
	(0.8)	(1.1)	(0.7)	(2.6)

SOURCE: SASS.
[a]In real 2000 dollars.

Table A.5

Description of Private School Principals, by Grade Level, 1999–2000

	Elementary	Middle	High	Combined
Number of principals	8,306	274	2,602	15,050
Average age	49.7	58.0	49.8	49.8
	(0.4)	(1.7)	(0.5)	(0.3)
Average annual salary ($)[a]	41,876	33,559	54,446	39,470
	(1,342)	(10,111)	(1,564)	(597)
Average years of experience as principal	10.1	10.0	9.6	10.4
	(0.4)	(2.4)	(0.4)	(0.2)
Average years of teaching experience	13.6	18.3	16.6	14.6
	(0.5)	(3.6)	(0.4)	(0.3)
Average unadjusted salary ratio	0.62	0.39	0.77	0.60
	(0.1)	(0.6)	(0.03)	(0.05)
Percent new principals	30.0	9.0	25.8	28.9
	(2.3)	(5.0)	(2.4)	(1.4)
Percent women	67.0	24.9	37.9	51.2
	(2.1)	(11.0)	(3.5)	(1.2)
Percent minority	15.8	21.3	4.9	9.4
	(1.9)	(13.1)	(1.5)	(0.9)

SOURCE: SASS.
[a]In real 2000 dollars.

Table A.6

Description of New School Principals, 1987–1988 Through 1999–2000

	Public School				Private School			
	87–88	90–91	93–94	99–00	87–88	90–91	93–94	99–00
Number of principals	19,749	22,335	24,445	25,115	8,397	7,590	8,268	7,540
Average age	43.1	44.0	45.4	45.7	42.5	42.3	42.9	44.1
	(0.2)	(0.2)	(0.2)	(0.2)	(0.5)	(0.5)	(0.5)	(0.5)
Average annual salary ($)[a]	56,777	59,207	61,105	62,772	25,763	29,536	30,753	36,839
	(392)	(330)	(334)	(327)	(865)	(1,185)	(959)	(854)
Percent women	40.6	45.0	47.5	53.9	53.7	51.2	56.1	59.7
	(1.4)	(1.4)	(1.3)	(1.2)	(2.6)	(2.4)	(2.5)	(2.1)
Percent minority	15.6	16.2	18.2	20.5	6.6	5.2	6.9	14.1
	(0.8)	(1.1)	(1.0)	(1.1)	(1.2)	(1.0)	(1.1)	(1.8)

SOURCE: SASS.
[a]In real 2000 dollars.

Figure A.1 presents private and public sector cumulative age distributions for 1999–2000. This figure illustrates a striking difference between the age distributions of public and private school teachers. The private school line has a much more consistent slope, indicating that private school principals are more evenly distributed across the entire age range. A higher proportion of public school principals are between the ages of 46 and 55. The private sector has a much higher proportion

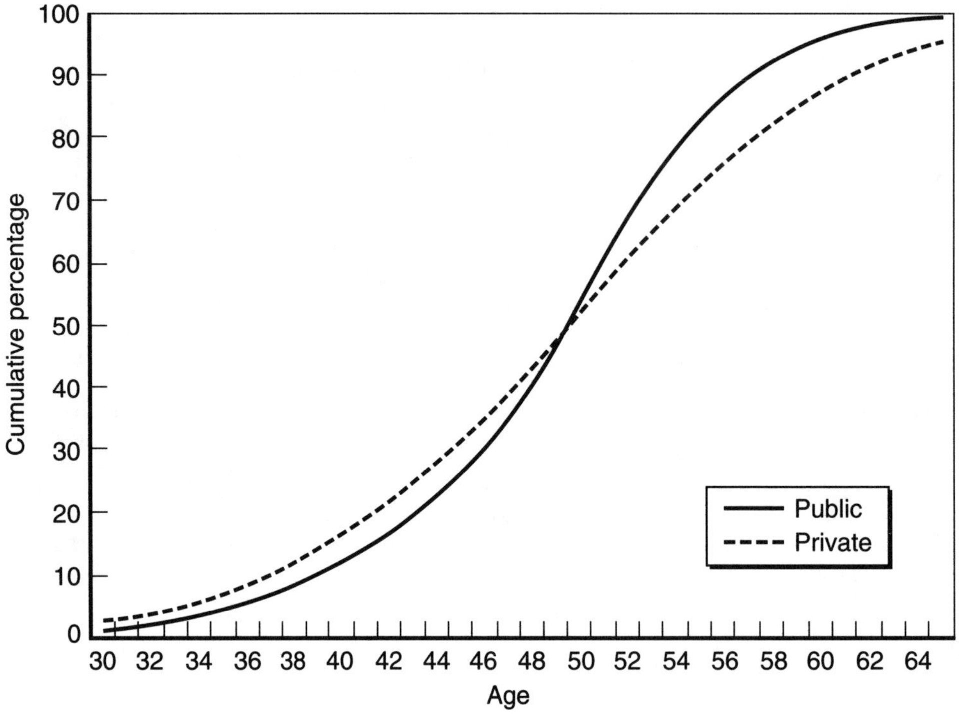

Figure A.1—Cumulative Age Distribution of Public and Private School Principals, 1999–2000

of principals over age 55. Whereas 28 percent of private school principals are over age 55, only 17 percent of public school principals are.

Figures A.2 and A.3 show that the age profiles of both public and private school principals shifted between 1987–1988 and 1999–2000. In the public sector, the shift increased the concentration of principals in the 46 to 55 range (as evidenced by the line getting steeper in that age range) and diminished the representation of younger individuals, particularly those between 40 and 45. In the private sector, similar shifts diminished the representation of younger individuals.

Part of the shift in the overall age distribution of principals can be explained by a shift in the distribution of new principals. As illustrated by Figure A.4, between 1987–1988 and 1999–2000, the proportion of new principals under 40, 45, and even 50 years of age decreased markedly in the public sector. Whereas 67 percent of new public school principals in 1987–1988 were 45 or younger, by 1999–2000 only 44 percent of new public school principals were. A similar, but much less dramatic shift occurred in the age distribution of new private school principals. In 1987–1988, 67 percent of them were 45 or younger; by 1999–2000, 57 percent were.

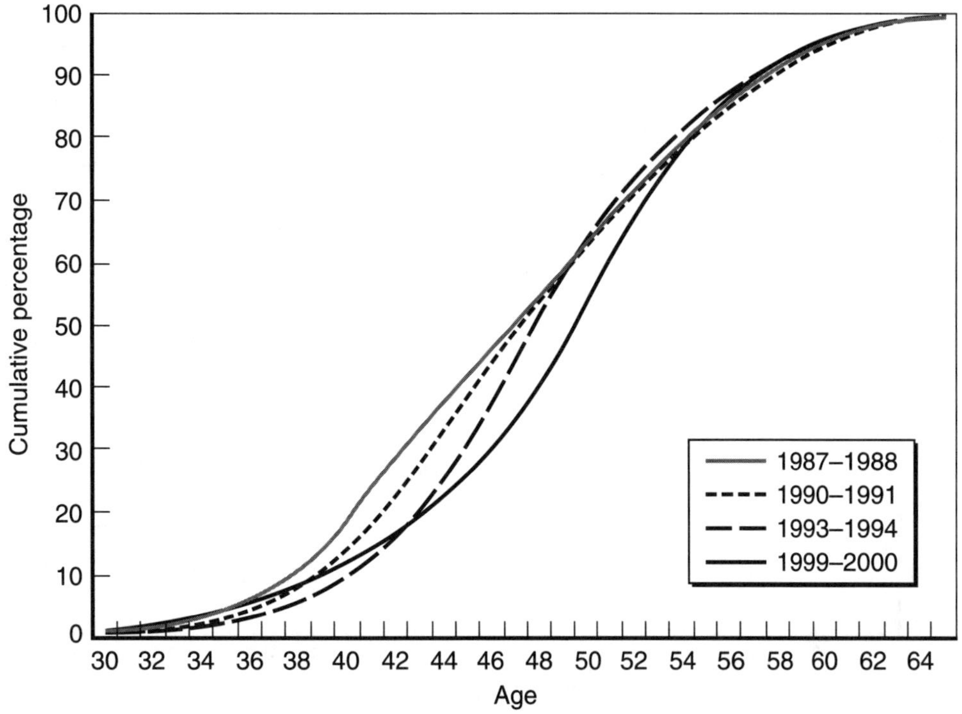

Figure A.2—Cumulative Age Distribution of Public School Principals, 1987–1988 Through 1999–2000

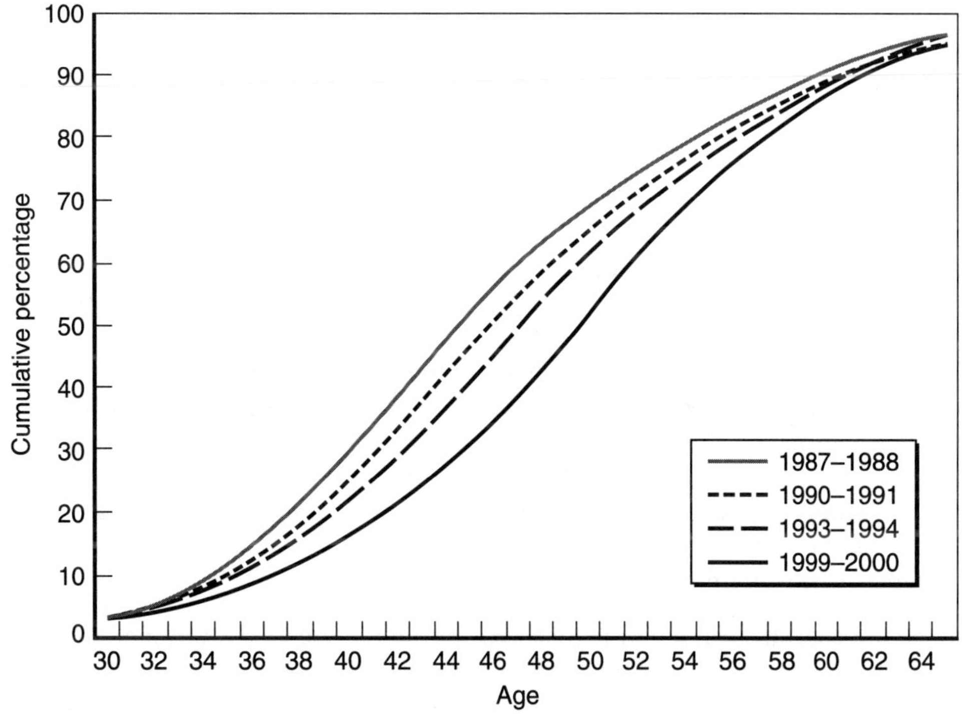

Figure A.3—Cumulative Age Distribution of Private School Principals, 1987–1988 Through 1999–2000

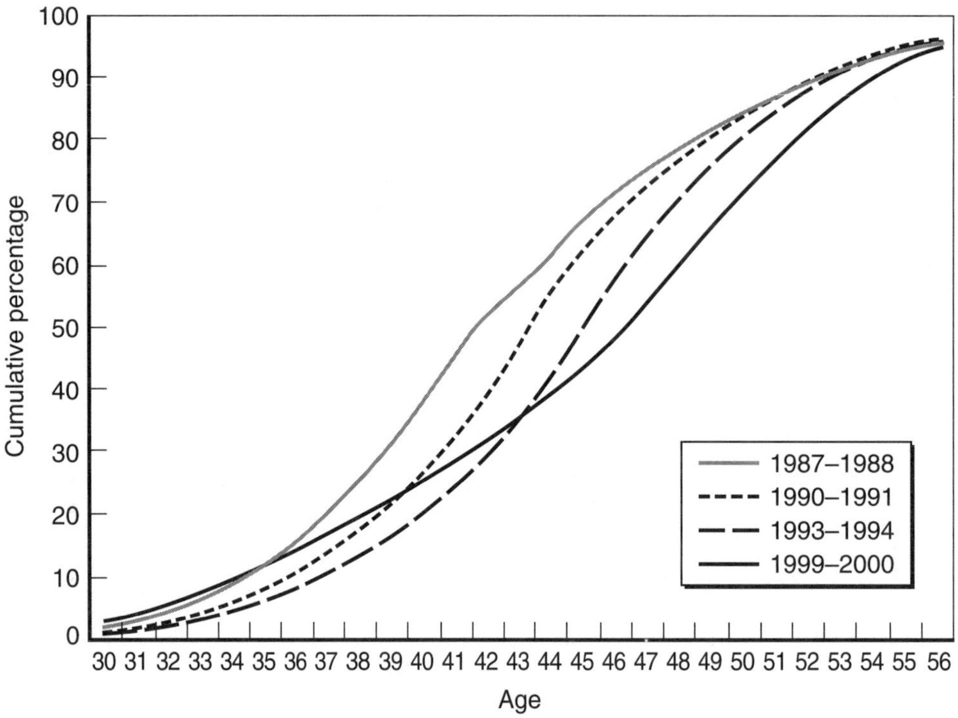

Figure A.4—Cumulative Age Distribution of New Public School Principals, 1987–1988 Through 1999–2000

EXPERIENCE OF PRINCIPALS

Information on the distribution of principals' experience as a principal reveals different trends for the public and private sectors, as shown in Figures A.5, A.6, and A.7.

As reflected in Table A.1 (see above), since 1988 the average experience of principals has decreased in the public sector and increased in the private sector. In addition, the distribution of experience among public school principals has not changed much since 1987–1988 (see Figure A.5), whereas private school principals have become more experienced, as evidenced by the consistent shift to the lower right in Figure A.6. This suggests that among public school principals, the increase in age does not stem from a tendency of these principals to stay on the job longer, but, rather, that the increase in age has brought with it an increase in experience. The proportion of public school principals with more than 10 years of experience as principals decreased from 38 percent in 1987–1988 to 30 percent in 1999–2000 (see Figure A.5). Meanwhile, the proportion of private school principals with more than 10 years of experience increased from 25 to 38 percent (see Figure A.6).

Overall, the data suggest that principals are an aging population. Although the public and private sectors are both witnessing the age increase (see Figure A.7), it appears to take different forms in the two sectors. Importantly, private, but not public, schools have experienced a concurrent increase in experience levels. It

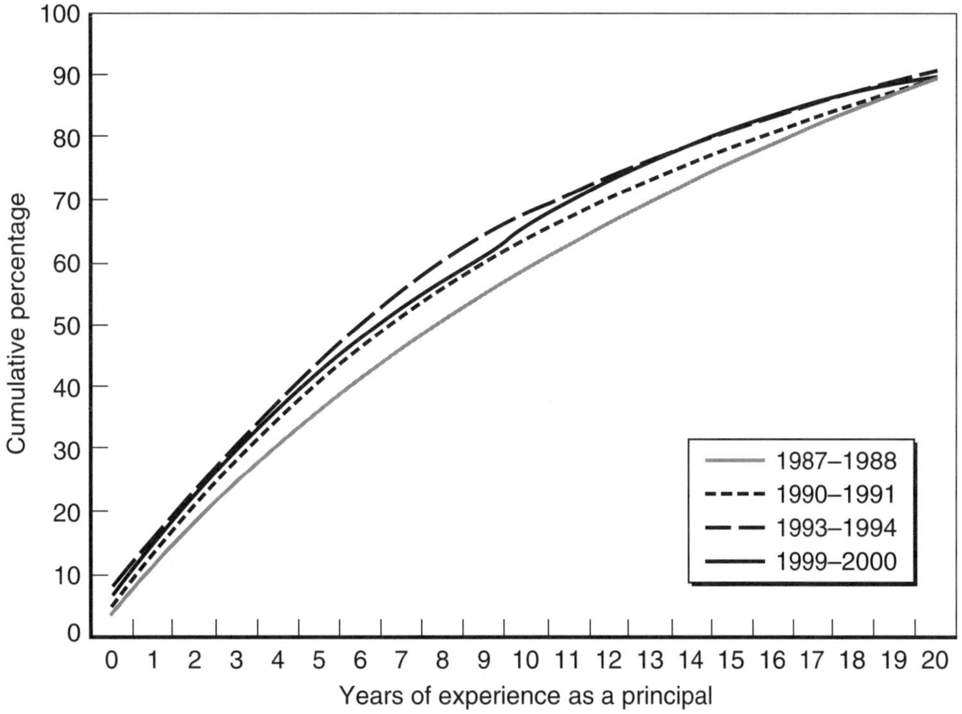

Figure A.5—Experience Distribution of Public School Principals, 1987–1988 Through 1999–2000

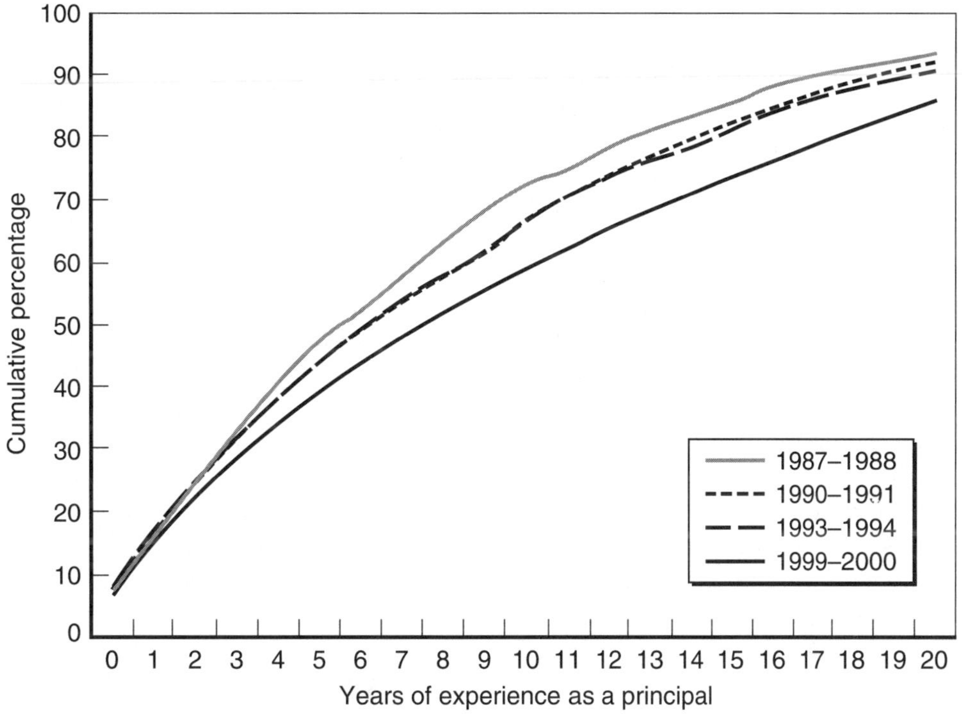

Figure A.6—Experience Distribution of Private School Principals, 1987–1988 Through 1999–2000

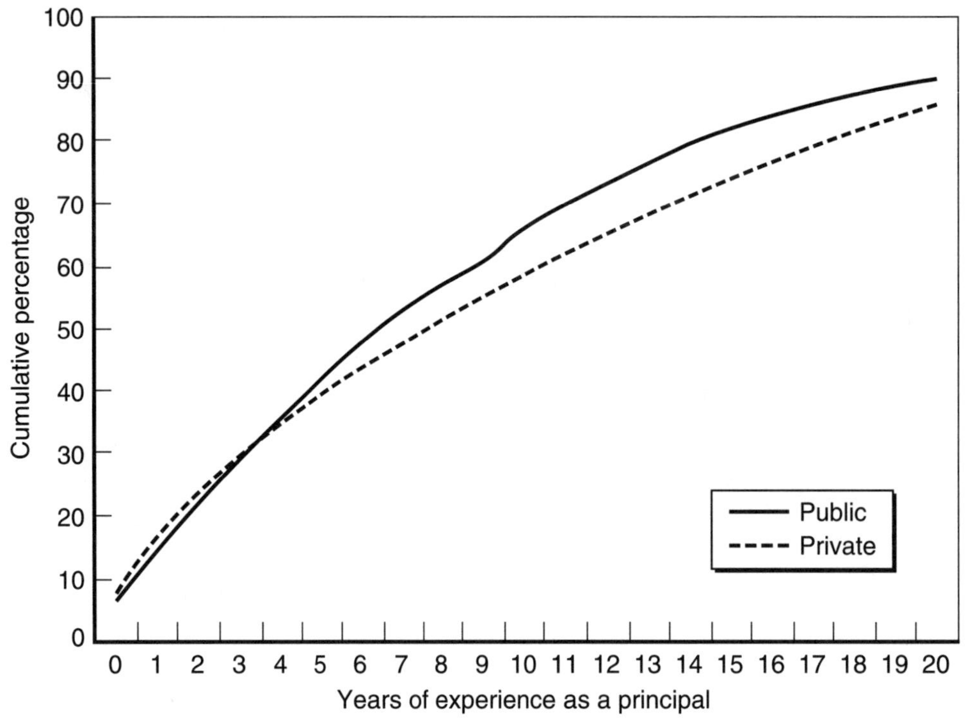

Figure A.7—Experience Distribution of Public and Private School Principals, 1999–2000

appears that both public and private schools are hiring new principals at increasingly older ages. In the public sector, principals still tend not to stay much beyond age 55, suggesting that they have shorter careers. In the private sector, however, it is far more common for principals to stay to age 60 or 65.

In an analysis of data on New York public school principals, Papa, Lankford, and Wyckoff (2002) found trends that were similar but have only continued since 1994. As of 2000, the average age of principals in New York state was nearly 51. The proportion of principals over 55 was nearly 20 percent, while the proportion over 50 was almost 60 percent. The authors show that the age distribution in New York shifted dramatically after 1990, and that principals were, as a whole, much older in 2000 than they were 10 years earlier. The same is true of first-time principals in New York. Comparing first-time principals in 1999–2000 with first-time principals in 1989–1990, the authors found that the average age of first-time principals was substantially higher (47 versus 43), and that the number of years of total experience was lower by two years. The age distribution of first-time principals shifted dramatically as well. The modal age of new principals was 43 in 1990 and 53 in 2000, and 66 percent of first-time principals were 50 or older.

THE MOVES PRINCIPALS MAKE

The 1993–1994 SASS asked principals who had held more than one principalship to characterize the school in which they previously served according to its highest grade level and whether it was private or public, within state or out of state, and within or outside of the district.[2] Forty-nine percent of public school principals and 37 percent of private school principals fell into this category.

The answers to these questions can shed some light on the moves that principals make during their careers as principals.[3] Of course, it is important to keep in mind that a majority of principals in both public and private schools have served as principal in only one school and thus are not included in our analysis.

The results of our examination of these answers for public and private school principals are described in Figure A.8. As the figure shows, most public school principals did not move very far for their most recent job change. Ninety percent remained in the same state, and 60 percent moved between schools in the same district. Seven percent moved from a public school in another state, and only 2 percent moved from a private school.

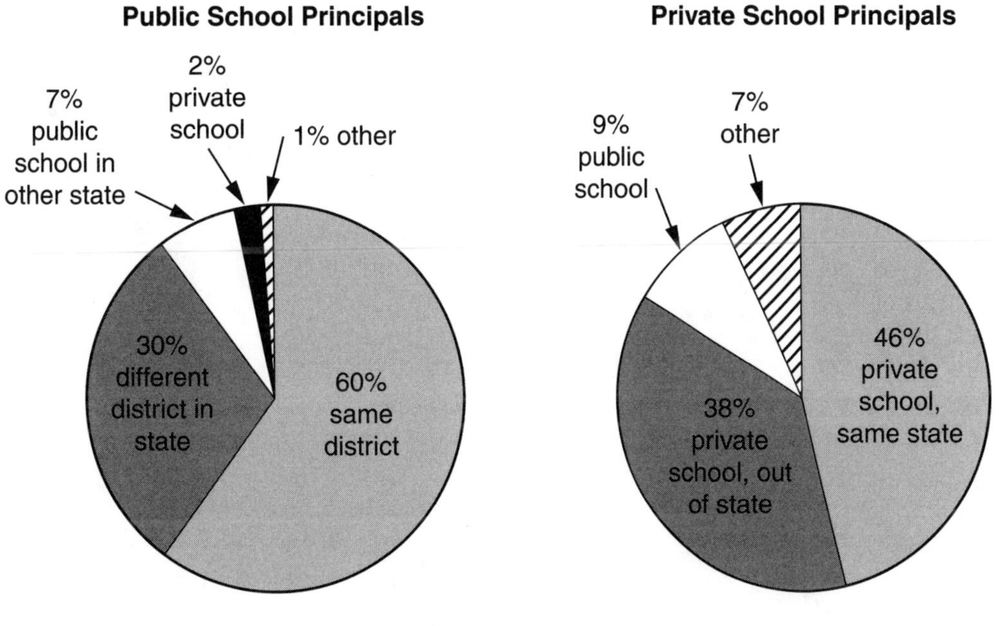

Figure A.8—Location of Previous Principalship for Public and Private School Principals Who Had Held More Than One Principalship

[2]It is worth noting that these questions were omitted from the 1999–2000 SASS.

[3]Unfortunately, the survey does not ask about the size of the previous school. We also do not know the total number of principalships an individual has held, so the responses may represent moves from the first to the second principalship or from the tenth to the eleventh.

The moves made by private school principals look different, however. Nearly half of the private school principals moved from a private school in the same state, while 38 percent moved across state lines for the new job. Nine percent came from a public school principalship.[4]

Among both public and private principals, a vast majority (70 percent) moved to schools serving the same grade levels, as illustrated in Figure A.9. Movement to a school serving lower grades (e.g., from a high school to a middle or elementary school) was more common among public school principals, and movement to a school serving higher grades was more common among private school principals.

In the case of private school moves, over 60 percent were from one combined school to another, 6 percent were from one high school to another, and 6 percent were from one elementary to another. The patterns are similar for both in-state and out-of-state moves between private schools.

Figure A.10 focuses on the moves made by public school principals, distinguishing between within-district and between-district moves. In both cases, most moves kept principals in a school serving the same grade levels. As indicated, most of the within-district public school moves involved a move from one elementary school to another.

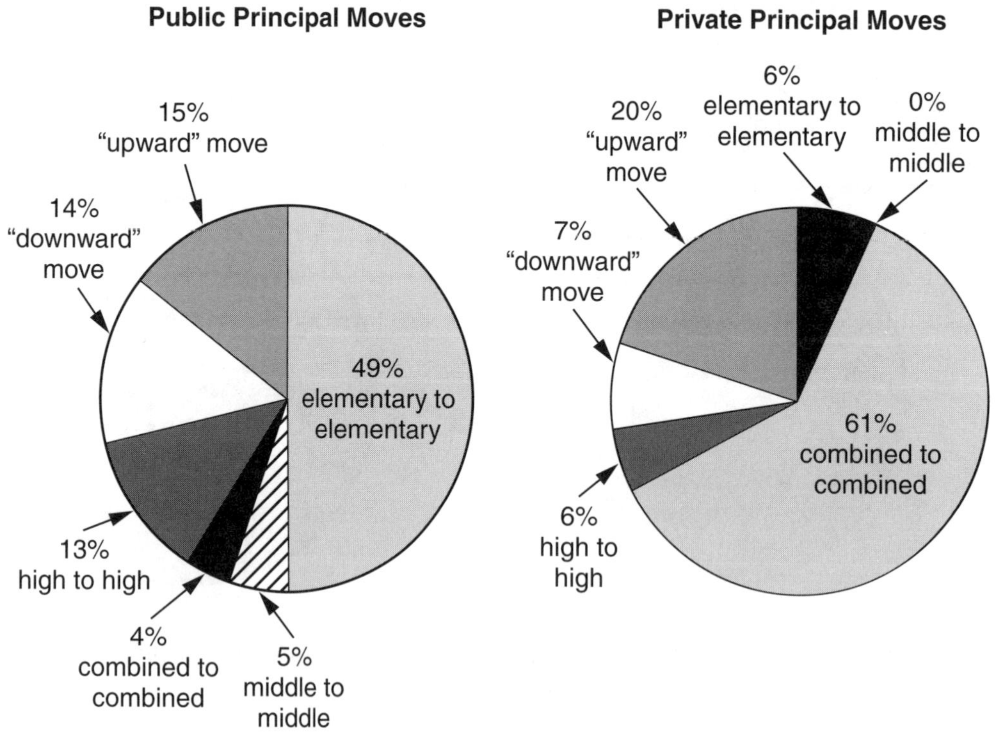

Figure A.9—Public and Private School Principals' Moves

[4]The survey did not ask whether the public school was in the same state.

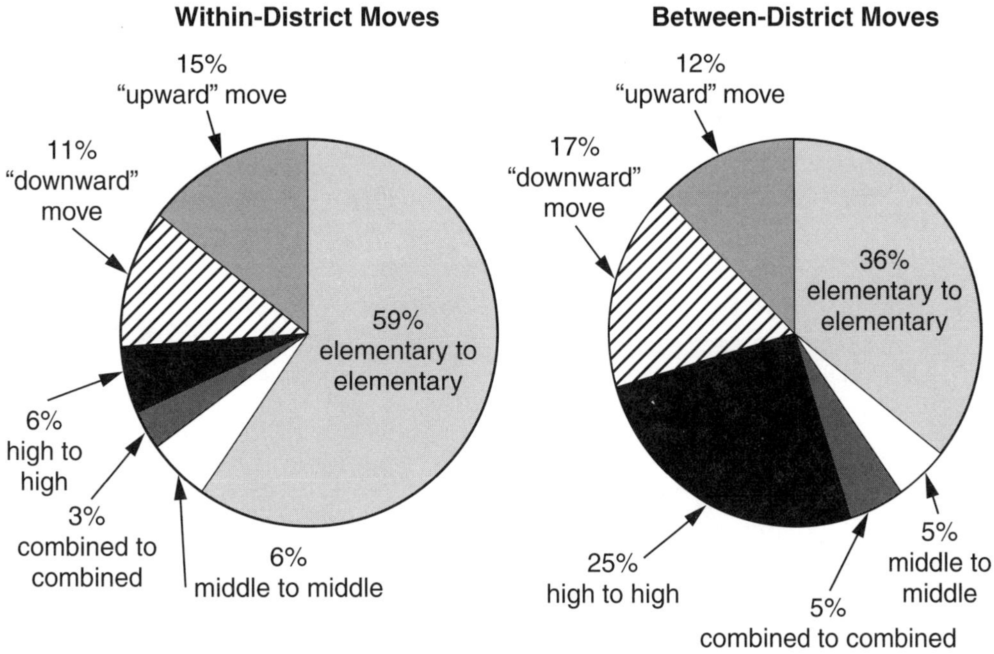

Figure A.10—Public School Within-District and Between-District Moves

Moves between districts were more evenly divided among grade levels, suggesting that some principals must move to another district if they are seeking a new principalship at higher grade levels.

This simple examination of principals' moves suggests several interesting features of principals' careers. First, labor mobility across state lines is low for public school principals but moderate for private school principals. Indeed, experienced public school principals are most likely to have moved from a school in their current district. Second, mobility between the public and private sectors appears to be limited. To the extent that such mobility exists, principals appear more likely to move from the public to the private sector than the other way around. Third, principals who change jobs are likely to move to a school serving the same grade levels—that is, there appears to be limited mobility across school type defined in this way.

An examination of principals' moves by gender reveals less mobility among female principals. For example, of the female public school principals who moved, 70 percent stayed in the same public school district, compared with 57 percent of their male counterparts who moved. Among female private school principals who moved, 54 percent moved from a private school in the same state, compared with 37 percent of their male counterparts. Fourteen percent of male private school principals who moved came from a private school in a different state, while only 5 percent of female private school principals did.[5]

[5] All of these differences are statistically significant at the 5 percent level.

Appendix B

ANALYSES OF SCHOOLS AND STAFFING SURVEY DATA ON PRINCIPALS' EARNINGS AND EXPERIENCE

This appendix presents the results of regression analyses we conducted, using the Schools and Staffing Survey (SASS) data described in Appendix A, to shed light on important questions:

- Do certain types of principals at certain types of schools earn more than others?
- Is the pay gap between principals and teachers larger at certain types of schools or for principals with certain characteristics?
- Do experienced principals gravitate toward certain types of schools?

We conducted three sets of regression analyses. In the first one, we examined the relationship between school and individual principal characteristics and the salary of the principal. In the second, we explored the relationship between those characteristics and the salary differential between principals and teachers. In the third, we looked at the relationship between school characteristics and a principal's experience.

Within these three sets of analyses, we generated separate parameter estimates for public and private schools using three waves of SASS results: 1990–1991, 1993–1994, and 1999–2000. We also ran separate models by gender and racial/ethnic group of the principal to examine whether the relationships were the same for these groups. Not all details of the regression analyses are presented here; instead, we present detailed results for 1999–2000 and discuss important differences between these results and those for the 1993–1994 SASS data.[1]

For each analysis described here, we used SAS with the SUDAAN statistical software package, using Balance Repeated Replication (BRR) techniques to produce correct standard errors.[2]

[1]Additional details and regression results are available from the authors upon request.

[2]SPSS and SAS are inappropriate for complex survey data, because they assume independent, identically distributed observations or simple random sampling with replacement. That is why, for SASS data, NCES recommends using software packages that can estimate variances with complex survey data using specialized methods such as Taylor linearization and replication (NCES, 2000).

CONTRACT LENGTH FOR 1999–2000 SASS WAVE

Although earlier SASS waves asked principals to report their annual salary and the number of months per year they were employed in their position, the 1999–2000 survey did not include the second question. As a result, it is not possible to adjust principals' salaries to account for the length of their contracts. From an analytical perspective, it is preferable to adjust annual salary for the number of months employed, since a person paid $50,000 for 10 months of work is receiving a higher effective salary than someone paid $50,000 for 12 months of work.

To analyze the link between observable school characteristics and principals' contract lengths, we specified the following equation:

$$PCONLEN_j = \alpha + \beta S_j + \varepsilon_j \tag{B.1}$$

where j = the school, and the dependent variable, PCONLEN, is the contract length of the principal. S is a vector of the school's observable characteristics (such as percentage of students eligible for free and reduced-price lunch programs, percentage of minority enrollment, urbanicity, school type, and school size). An analysis of principals' contract lengths suggests that they vary systematically by state, grade level served by the school, and urbanicity and other school characteristics for both public and private schools (see Tables B.1 and B.2). Elementary school principals had the shortest contracts; high school principals had the longest. Compared with elementary school principals of similar schools, public high school principals worked two-thirds of a month longer, and private high school principals worked about one-quarter of a month longer. Enrollment had a nonlinear relationship with contract length. Larger schools had longer contracts up to enrollment levels of just over 1,640 for public schools and 81 for private schools;[3] beyond that, contract length declined with enrollment. Bureau of Indian Affairs (BIA) schools had longer contracts, by a little over one-half of a month. Rural principals had slightly shorter contracts (by 0.1 month) compared with urban principals. Principals in certain states (e.g., Alaska, Hawaii, Idaho) had substantially shorter contracts than did principals in other states (e.g., North Carolina, Virginia, Maryland) and the District of Columbia. Of the private schools, the religiously affiliated ones tended to have shorter contracts.

Because of these relationships, we were concerned that an analysis of unadjusted salary information would yield skewed results. Obviously, it would be preferable to know the number of months per year each principal was employed, and we hope that this question will be included in future waves of the SASS. Here, we report only the regression results that utilize adjusted salary figures, with the adjustment for 1999–2000 based on imputed contract length. However, we did run the same analyses on salary and salary ratio using unadjusted salary figures as well. We adjusted the salary data by imputing a contract length for principals in the 1999–2000 survey wave

---

[3]A principal of a public school with this level of enrollment had a contract length about one-half of a month longer than that of a principal in a very small school; the relationship for private schools was very small.

Table B.1

Regression Results of Public School Characteristics on Contract Length, 1993–1994

Variable Name	Parameter Estimate	Standard Error
INTERCEPT	11.13[a]	0.09
ELEMENT	–0.38[a]	0.03
MIDDLE	–0.18[a]	0.03
COMBINED	–0.15[a]	0.04
ENROL	0.0067[a]	0.0008
ENRSQ	–0.000020[a]	0.000003
PCTLUNCH	0.0002	0.0015
PCTLEP	0.002	0.001
PCMINENR	0.006	0.006
PCTMINSQ	–0.00007	0.00005
DIVINDEX	0.09	0.28
DIVINDSQ	–0.36[b]	0.21
RURAL	0.13[a]	0.04
SUBURBAN	0.11[a]	0.04
ALABAMA	0.19	0.09
ALASKA	–1.15	0.09
ARIZONA	0.10	0.10
ARKANSAS	0.36	0.07
COLORADO	–0.62	0.08
CONNECTICUT	0.35	0.08
DELAWARE	0.60	0.07
DC	1.03	0.09
FLORIDA	0.60	0.06
GEORGIA	0.10	0.08
HAWAII	–1.12	0.08
IDAHO	–0.98	0.10
ILLINOIS	–0.07	0.08
INDIANA	–0.39	0.11
IOWA	–0.25	0.08
KANSAS	–0.46	0.08
KENTUCKY	0.25	0.09
LOUISIANA	–0.30	0.09
MAINE	0.02	0.13
MARYLAND	0.68	0.07
MASSACHUSETTS	0.04	0.09
MICHIGAN	–0.45	0.11
MINNESOTA	–0.37	0.10
MISSISSIPPI	0.03	0.09
MISSOURI	–0.22	0.09
MONTANA	–0.51	0.10
NEBRASKA	–0.62	0.09
NEVADA	–0.23	0.07
NEW HAMPSHIRE	0.33	0.11
NEW JERSEY	0.46	0.09
NEW MEXICO	–0.79	0.07
NEW YORK	0.08	0.10
NORTH CAROLINA	0.70	0.07
NORTH DAKOTA	–0.90	0.09
OHIO	–0.46	0.10
OKLAHOMA	–0.30	0.08

Table B.1 (continued)

Variable Name	Parameter Estimate	Standard Error
OREGON	–0.29	0.14
PENNSYLVANIA	0.38	0.12
RHODE ISLAND	0.03	0.09
SOUTH CAROLINA	0.42	0.08
SOUTH DAKOTA	–0.80	0.08
TENNESSEE	0.002	0.091
TEXAS	–0.02	0.08
UTAH	–0.16	0.08
VERMONT	0.18	0.14
VIRGINIA	0.72	0.07
WASHINGTON	–0.07	0.08
WEST VIRGINIA	–0.24	0.09
WISCONSIN	–0.17	0.11
WYOMING	–0.58	0.09
BIA	0.56	0.07
R-squared	0.28	

[a]Significant at 95 percent confidence level.
[b]Significant at 90 percent confidence level.

Table B.2

Regression Results of Private School Characteristics on Contract Length, 1993–1994

Variable Name	Parameter Estimate	Standard Error
INTERCEPT	11.45[a]	0.09
ELEMENT	–0.24[a]	0.06
MIDDLE	–0.15	0.11
COMBINED	–0.31[a]	0.04
ENROL	0.018[a]	0.002
ENRSQ	–0.0011[a]	0.00002
PCTLUNCH	0.0007	0.0011
PCTLEP	0.004	0.002
PCMINENR	–0.02[a]	0.01
PCTMINSQ	0.0002[a]	0.0001
DIVINDEX	2.06[a]	0.56
DIVINDSQ	–1.35[a]	0.46
RURAL	0.01	0.06
SUBURBAN	0.22[a]	0.08
MIUNION	–0.13	0.09
LOUNION	0.10	0.07
CATHOLIC	–0.50[a]	0.05
OTHAFFIL	–0.33[a]	0.07
R-squared	0.13	

[a]Significant at 95 percent confidence level.

based on the characteristics of their schools in that year and the contract length regression parameter estimates. We then used the imputed contract length to adjust the annual reported salary for that year. The regression results using the imputed contract length differed in expected ways from the unadjusted regression results: the significance of the school's grade level and of urbanicity was reduced, and some of the state effects were altered.[4]

ANALYSIS OF FACTORS RELATED TO PRINCIPALS' SALARIES

A primary purpose of our analysis was to understand the factors related to variation in the compensation of the nation's principals. Are principals of large schools paid more than principals of small schools? Are experienced principals paid more than inexperienced principals? Are principals in urban schools or in low-income schools paid more or less than principals in other types of schools? The SASS contains information on the salary paid to each principal surveyed, the individual characteristics of that principal (such as age, race/ethnicity, gender, and experience), and the characteristics of the school (and in the case of public schools, the district) in which that principal is employed. We analyzed this information to examine whether certain types of principals at certain types of schools systematically earned more or less than other principals did.

Methodology

To analyze the link between principals' salaries and observable school characteristics, we specified the following equation:

$$\mathrm{PADJSAL}_i = \alpha + \beta_1 X_i + \beta_2 S_j + \varepsilon_{ij} \qquad \text{(B.2)}$$

where i = the principal, j = the school, and the dependent variable, PADJSAL, is the salary of the principal (adjusted for the number of months in the principal's contract). X is a vector of the principal's characteristics (such as experience, age, and race/ethnicity); S is a vector of the school's observable characteristics (such as percentage of students eligible for free and reduced-price lunch programs, percentage of minority enrollment, urbanicity, school type, and school size). Table B.3 summarizes the variables used in this and the other regressions. For public schools, the 1999–2000 analysis also included a dummy variable equaling 1 if the school was a charter school.

A few caveats regarding the variables used in the analysis are worth noting. For the public school analysis of the full sample of principals, we included state-level dummy variables to capture differences across states. However, for the private school analysis, and for some analyses of subgroups of the public school sample (e.g., small racial/ethnic groups), the number of observations could not support the use of state-level dummy variables.[5] In these cases, we included a dummy variable that reflected the proportion of public school teachers in the state who were unionized. We hypothesized that states with high rates of unionization for teachers would have

[4]Results obtained using the unadjusted salary figures are available from the authors upon request.

[5]Whereas the public school sample was designed to be representative at the state level, the private school sample was not.

higher salaries for public school teachers and that this, in turn, would lead to higher salaries for public school principals. If there are spillover effects between the public and private sectors, we would also expect private school principals' salaries to be higher in states with high unionization.

For private schools, the vector S also includes a dummy variable equal to 1 for Catholic schools, and another dummy variable equal to 1 if the school has some other religious affiliation.

Table B.3

Description of Variables Used in Regression Analyses

Variable Label	Description	Public	Private
Principal Characteristics			
FEMALE	Principal's gender: Dummy variable 0 = male; 1 = female	X	X
TEXP	Years of teaching experience	X	X
PEXP	Years of experience as a principal	X	X
PASIAN PBLACK PHISP PNA	Principal's race/ethnicity: For public schools, dummy variables set to 1 if principal is member of designated minority group: Asian, black, Hispanic, Native American (omitted category = white)	X	X
School Characteristics			
ELEMENT MIDDLE COMBINED	Grade level: Dummy variable ELEMENT = 1 for elementary school; MIDDLE = 1 for middle school; COMBINED = 1 for combined school (see Appendix A for definitions)	X	X
ENROL	(0.1) multiplied by number of students enrolled in school	X	X
ENRSQ	ENROL squared	X	X
PCTLUNCH	Percentage of students on free and reduced-price lunch	X	X
PCTLEP	Percentage of students who are limited English proficient (LEP)	X	
PCMINENR PCTMINSQ	Percentage of minority students enrolled; squared	X	X
DIVINDEX	Student diversity: Normalized integration index (see text)	X	X
DIVINDSQ	Student diversity squared	X	X
RURAL SUBURBAN	Urbanicity: Dummy variable RURAL = l for rural school; SUBURBAN = 1 for suburban school (omitted category = urban)	X	X
MIUNION HIUNION	Unionization: State-based dummy variable reflecting level of unionization of public school teachers in each state (see Table B.6). Dummy variable MIUNION = 1 for schools in states with rates of public school teacher unionization between 54 and 83 percent; HIUNION = 1 for schools in states with rates of public school teacher unionization between 92 and 100 percent (omitted category = low unionization; used when not practical to include state-level dummy variables due to sample size concerns)	X	X

Table B.3 (continued)

Variable Label	Description	Public	Private
State (state names are variable labels)	Dummy variables for each state (CA = omitted state)[a]	X	
BIA	Dummy variable BIA = 1 if school is Bureau of Indian Affairs school	X	
CHARTER	Dummy variable CHARTER = 1 if school is a charter school (for 2000 only)	X	
CATHOLIC OTHAFFIL	Dummy variable CATHOLIC = 1 if school is Catholic; OTHAFFIL = 1 for other religious affiliations (omitted category = nonsectarian)		X
POVFAMPROB INDPROB CONFLICT	Constructed school-level variables based on principals' reports of school problems: POVFAMPROB reflects average score on poverty and family-related problems; INDPROB, on individual student problems; CONFLICT, on school conflict problems (see Appendix C for more details on these variables)	X	X

[a]The parameter estimates on the state dummy variable thus reflect the difference between the state in question and California (the omitted category). Although most of the states' parameter estimates are statistically significantly different from California's at the 5 percent level, we do not note this in the table. Instead, the magnitude of the parameter estimates should be viewed along with the standard error estimates to facilitate comparisons across states.

We examined the relationship between principals' salaries and the racial/ethnic composition of the student body by including two different variables and their square terms in the regression model. The first variable is simply the percentage of minority students in the school; the second is a normalized index of integration for n groups, which we describe as the diversity index (see details in Appendix A).

Equation B.2, above, was then estimated using linear regression.

Findings

The results of estimating Equation B.2 can be found in Tables B.4 (for public schools) and B.5 (for private schools). In the private school analysis, we did not use state-level dummy variables, but we did include dummy variables reflecting the unionization of public school teachers in the state in which the school was located. The explanatory power of the model was substantially higher for the public school analysis (multiple $R^2 = 0.59$ versus 0.29), and there were differences in some of the parameter estimates, suggesting that there is a different relationship between salary and the independent variables in public versus private schools.

Experience of Principal. We controlled for a principal's experience both as a teacher and as a principal. In public schools, each additional year of experience as a principal was associated with an additional $350; in private schools, each additional year was worth an additional $175. These relationships are significant at the 5 percent level. The parameter estimates suggest that all other things being equal, a public school principal with 10 years of experience as a principal earns only $3,500 per year more than a principal with no experience as a principal.

Table B.4

Regression Results of Public School Characteristics on 1999–2000 Salary (adjusted for contract length)

Variable Name	Parameter Estimate	Standard Error
INTERCEPT	68800.17[a]	1175.31
FEMALE	238.87	312.01
TEXP	0.21	22.32
PEXP	352.46[a]	21.51
PASIAN	2287.52	1933.14
PBLACK	84.83	527.06
PHISP	–417.51	1122.95
PNA	–2630.29[a]	856.27
ELEMENT	–1190.58[a]	391.77
MIDDLE	–730.59[a]	377.31
COMBINED	–1249.33[b]	744.67
ENROL	91.41[a]	10.89
ENRSQ	–0.09[a]	0.04
PCTLUNCH	–60.33[a]	7.26
PCTLEP	43.84[a]	14.54
PCMINENR	100.45[b]	52.32
PCTMINSQ	–0.36	0.50
DIVINDEX	12918.27[a]	3404.07
DIVINDSQ	–12263.71[a]	2908.41
RURAL	–7307.02[a]	399.15
SUBURBAN	–211.00	433.36
ALABAMA	–13785.96	827.13
ALASKA	12017.34	994.75
ARIZONA	–15260.60	1213.35
ARKANSAS	–17136.04	1390.12
COLORADO	–4003.57	885.83
CONNECTICUT	11796.25	925.56
DELAWARE	915.59	828.84
DC	–5002.15	957.03
FLORIDA	–13958.31	857.64
GEORGIA	–672.76	891.90
HAWAII	–6121.36	1924.65
IDAHO	–4292.40	845.54
ILLINOIS	1583.89	1117.38
INDIANA	–2422.62	1125.53
IOWA	–5352.09	764.09
KANSAS	–6881.60	810.31
KENTUCKY	–6225.80	833.54
LOUISIANA	–18869.53	1190.00
MAINE	–8001.16	963.76
MARYLAND	–4545.96	904.10
MASSACHUSETTS	2233.78	1699.72
MICHIGAN	6508.07	908.97
MINNESOTA	4321.45	1154.20
MISSISSIPPI	–16214.21	908.97
MISSOURI	–7831.15	1283.33
MONTANA	–11398.34	1077.85
NEBRASKA	–9102.88	998.52
NEVADA	–1040.22	796.02

Table B.4 (continued)

Variable Name	Parameter Estimate	Standard Error
NEW HAMPSHIRE	–9502.58	1086.47
NEW JERSEY	13617.40	1068.85
NEW MEXICO	–12755.60	1369.58
NEW YORK	8785.91	1099.62
NORTH CAROLINA	–13570.90	1003.34
NORTH DAKOTA	–16874.89	904.53
OHIO	–3321.29	1044.94
OKLAHOMA	–19185.90	884.80
OREGON	–171.84	1186.03
PENNSYLVANIA	–422.75	1054.51
RHODE ISLAND	–1427.84	704.29
SOUTH CAROLINA	–10451.89	983.13
SOUTH DAKOTA	–14548.65	986.27
TENNESSEE	–14962.65	1034.19
TEXAS	–12057.69	967.09
UTAH	–10363.03	903.26
VERMONT	–6612.18	1058.27
VIRGINIA	–11597.65	938.63
WASHINGTON	–543.53	836.48
WEST VIRGINIA	–14854.28	890.66
WISCONSIN	–1136.50	1013.64
WYOMING	–7004.12	840.52
BIA	6413.28[a]	992.29
CHARTER	–12539.64[a]	586.98
R-squared	0.59	

NOTE: Omitted categories are high school, principal is white, urban, and California.

[a]Significant at 95 percent confidence level.

[b]Significant at 90 percent confidence level.

Table B.5

Regression Results of Private School Characteristics on 1999–2000 Salary (adjusted for contract length)

Variable Name	Parameter Estimate	Standard Error
INTERCEPT	58709.07[a]	2791.44
FEMALE	–5899.95[a]	1047.91
TEXP	85.88[b]	50.57
PEXP	173.81[a]	70.95
PASIAN	–3430.20	4075.20
PBLACK	2738.14	3135.93
PHISP	–5138.78	3389.50
PNA	–9429.12	6434.32
ELEMENT	–5612.98[a]	2674.22
MIDDLE	–6299.61	8978.06
COMBINED	–6451.61[a]	1545.03
ENROL	586.87[a]	42.19
ENRSQ	–2.15	0.30
PCTLUNCH	–19.74	29.11
PCTLEP	153.58[a]	61.92

Table B.5 (continued)

Variable Name	Parameter Estimate	Standard Error
PCMINENR	151.72	169.02
PCTMINSQ	–1.81	1.59
DIVINDEX	–8319.79	10217.03
DIVINDSQ	4580.63	8967.78
RURAL	–6376.75[a]	1386.87
SUBURBAN	–2987.09[a]	1059.54
MIUNION	–1462.48	2319.75
LOUNION	–5093.21[a]	1444.95
CATHOLIC	–19952.77[a]	1486.90
OTHAFFIL	–19176.87[a]	1915.99
R-squared	0.27	

NOTE: Omitted categories are high school, principal is white, urban, nonsectarian, and high union.

[a]Significant at 95 percent confidence level.

[b]Significant at 90 percent confidence level.

We found no statistically significant relationship between salary and teaching experience in the public sector. In the private sector, the relationship is small ($85 per year of teaching experience) and is significant at the 10 but not the 5 percent level.

Grade Level and Size of School. When we controlled for other characteristics of the school, including enrollment, our analysis revealed that a school's grade level relates to a principal's salary in both sectors.[6] High school principals earned more, all things being equal, than principals of other types of schools did. In public schools, they earned about $1,200 per year more than principals of elementary and combined schools did, and over $700 per year more than middle school principals did. In private schools, grade level had a larger impact, with high school principals earning about $6,000 per year more than principals of elementary and combined schools did.

A principal's salary increased up to enrollment levels of about 5,000 in public schools and 1,350 in private schools, and declined thereafter. At the average school, the effect of enrollment on salary was about $4,500 per year in the public sector and $12,000 per year in the private sector evaluated at the respective sample means.[7] The relationship between salary and enrollment is a substantial one, with principals of public schools with enrollments of about 5,000 earning over $23,000 per year more than principals of very small schools, and principals of private schools with enrollments of 1,350 earning nearly $40,000 per year more.[8]

Our analysis suggests that the relationship between school enrollment and salary is not linear. Principals in both sectors were paid more to lead larger schools up to a point, beyond which their salaries decreased with size (as discussed in the main body

[6]Note that for this characteristic, contract length affects the regression results. A comparison of the 1994 adjusted and unadjusted results suggests that the school's grade level has a much smaller effect on salary once one controls for contract length.

[7]Average school size was 532 in the public sector and 221 in the private sector.

[8]These relationships with grade level and enrollment are similar to what was observed for 1994.

of the report). The parameter estimates are highly significant in both sectors and of larger magnitude for private schools.

Low-Income and LEP Students. The proportion of students receiving free and reduced-price lunches (i.e., low-income students) is statistically significantly related to the salary of public but not private school principals. This finding indicates that compared to other public school principals, those who work in schools with a higher proportion of low-income children receive lower compensation. When we controlled for other characteristics, the effect was $2,200 per year evaluated at the sample mean, and principals at schools with 100 percent of students in the programs earned $6,000 per year less than did principals in schools with no students in the program.[9]

We found that the percentage of limited English proficient (LEP) students had a positive relationship to the salary of both public and private school principals. When other characteristics were controlled for, principals of schools with all LEP students earned about $5,000 (public) and $15,000 (private) per year more than principals in schools with no such students did. Because the average school has a very low percentage of LEP students (5 percent in the public sector and less than 1 percent in the private sector), the average effect on a principal's salary was only $222 per year in the public sector and just over $100 per year in the private sector.

Minority Enrollment and Student Diversity. Minority student enrollment and student diversity have nonlinear and statistically significant relationships with the salary of a principal in the public sector only. In public schools, a principal's salary increased as the percentage of minority students increased, such that principals of schools with 100 percent minority enrollment earned about $6,500 per year more than principals of comparable all-white schools did.[10] Although the relationship is nonlinear, salary increased over the entire range of the data.

The impact of diversity evaluated at the sample mean was about $3,000 per year. The diversity factor was found to add up to $3,500 per year to the principal's salary at moderate levels of diversity (DIVINDEX = 0.53). Beyond this point, salary declined as diversity increased, but principals of the most diverse schools still earned more than principals of completely homogeneous schools did.

Urbanicity. The regression results suggest that urbanicity is related to a principal's salary in both public and private schools. Rural principals earned less than urban principals did. Relative to principals in public urban schools, those in public rural schools earned about $7,300 less per year. In private schools, the rural principals received about $6,400 less than their urban counterparts.

There was no statistically significant difference between the salaries of urban and suburban principals in the public sector. In the private sector, however, suburban principals earned nearly $3,000 per year less than their urban counterparts did.

---

[9]This relationship was not significant in 1994.

[10]These relationships between salary and school characteristics appear to be stronger than they were in 1994.

The relationship between urbanicity and principals' salaries appears to have changed between 1994 and 2000. In 1994, rural and suburban principals in the private sector earned about $2,500 per year more than private urban principals did, and public suburban principals earned about $2,000 per year more than their urban counterparts. Thus, it appears that urban principals made gains between 1994 and 2000.

State Differences. For our analysis of public schools, the sample size was large enough to support the use of state fixed effects along with all the other control variables used in the model. However, for our analysis of private schools, as well as of smaller subgroups of public school principals, we could not include all the state dummy variables. Instead, we ran the regressions with dummy variables LOUNION and MIUNION to reflect states with, respectively, low and moderate levels of unionization among public school teachers.[11] The private school analysis yielded a statistically significant negative estimate on LOUNION, with principals in low unionization states receiving about $5,000 per year less than principals in high union states did. This might reflect spillover effects in the wages of public and private school educators.

In the public school analysis, the parameter estimates on the state dummy variables reflected the differences between a typical principal's salary in the identified state relative to one in California (CA was the reference category for the regression). For example, all other things being equal, a principal in Connecticut earned nearly $12,000 per year more than a principal in California did, whereas a principal in Louisiana earned about $19,000 less. The parameter estimates thus aid in identifying those states in which principals are relatively well paid and those in which they are relatively poorly paid, as discussed in the main text. Table B.6 presents information on the cost-of-living index in each state. It is important to consider the state salary results in view of cost-of-living differences.

Charter School Status. Charter school principals earned substantially less—over $12,500 per year less—than principals in comparable traditional public schools, even when we controlled for school size and school grade level. This is interesting, given the conventional wisdom that charter school principals have more administrative responsibilities and greater time demands.

Religious Orientation of School. As expected, the religious orientation of a private school had a strong negative relationship to the salary of principals. Principals of Catholic and other religiously affiliated schools earned about $20,000 less per year than principals of comparable nonsectarian private schools did.

---

[11]We ran the pubic school regression with HIUNION and MIUNION in place of the state dummies. The explanatory power of the model was, not surprisingly, lower (0.47), but the parameter estimates were large and highly significant, with principals in low union states earning less than principals in high union states. The parameter estimates on the other variable were not substantially different for the two models.

Table B.6

State Unionization and Cost-of-Living Information

State	Percentage of Teachers with Collective Bargaining Contract (1994)	Interstate Cost-of-Living Index (1999)
HI	100	133.8
NJ	100	114.8
RI	100	105.6
WI	100	92.7
PA	100	97.7
MD	100	105.3
FL	100	94.4
NY	99.7	109.2
MA	99.6	114.2
ME	99.4	95.6
NH	99.3	105.6
CT	99	120.2
IN	99	90.6
OR	98.7	94.6
CA	98.5	122.7
AK	98.3	125.0
WA	98.2	100.9
OH	98.1	94.3
IA	97.3	88.9
MI	96.7	92.4
IL	96.4	98.1
VT	95.7	97.4
DE	95	102.8
NV	94.4	98.4
MT	93	92.5
MN	92.6	95.2
ID	83	91.4
NE	82.3	89.0
SD	78.9	87.6
KS	76.4	89.8
UT	76.4	93.8
TN	74.7	90.0
CO	69.3	98.1
ND	66.3	90.7
OK	58.4	87.7
NM	54.5	94.7
WY	34	93.3
KY	20.9	88.4
AR	17.3	87.4
LA	16	90.4
AZ	15.1	95.9
MO	7.7	91.8
AL	1.8	89.2
GA	1.7	93.0
WV	0	88.1
VA	0	97.8
TX	0	90.0
MS	0	87.5
SC	0	90.8
NC	0	91.6
National average	68.1	100

SOURCE: Nelson, Drown, and Gould, 2000. Data on teachers subject to a collective bargaining contract are from the 1993–1994 SASS.

Characteristics of Principals. The analysis of principals' salaries also controlled for the gender and race/ethnicity of a principal. Although much has been made of the difference between the average salaries of male and female principals, our analysis revealed a statistically significant relationship between the salaries of male and female principals in the private sector but not the public sector. After we controlled for the characteristics of the schools they were leading, female principals appeared to earn the same amount as male principals in public schools. In private schools, women earned almost $6,000 per year less than did men with similar characteristics leading comparable schools. Thus, evidence of possible gender-based salary discrimination was found for private but not public schools.[12]

With the exception of Native American principals, who earned about $2,600 per year less in the public sector than their white counterparts did, we found no statistically significant relationships between race/ethnicity and principals' salaries in 1999–2000. This is in contrast to what we found for 1993–1994, which were observable differences among public school principals of different races/ethnicities. In 1993–1994, Asian, Native American, and Hispanic principals earned slightly less than their white counterparts in similar schools did, while black principals earned slightly more. Among private school principals, we found a similar but larger positive effect for black principals (over $6,000 per year more) in 1993–1994, but the effects for other racial/ethnic groups were not statistically significantly different from zero.

ANALYSIS OF FACTORS RELATED TO SALARY DIFFERENTIAL BETWEEN PRINCIPALS AND TEACHERS

We were interested in whether the characteristics of schools impact the differential between the compensation of principals and teachers at the same school. In other words, is the pay of a principal proportional to the pay of teachers at the same school across the board, or do principals of certain types of schools experience more of a premium? This is an interesting question to examine in light of current concerns that the principal-teacher pay difference is not large enough to attract people from teaching into the principalship or to keep principals from returning to teaching. In the regression analysis we describe here, we focus on the differential when the salary of experienced teachers—i.e., those with 10 or more years of experience—is used as a baseline. As discussed in Appendix A, use of a more strict definition of *experienced* (e.g., 25 years of experience) caused us to lose a substantial number of observations (i.e., schools) in the private sector and in some states' public sector.

Methodology

To analyze the link between observable principal and school characteristics and the salary differential between principals and teachers, we specified the following:

$$\mathrm{DIFF100}_{ij} = \alpha + \beta_1 X_i + \beta_2 S_j + \varepsilon_{ij} \qquad \text{(B.3)}$$

[12]Similar relationships were observed in the 1994 results.

where i = the principal and j = the school. The analysis was conducted separately for public schools and private schools. The dependent variable is a measure of how much more, in percentage terms, principals earn relative to experienced teachers (again, those with ≥10 years of experience) in the same school.[13] The independent variables are the same ones used in the salary regression (see above).

Equation B.3 was then estimated using linear regression. We used the SUDAAN statistical software with Balance Repeated Replication (BRR) techniques to produce correct standard errors.

Findings

Compared to the salary regression model, this model had extremely low explanatory power on the salary differential (multiple $R^2 = 0.13$ for public schools, 0.08 for private). For the public school analysis, about half of the variation was explained by the state dummy variables. The results of estimating Equation B.3 can be found in Tables B.7 (for public schools) and B.8 (for private schools).

Table B.7

Regression Results of Public School Characteristics on 1999–2000 Salary Differential (adjusted for contract length)

Variable Name	Parameter Estimate	Standard Error
INTERCEPT	23.45[a]	4.63
FEMALE	–3.28[a]	1.16
TEXP	0.07	0.09
PEXP	0.46[a]	0.06
PASIAN	–2.46	4.78
PBLACK	1.66	1.68
PHISP	–3.30	2.82
PNA	5.45	4.06
ELEMENT	–5.70[a]	2.19
MIDDLE	–2.66[b]	1.62
COMBINED	–2.40	2.68
ENROL	0.02	0.04
ENRSQ	0.0001	0.0001
PCTLUNCH	–0.03	0.03
PCTLEP	–0.02	0.06
PCMINENR	–0.25	0.16
PCTMINSQ	0.003[b]	0.001
DIVINDEX	4.27	12.40
DIVINDSQ	12.24	12.65
RURAL	–6.10[a]	1.52

[13]DIFF100 is 100 multiplied by the difference between the salary of principal i in school j and the average salary of experienced teachers in school j, divided by the average salary of experienced teachers in school j. The salaries of both the principals and the teachers are adjusted by the length of contract.

Table B.7 (continued)

Variable Name	Parameter Estimate	Standard Error
SUBURBAN	–0.05	1.35
ALABAMA	–1.44	2.33
ALASKA	4.77	3.43
ARIZONA	8.38	2.52
ARKANSAS	1.84	5.02
COLORADO	19.55	3.45
CONNECTICUT	10.02	2.88
DELAWARE	6.32	3.01
DC	–15.32	2.62
FLORIDA	9.45	2.90
GEORGIA	11.44	3.09
HAWAII	62.24	5.98
IDAHO	8.18	3.13
ILLINOIS	11.99	3.34
INDIANA	–0.62	3.28
IOWA	29.18	4.97
KANSAS	23.16	3.79
KENTUCKY	15.51	2.98
LOUISIANA	3.98	4.63
MAINE	19.70	4.18
MARYLAND	5.25	2.73
MASSACHUSETTS	4.75	2.61
MICHIGAN	–0.65	3.03
MINNESOTA	15.84	3.69
MISSISSIPPI	0.48	2.82
MISSOURI	20.84	4.39
MONTANA	16.34	5.00
NEBRASKA	49.19	4.58
NEVADA	20.71	3.37
NEW HAMPSHIRE	4.46	3.60
NEW JERSEY	13.75	6.91
NEW MEXICO	6.33	3.14
NEW YORK	10.27	3.25
NORTH CAROLINA	11.88	4.30
NORTH DAKOTA	25.21	3.45
OHIO	6.55	5.02
OKLAHOMA	14.61	3.61
OREGON	11.44	3.64
PENNSYLVANIA	–9.59	3.51
RHODE ISLAND	12.33	2.03
SOUTH CAROLINA	2.11	2.44
SOUTH DAKOTA	25.42	3.62
TENNESSEE	6.49	2.90
TEXAS	11.05	3.18
UTAH	–2.05	3.30
VERMONT	26.74	6.97
VIRGINIA	7.45	2.96
WASHINGTON	10.52	2.80
WEST VIRGINIA	–0.40	2.82
WISCONSIN	5.93	3.45
WYOMING	29.85	4.35
BIA	4.09	3.83

Table B.7 (continued)

Variable Name	Parameter Estimate	Standard Error
CHARTER	–8.15[a]	2.54
R-squared	0.13	

NOTE: Omitted categories are high school, principal is white, urban, and California.

[a]Significant at 95 percent confidence level.

[b]Significant at 90 percent confidence level.

Table B.8

Regression Results of Private School Characteristics on 1999–2000 Salary Differential (adjusted for contract length)

Variable Name	Parameter Estimate	Standard Error
INTERCEPT	93.86[a]	14.48
FEMALE	–21.08[a]	6.85
TEXP	–0.36	0.28
PEXP	–0.48	0.31
PASIAN	–1.62	14.80
PBLACK	34.69	29.38
PHISP	–3.20	10.30
PNA	12.99	55.35
ELEMENT	–5.86	12.31
MIDDLE	–12.54	40.43
COMBINED	–0.70	4.72
ENROL	0.41[a]	0.21
ENRSQ	–0.002	0.002
PCTLUNCH	–0.26	0.18
PCTLEP	0.73	0.93
PCMINENR	–1.57	1.26
PCTMINSQ	0.01	0.01
DIVINDEX	62.70	66.38
DIVINDSQ	–29.66	49.66
RURAL	–8.58	10.48
SUBURBAN	–7.36	6.94
MIUNION	3.78	10.85
LOUNION	–3.39	6.65
CATHOLIC	–34.42[a]	5.85
OTHAFFIL	–33.30[a]	10.93
R-squared	0.08	

NOTE: Omitted categories are high school, principal is white, urban, nonsectarian, and high union.

[a]Significant at 90 percent confidence level.

Experience of Principal. In the public sector, a principal's experience as a principal was positively related to salary differential, although the effect was small (about half a percentage point for each year of experience) once we controlled for other characteristics of the school and principal. A principal's teaching experience was not related to the salary differential in the public sector, however. In the private sector, neither type of experience was related to the salary differential.

Grade Level and Size of School. We found grade level to be related to the salary differential in public schools, where it was five percentage points lower in elementary schools than in high schools. In other words, the salary differential for elementary school principals was five percentage points smaller than that for high school principals. There was no statistically significant difference in the ratio by grade level in private schools. School size had a slight and nonlinear impact on the salary ratio in both public and private schools.

Low-Income and LEP Students. Neither the percentage of students enrolled in free and reduced-price lunch programs nor the percentage of LEP students had a statistically significant relationship to the salary differential between principals and teachers in either sector.

Minority Enrollment and Diversity. The analysis revealed no statistically significant relationship between minority enrollment or diversity and the salary ratio in either sector.

Urbanicity. The regression results suggest that urbanicity has a minor impact on the relative compensation of public but not private school principals. Public school principals in rural areas received a salary differential about six percentage points smaller than that of their counterparts in comparable urban schools, and we saw no difference between suburban and urban schools on this score.

State Differences. The ratio between the salaries of public school principals and teachers appears to vary substantially by state. The parameter estimates on the state dummy variables in this regression provided a sense of the states where it is more or less financially advantageous to be a principal rather than a teacher. In states with a large, positive parameter estimate, principals received a larger salary bump relative to teachers than did principals in other states. It is interesting to compare the relationship between state and principal salary (Tables B.4 and B.5) with the relationship between state and salary ratio (Tables B.7 and B.8). Notice that for some states, the effect on salary is not in the same direction in the two regressions:

- *Positive relationship with both salary and salary ratio.* In these states, principals are highly paid relative to both principals in other states and teachers in their own state. Examples: Connecticut, New York.
- *Negative relationship with salary but positive relationship with salary ratio.* In these states, principals are paid poorly relative to principals in other states but well relative to teachers in their own state. Examples: Hawaii, North Carolina, Oklahoma.
- *Positive relationship with salary but negative relationship with salary ratio.* In these states, principals are paid well relative to principals in other states but poorly relative to teachers in their own state. Example: Michigan.
- *Negative relationship with both salary and salary ratio.* In these states, principals are paid poorly relative to both principals in other states and teachers in their own state. Examples: Arkansas, Utah.

Charter School Status. The salary differential for charter school principals was eight percentage points smaller than that for traditional public school principals in schools with similar characteristics.

Religious Orientation of School. The salary differential between principals and teachers was about 35 percentage points smaller in religiously affiliated private schools than it was in nonsectarian private schools. This suggests that religiously affiliated schools may have a more egalitarian culture that encourages greater wage compression between teachers and principals.

Characteristics of Principals. A principal's race/ethnicity had no relationship with the relative salary between principals and teachers in either the public or the private sector. In both sectors, there appears to be a gender effect on the salary ratio, with male principals earning more than female principals relative to teachers in the same school. In the public sector, the gender relationship is small—three percentage points; in the private sector, however, it is quite large—over 20 percentage points.

ANALYSIS OF FACTORS RELATED TO EXPERIENCE OF PRINCIPAL

Sorting is one possible indicator of shortage in a market where employers are not free to adjust the salary they offer to potential employees and where working conditions vary across sites. If it is true that (a) more-experienced principals are "better" or more desirable in some sense, (b) schools have limited ability to pay more to those who are willing to work in more challenging environments, and (c) principals have systematic preferences in the types of schools they are willing to work in, then we should see systematic patterns in principals' experience across schools with different characteristics.

Methodology

To analyze the link between a principal's experience and school characteristics, we specified the following equation:

$$\text{PRNEXPER}_{i} = \alpha + \beta S_{j} + \varepsilon_{ij} \qquad \text{(B.4)}$$

where i = the principal and j = the school. The dependent variable, PRNEXPER, is the principal's experience. S is a vector of the school's observable demographic characteristics. The school observable characteristics used in this regression were the same ones used in the previous regressions plus three measures of school problems (as discussed in Appendix C). Although we included a principal's personal characteristics in the salary and salary ratio regressions, we omitted them from this regression because we were focusing on the relationship between a principal's experience and school characteristics. In other words, we were working from the hypothesis that experience matters and were trying to determine whether principals are sorting among schools on the basis of that experience.

Our analysis was conducted separately for public schools and private schools.

Findings

The results of estimating Equation B.4 are in Tables B.9 (for public schools) and B.10 (for private schools). Our hypothesis was that experienced principals would choose to work in "easier" schools (those with fewer problems) and that schools with high-minority, diverse, low-income student populations would thus have principals with less experience. We found little support for a relationship between a school's racial/ethnic and other demographic characteristics and a principal's experience. Indeed, the only such characteristic with a statistically significant relationship to a principal's experience was the percentage of students enrolled in free and reduced-price lunch programs, and that relationship was statistically significant only for private schools. We found that private schools with a higher proportion of students receiving free and reduced-price lunches had principals with less experience. We also found that principals in public elementary schools and principals in private combined schools tended to have slightly more experience than did principals in high schools in the respective sectors, but the results here were significant only at the 10 percent level. Experience was related to enrollment in a nonlinear way, but continued to increase up to fairly high enrollment levels (over 3,000 in the public sector and 1,700 in the private sector).

Table B.9

Regression Results of Public School Characteristics on Experience

Variable Name	Parameter Estimate	Standard Error
INTERCEPT	9.30[a]	0.80
POVFAMPROB	–0.23	0.20
INDPROB	–0.36	0.33
CONFLICT	–0.65[a]	0.30
ELEMENT	0.81[a]	0.36
MIDDLE	–0.37	0.31
COMBINED	0.67	0.42
ENROL	0.01[a]	0.01
ENRSQ	–0.00003	0.00002
PCTLUNCH	–0.01	0.01
PCTLEP	0.003	0.010
PCMINENR	0.03	0.04
PCTMINSQ	–0.0004	0.0004
DIVINDEX	–0.58	2.47
DIVINDSQ	–1.96	2.09
RURAL	0.34	0.39
SUBURBAN	0.17	0.31
ALABAMA	–0.94	0.88
ALASKA	–1.64	0.66
ARIZONA	–0.38	0.76
ARKANSAS	1.33	0.80
COLORADO	–0.08	0.73
CONNECTICUT	0.27	0.81
DELAWARE	–1.44	1.00
DC	–1.72	0.68
FLORIDA	–1.05	0.69

Table B.9 (continued)

Variable Name	Parameter Estimate	Standard Error
GEORGIA	–2.16	0.78
HAWAII	–1.30	0.77
IDAHO	1.63	0.70
ILLINOIS	1.16	0.78
INDIANA	–0.26	0.92
IOWA	2.29	0.97
KANSAS	–0.85	0.81
KENTUCKY	–1.65	0.74
LOUISIANA	–1.56	0.84
MAINE	–0.09	0.87
MARYLAND	–2.08	0.83
MASSACHUSETTS	–0.55	0.77
MICHIGAN	–0.13	0.80
MINNESOTA	–0.64	0.81
MISSISSIPPI	–0.20	0.68
MISSOURI	–1.50	0.76
MONTANA	0.32	0.73
NEBRASKA	3.29	0.95
NEVADA	–1.12	0.73
NEW HAMPSHIRE	1.73	1.13
NEW JERSEY	–0.29	0.88
NEW MEXICO	–0.99	0.76
NEW YORK	–0.48	0.74
NORTH CAROLINA	–0.97	0.79
NORTH DAKOTA	1.47	0.72
OHIO	0.87	0.95
OKLAHOMA	0.53	0.75
OREGON	–1.36	0.87
PENNSYLVANIA	2.66	1.00
RHODE ISLAND	–1.41	0.69
SOUTH CAROLINA	1.07	0.96
SOUTH DAKOTA	1.27	0.70
TENNESSEE	0.78	1.02
TEXAS	–0.81	0.66
UTAH	–0.98	0.71
VERMONT	–0.59	0.84
VIRGINIA	–0.90	0.82
WASHINGTON	0.08	0.69
WEST VIRGINIA	4.45	0.91
WISCONSIN	1.39	0.84
WYOMING	0.86	0.83
BIA	1.07[b]	0.58
CHARTER	–1.54[a]	0.30
R-squared	0.05	

NOTE: Omitted categories are high school, principal is white, urban, and California.

[a]Significant at 95 percent confidence level.

[b]Significant at 90 percent confidence level.

Table B.10

Regression Results of Private School Characteristics on Experience

Variable Name	Parameter Estimate	Standard Error
INTERCEPT	9.80[a]	0.99
POVFAMPROB	0.59	0.53
INDPROB	–0.34	0.84
CONFLICT	–1.00	0.93
ELEMENT	1.20	0.94
MIDDLE	1.83	2.41
COMBINED	1.07[b]	0.60
ENROL	0.07[a]	0.02
ENRSQ	–0.0002	0.0001
PCTLUNCH	–0.03[b]	0.02
PCTLEP	–0.02	0.03
PCMINENR	–0.04	0.07
PCTMINSQ	0.0002	0.0006
DIVINDEX	4.80	4.10
DIVINDSQ	–5.85	4.06
RURAL	–0.69	0.57
SUBURBAN	–0.14	0.47
MIUNION	–0.075	0.73
LOUNION	–0.55	0.53
CATHOLIC	–1.54[a]	0.68
OTHAFFIL	–0.34	0.97
R-squared	0.03	

NOTE: Omitted categories are principal is white, high school, urban, and high unionization.

[a]Significant at 95 percent confidence level.

[b]Significant at 90 percent confidence level.

School Problems. We did find a statistically significant relationship in the public sector between one category of school problems—school conflict problems—and a principal's experience. In the private sector, school problems were not found to be related to a principal's experience. What we found was that public school principals who reported more school conflict problems had less experience. This relationship is difficult to interpret. On the one hand, it may reflect the fact that principals move out of problematic schools as soon as they have enough seniority to do so. On the other hand, it may reflect the fact that principals with less experience are more likely to rate their schools as problematic.

State Differences. The parameter estimates on the state dummy variables suggest that some states (in particular, Nebraska, Iowa, and West Virginia) have a more experienced group of principals than do others (in particular, Georgia and Maryland). The relative experience level of principals in a particular state may be influenced by a combination of factors, such as salary, salary ratio, labor market conditions, and growth in the number of schools in the state. We did not find that the low-paying states had the least-experienced principals. Indeed, Nebraska and West Virginia had some of the lowest principal salaries and yet had the most-experienced principals.

Religious Orientation of School. Principals at Catholic schools had less experience (about 1.5 years) than did principals of nonsectarian private schools.

Appendix C

ANALYSIS OF PRINCIPALS' REPORTS OF SCHOOL PROBLEMS

In this appendix, we use information on principals' reports of school problems to examine an important aspect of the working conditions principals face. Most existing research on school working conditions focuses on teachers. Using data from New York state, Loeb (2000) found that most of the variation in teacher attributes across schools was within, rather than between, districts. She argues that sorting within districts reflects a preference on the part of teachers for students that are high achieving and high in socioeconomic status or for the working conditions found in schools attended by such students. Urban schools and schools with higher proportions of black or Hispanic students had less-qualified teachers on average than did rural, suburban, and white schools. Walden and Sogutlu (2001) studied intrastate variations in teacher salaries for North Carolina in the 1993–1994 school year. They found that teachers in schools with larger enrollment and in secondary schools received relatively higher compensation than teachers in other schools did. Research has also revealed that teachers often leave schools with higher proportions of low-income, limited English proficient (LEP), and non-white students (Boyd et al., 2001; Carroll, Reichardt, and Guarino, 2000).

It is plausible that similar drivers are at work for school principals. In the school leadership literature, urban schools are thought to differ substantially from suburban schools. According to Portin (2000), the urban principalship seems to have a number of characteristics that make it more challenging, such as larger bureaucratic districts, less local revenue, and higher percentages of students at risk for school failure, living in poverty, and with LEP status. Portin also sees the role of principal in these districts as demanding more political leadership, social complexity management, and fund-raising skills than are expected in suburban settings. Although we have been able to find no study that explicitly examines the effects of school characteristics on school principals' career choices, we hypothesize that what holds for teachers also holds for principals: If given some flexibility to select the school they work in or to leave their position if unhappy with the work setting, many (although certainly not all) will try to avoid schools that present greater challenges and will favor schools that are less difficult—unless they are adequately compensated for the additional hassle.[1]

[1]Because career decisions are often based on incomplete information, the observable characteristics of schools may have a lot to do with them. For example, a principal that perceives his or her school to have many serious problems may indirectly create a bad reputation for that school. When an administrative vacancy opens up there, that reputation may influence other administrators' decisions about applying for

As part of its principals' survey, the National Center for Education Statistics (NCES) Schools and Staffing Survey (SASS) asks questions about school problems. It asks principals to rate the degree to which various things—student drug abuse, students cutting class, lack of parental involvement, physical conflict among students, and student poverty, etc.—are a problem in their school. However, few studies have actually tried to link qualitative measures of school climate with observable socioeconomic or demographic characteristics of schools.[2] We analyzed this relationship to help us determine whether some observable characteristics of schools make a principal's job more difficult.

METHODOLOGY

The 1993–1994 and 1999–2000 SASSs both included questions designed to obtain principals' perceptions of school problems. Tables C.1 and C.2 provide the means and standard deviations for these questions in the 1999–2000 and 1993–1994 SASSs for, respectively, the public and private school sectors.[3]

To simplify our analysis and make our results easier to interpret, we applied principal factor analysis[4] with a varimax rotation to the responses of public school principals to 17 "problem" questions in the 1999–2000 SASS.[5] Factor analysis allows us to group questions that are highly correlated with each other. The analysis yielded three independent groups, each with an eigenvalue above 1. The items within each group made intuitive sense, and it was fairly clear how they should be labeled. Each factor included eight questions, and most questions loaded fairly high on a single factor. We then took all the items grouped in each factor and produced average scores for each principal. This eased the interpretation of the scores as well as the regression results because the original scale was retained.

---

the job. This effect may be particularly important in larger districts, where potential administrators may rely more frequently on informal information channels in making career move decisions.

[2]In its *Condition of Education*, the National Center for Education Statistics (1996) linked a few qualitative school variables (such as teachers' perceptions of their influence as well as student tardiness and absenteeism) to observable school characteristics. For example, it found that teachers in schools with few low-income students (5 percent or fewer eligible for free and reduced-price lunches) were generally more likely to report that they had a great deal of influence over their school's policies. In contrast, teachers in schools with large proportions of low-income students were found to be more likely to perceive student absenteeism and tardiness as serious problems.

[3]All the questions in Tables C.1 and C.2 appeared in the 1999–2000 SASS. To foster comparison, we did not include six questions that appeared in the 1993–1994 SASS but not in the 1999–2000 SASS.

[4]It is recommended that principal factor or common factor analysis be used (instead of principal component factor analysis) when the observed variables are indicators of latent constructs to be measured, such as attitudes or organizational problems. The reason is that when looking at latent constructs, one is more interested in their common variance or covariation among variables than in the total variance accounted for in principal component analysis (Widaman, 1993).

[5]The 1999–2000 SASS also asks principals the extent to which teacher absenteeism is a problem. We excluded this problem from the analysis because it is conceptually distinct from the others, all of which have to do with students. When we performed the same analysis using the 1993–1994 data, the groupings in both years were almost identical. The most relevant trends and changes are discussed in this appendix; the full 1993–1994 results, not shown here, are available upon request.

Table C.1

Public School Principals' Perceptions of SASS Items on School-Problems Rating Scale

	1999–2000 SASS		1993–1994 SASS	
Questionnaire Item: *To what extent is . . . a problem?*	Mean	Std. Dev.	Mean	Std. Dev.
Students unprepared to learn	1.58	1.08	1.42	1.19
Student poverty	4.57	1.23	1.48	1.14
Lack of parental involvement	1.34	1.41	1.32	1.12
Student tardiness	1.21	0.88	1.02	1.07
Student absenteeism	1.16	0.75	1.06	1.05
Student apathy	1.01	1.06	0.73	0.98
Disrespect for teachers	0.97	0.82	0.91	1.10
Poor student health	0.90	0.85	0.85	0.01
Physical conflicts	0.86	0.73	0.96	1.05
Vandalism	0.58	0.80	0.66	0.93
Use of alcohol	0.53	0.67	0.55	0.72
Theft	0.52	0.76	0.55	0.72
Drug abuse	0.52	0.65	0.46	0.01
Dropouts	0.39	0.54	1.09	1.13
Student pregnancy	0.36	0.59	0.41	0.01
Class cutting	0.35	0.57	0.35	0.56
Possession of weapons	0.27	0.48	0.32	0.01
N (sample size, weighted size)	9,526	83,909	9,098	79,618

SOURCE: 1999–2000 and 1993–1994 SASS, public school principal files.
NOTE: Items have been re-coded and thus do not correspond to SASS.
SCALE: 0 = not a problem, 1 = minor, 2 = moderate, 3 = serious problem.

Table C.2

Private School Principals' Perceptions of SASS Items on School-Problems Rating Scale

	1999–2000 SASS		1993–1994 SASS	
Questionnaire Item: *To what extent is . . . a problem?*	Mean	Std. Dev.	Mean	Std. Dev.
Students unprepared to learn	0.85	0.85	0.61	0.95
Student poverty	0.72	0.99	0.59	1.10
Lack of parental involvement	0.74	1.09	0.62	1.06
Student tardiness	0.91	0.78	0.74	0.98
Student absenteeism	0.60	0.83	0.50	0.74
Student apathy	0.67	0.84	0.32	0.64
Disrespect for teachers	0.62	0.69	0.50	0.86
Poor student health	0.37	0.67	0.27	0.65
Physical conflicts	0.47	0.66	0.42	0.64
Vandalism	0.29	0.63	0.36	0.72
Use of alcohol	0.24	0.55	0.22	0.67
Theft	0.26	0.55	0.24	0.57
Drug abuse	0.21	0.50	0.16	0.62
Dropouts	0.17	0.59	0.13	0.56
Student pregnancy	0.09	0.47	0.08	0.37
Class cutting	0.10	0.38	0.09	0.34
Possession of weapons	0.05	0.26	0.05	0.28
N (sample size, weighted size)	2,734	26,231	2,732	24,964

SOURCE: 1999–2000 and 1993–1994 SASS, private school principal files.
NOTE: Items have been re-coded and thus do not correspond to SASS.
SCALE: 0 = not a problem, 1 = minor, 2 = moderate, 3 = serious problem.

We labeled the first factor "individual student problems" and included in it all questions about student drug and/or alcohol abuse, pregnancy, dropping out, cutting class, and student apathy. We labeled the second factor "poverty and family-related problems"; it includes ratings on students coming to school unprepared to learn, student absenteeism, student tardiness, poverty, lack of parental involvement, and poor student health. Finally, we labeled the third factor "school conflict." It includes items on vandalism of school property, physical conflict among students, robbery or theft, student disrespect of teachers, and possession of weapons. Table C.3 provides the results of the factor analysis for the public school principals' responses.

When we applied the same factor analysis to the responses of private school principals to the same 17 questions included in the 1999–2000 SASS, a different set of three factors resulted: (1) poverty, (2) family-related problems, school conflict, and individual problems, and (3) tardiness and absenteeism. However, to allow public-private comparisons, we decided to use the original three groups for further analysis.[6]

Table C.3

Factor Analysis Results for School Problems

	Factor		
Questionnaire Item: *To what extent is . . . a problem?*	1	2	3
Student use of alcohol	0.85		
Student drug abuse	0.85		
Student pregnancy	0.81		
Student dropping out	0.78		
Student cutting class	0.72		
Student apathy	0.47		
Poverty		0.81	
Students unprepared to learn		0.82	
Poor student health		0.70	
Lack of parent involvement		0.72	
Student tardiness		0.41	
Student absenteeism		0.55	
Vandalism of school property			0.74
Robbery or theft			0.73
Physical conflict among students			0.72
Student possession of weapons			0.60
Student disrespect for teachers			0.55

NOTE: Eigenvalues for the three factors were all greater than 1. Total variance explained is 60 percent. Method used was principal component factor analysis with a varimax rotation.

[6]To test whether using different factors would significantly alter the results, we estimated Equation C.1 (shown later in this section) using both sets of groupings. The results were quite similar. Even though the coefficients varied in magnitude for the different factors (e.g., poverty and family-related problems in the public principals case versus poverty, family-related, and school conflict problems in the private principals case), the signs of the coefficients were almost always in the same direction.

For each of the three problem groups, we calculated an average score variable for each school by averaging the rating attributed to each problem within that group. Table C.4 provides the mean and standard errors of the average score for each problem group for public and private principals in 1993–1994 and 1999–2000.[7]

In 2000, public school principals perceived on average fewer poverty and family-related problems than they did in 1994, but there was no statistically significant difference in terms of their average ratings of individual student and school conflict problems.[8]

Private school principals perceived the three types of school problems as less serious than their public counterparts did in both 1993–1994 and 1999–2000 (see Table C.4). Their worst rating was given to poverty and family-related problems—just as was the case for public school principals—but their mean rating for this problem was only 0.60, somewhere between "not a problem" and "minor."

Whereas the average problem ratings of public school principals dropped or remained constant between 1994 and 2000, private principals' ratings of all three types of problems rose on average from 1994 to 2000. This suggests that working conditions may have worsened in private schools relative to public schools during this period.

Using this information, we looked to see whether there was a statistical relationship between observable school characteristics and principals' perceptions of school problems.

Table C.4

Mean Scores of Constructed School Problem Variables

	Public Schools		Private Schools	
Factor	1999–2000	1993–1994	1999–2000	1993–1994
1. Individual student problems	0.52	0.54	0.25	0.22
	(0.005)	(0.01)	(0.01)	(0.01)
2. Poverty and family-related problems	1.2	1.1	0.61	0.47
	(0.01)	(0.01)	(0.01)	(0.01)
3. School conflict problems	0.61	0.65	0.34	0.29
	(0.005)	(0.01)	(0.01)	(0.01)

SOURCE: 1999–2000 and 1993–1994 SASS, public and private school principal files.
NOTE: Standard errors are in parentheses.
SCALE: 0 = not a problem, 1 = minor, 2 = moderate, 3 = serious problem.

[7]For easier interpretation of the regression results, we used average scores instead of factor scores. To ensure this measure was robust, the analysis was done with both composite and factor scores. We found no significant differences in the signs of the coefficients (results are available upon request).

[8]All statistically significant differences across years and between private and public school principals discussed in the text are significant at the 5 percent level.

To analyze the link between observable school characteristics and school problems, we specified the following equation:

$$MEANSC_{ij} = \alpha + \beta_1 X_i + \beta_3 S_j + \varepsilon_{ij} \quad \text{(C.1)}$$

where i = the principal and j = the school. Equation C.1 was then estimated using linear regression. We used SAS with the SUDAAN statistical software package, using Balance Repeated Replication (BRR) techniques to produce correct standard errors.

The analysis was conducted separately for public and private schools and for each of the three problem groups. The dependent variable, MEANSC, is the average of principal i in school j's rating on each of the items in the relevant problem group. The scores range from 0 to 3, with increasing scores reflecting more-serious problems.[9] As shown earlier, in the tables, the scores are interpreted as follows: 0 = not a problem, 1 = minor problem, 2 = moderate problem, and 3 = serious problem. X is a vector of the principal's characteristics, such as experience, age, and race/ethnicity; S is a vector of the school's observable characteristics, such as percentage of low-income students (i.e., those enrolled in free and reduced-price lunch programs), percentage of minority enrollment, urbanicity, school type, and school size.

Table B.3 in Appendix B summarizes the variables used in this and other regressions. For public schools, the 1999–2000 analysis included a dummy variable equaling 1 if the school was a charter school. For private schools, the vector S also included a dummy variable equaling 1 if the school was nonsectarian. For the public school analysis of the full sample of principals, we included state-level dummy variables to capture differences across states. However, the number of observations could not support the use of state-level dummy variables for the private school analysis,[10] so we included a dummy variable reflecting the proportion of public school teachers in the state that were unionized.

To test the hypothesis that minority enrollment has an effect on principals' perceptions of school problems, we used two different measures of diversity. The first was simply the percentage of minority students in the school. The second was a normalized index of integration for n groups, following White (1986) (see Appendix A for a description). The model also included both of these variables' squared terms.

A full description of the variables used in the regression analyses, including means and standard deviations where relevant, is in Tables C.5 (for public schools) and C.6 (for private schools).

---

[9]For easier interpretation of this variable, the scores were re-coded from their original coding in SASS. SASS coded responses on a scale of 1 to 4, where 1 = serious problem, 2 = minor, 3 = moderate, and 4 = not a problem.

[10]Only the public school sample was designed to be representative at the state level.

Table C.5

Descriptive Statistics of Variables Used in Public School Analysis

Variable Name	Variable Definition	Mean	Std. Dev.	Min	Max
	Independent Variables				
School descriptors					
ELEMENT	School's highest grade is 7th	0.583		0	1
MIDDLE	School's highest grade is 8th or 9th	0.139		0	1
HIGHSCH	School has 10th grade or higher	0.201		0	1
COMBSCH	Combined school (see Appendix A)	0.077		0	1
ENROL1[a]	Number of students enrolled in school	53.7	37.8	0.2	538
PCMINENR	Percent minority students	32.8		0	100
DIVINDEX	Normalized interaction index	0.33		0	1
PCTLUNCH	Percent receiving free and reduced-price lunch	37.6		0	100
PCTLEP	Percent limited English proficient students	5.07		0	100
Principals' characteristics					
PEXP	Principal's years of principal experience	8.9	10.4	0	67
TEXP	Principal's years of teaching experience	14.0	10.1	0	44
FEMALE	Principal is female (=1)	0.43		0	1
PRAMIN	Principal is American Indian (=1)	0.085		0	1
PRASIAN	Principal is Asian (=1)	0.075		0	1
PRBLACK	Principal is black (=1)	0.110		0	1
PRWHITE	Principal is white (=1)	0.822		0	1
PRHISP	Principal is Hispanic (=1)	0.0516		0	1
Regional characteristics					
URBAN	School is in city	0.24		0	1
SUBURBAN	School is in urban fringe of large/mid-size city, large town (=1)	0.449		0	1
RURAL	Small town or rural (=1)	0.311		0	1
CHARTER	School is charter school (=1)	0.0117		0	1
BIA	Bureau of Indian Affairs school (=1)	0.014		0	1
HIUNION	State has rates of public teacher unionization between 92 and 100 percent (=1)			0	1
MIUNION	State has rates of public teacher unionization between 54 and 83 percent (=1)			0	1
	Dependent Variables[b]				
INDPROB	Individual student problems	0.52	0.47	0	3
POVFAMPROB	Poverty and family-related problems	1.23	0.73	0	3
CONFLICT	School conflict problems	0.67	0.47	0	3
Valid N (weighted)	77,477				

SOURCE: 1990–2000 SASS, public principal and school questionnaires.

[a]Enrollment figures have been multiplied by 0.1.

[b]The scores here are averages of principals' responses on the items included in the specific factor.

Table C.6

Descriptive Statistics of Variables Used in Private School Analysis

Variable Name	Variable Definition	Mean	Std. Dev.	Min	Max
	Independent Variables				
School descriptors					
ELEMENT	School's highest grade is 7th	31.7		0	100
MIDDLE	School highest grade is 8th or 9th	1.0		0	100
HIGHSCH	School has 10th grade or higher	9.9		0	100
COMBSCH	School is combined (see Appendix A)	57.4		0	100
ENROL1[a]	Number of students enrolled in school	22.1	18.3	0.4	281.7
PCMINENR	Percent minority students	22.7		0	100
DIVINDEX	Normalized interaction index	0.30		0	0.94
PCTLUNCH	Percent receiving free and reduced-price lunch	3.0		0	100
PCTLEP	Percent limited English proficient students	0.7		0	100
Principals' characteristics					
PEXP	Principal's years of principal experience	10.2	10.6	0	60
TEXP	Principal's years of teaching experience	14.5	11.4	0	59
FEMALE	Principal is female (=1)	0.54		0	1
PRAMIN	Principal is American Indian (=1)	0.06		0	1
PRASIAN	Principal is Asian (=1)	0.014		0	1
PRBLACK	Principal is black (=1)	0.06		0	1
PRWHITE	Principal is white (=1)	0.89		0	1
PRHISP	Principal is Hispanic (=1)	0.032		0	1
Regional characteristics					
URBAN	School is in city	0.429		0	1
SUBURBAN	School is in urban fringe of large/mid-size city, large town (=1)	0.393		0	1
RURAL	Small town or rural (=1)	0.178		0	1
CATHOLIC	School is Catholic (=1)	0.634		0	1
OTHAFFIL	School has other affiliation (–1)	0.072		0	1
NOAFFIL	School has no affiliation (=1)	0.294		0	1
	Dependent Variables[b]				
INDPROB	Individual problems	0.25	0.38	0	3
POVFAMPROB	Poverty and family-related problems	0.61	0.58	0	3
CONFLICT	School conflict problems	0.34	0.38	0	3
Valid N (weighted)	23,006				

SOURCE: 1990–2000 SASS, private principal and school questionnaires.

[a]Enrollment figures have been multiplied by 0.1.

[b]The scores here are averages of principals' responses on the items included in the specific factor.

FINDINGS

On average, public school principals rated their schools as having not serious or minor problems in all three problem groups, or categories. Looking at the standard deviations, we concluded that most of the public schools were rated like this, with only a small percentage being rated as having moderate and serious problems, particularly in category 1, poverty and family-related problems.

Tables C.7 and C.8 present the results of estimating Equation C.1 for public and private schools, respectively, using the results for the regression models with state

Table C.7

Regression Results of Public School Characteristics on School Problems

Variable Name	Individual	Poverty and Family-Related	Conflict
ELEMENT	–1.08[a]	–0.35[a]	–0.21[a]
	(0.014)	(0.017)	(0.016)
MIDDLE	–0.64[a]	–0.26[a]	0.02
	(0.018)	(0.020)	(0.017)
COMBSCH	–0.80[a]	–0.30[a]	–0.16[a]
	(0.024)	(0.026)	(0.020)
ENROL1	0.0011[a]	0.0011[b]	0.0031[a]
	(0.0003)	(0.0004)	(0.0003)
ENROLSQ1	–0.000001	–0.000004[a]	–0.00006[a]
	(0.0000001)	(0.000001)	(0.000001)
DIVINDEX	–0.09	–0.04	0.17
	(0.103)	(0.181)	(0.135)
DIVINDSQ	–0.02	0.27[a]	–0.06
	(0.082)	(0.135)	(0.119)
PCTLUNCH	0.0020[a]	0.0091[a]	0.0031[a]
	(0.0003)	(0.0004)	(0.0003)
PCTLEP	–0.0006	–0.0005	–0.0022[a]
	(0.0005)	(0.0008)	(0.0006)
RURAL	0.06[a]	0.03	0.03
	(0.015)	(0.022)	(0.019)
SUBURBAN	0.01	–0.00	–0.01
	(0.013)	(0.023)	(0.017)
PCMINENR	0.004[a]	0.004	0.001
	(0.002)	(0.003)	(0.002)
PCTMINSQ	–0.00003[b]	–0.00001	0.0001
	(0.000002)	(0.00003)	(0.00001)
PEXP	–0.002[a]	–0.004[a]	–0.0024[a]
	(0.001)	(0.001)	(0.0006)
PRASIAN	–0.09[b]	–0.18	–0.10
	(0.054)	(0.118)	(0.095)
PRBLACK	–0.09[a]	–0.12[a]	–0.04
	(0.017)	(0.034)	(0.024)
PRHISP	–0.05[b]	–0.11[a]	–0.07[a]
	(0.028)	(0.043)	(0.034)
PRAMIN	0.02	0.02	0.08[b]
	(0.034)	(0.047)	(0.043)
CHARTER	–0.08[a]	–0.08[a]	–0.10[a]
	(0.015)	(0.022)	(0.017)
BIA	0.12[a]	–0.05	0.13[a]
	(0.037)	(0.049)	(0.041)
R-squared	0.60	0.34	0.18

NOTE: Standard errors are in parentheses. Omitted categories are high school, principal is white, and rural. Coefficients for state dummies are not shown. Coefficients on female and PEXP are not shown (all were 0 or not significant).

[a]Significant at 95 percent confidence level.

[b]Significant at 90 percent confidence level.

Table C.8

Regression Results of Private School Characteristics on School Problems

Variable Name	Individual	Poverty and Family-Related	Conflict
ELEMENT	–0.49[a]	–0.27[a]	–0.09[a]
	(0.041)	(0.059)	(0.039)
MIDDLE	–0.35[a]	–0.10	–0.15
	(0.063)	(0.144)	(0.100)
COMBSCH	–0.41[a]	–0.14[a]	–0.08[a]
	(0.030)	(0.040)	(0.024)
ENROL1	0.001[a]	–0.004[a]	0.002[a]
	(0.0001)	(0.001)	(0.001)
ENROLSQ1	0.000005	0.000013[a]	–0.000004
	(0.000003)	(0.000004)	(0.000004)
DIVINDEX	0.00	0.45[a]	–0.31[b]
	(0.134)	(0.205)	(0.148)
DIVINDSQ	0.09	–0.03	0.58[a]
	(0.133)	(0.210)	(0.147)
PCTLUNCH	0.005[a]	0.006[a]	0.006[a]
	(0.001)	(0.001)	(0.001)
FEMALE	–0.08[a]	–0.05[a]	–0.03[b]
	(0.015)	(0.023)	(0.018)
RURAL	0.04[b]	0.04	0.00
	(0.021)	(0.031)	(0.027)
SUBURBAN	0.02	0.002	0.001
	(0.016)	(0.024)	(0.019)
PCMINENR	–0.003	–0.005	–0.005
	(0.003)	(0.004)	(0.0025)
PCTMINSQ	0.00	0.00010[a]	0.00
	(0.000)	(0.00004)	(0.000)
PEXP	–0.00	–0.00	0.00
	(0.001)	(0.001)	(0.001)
PRASIAN	–0.04	–0.21[a]	–0.01
	(0.039)	(0.071)	(0.046)
PRBLACK	–0.06	–0.20[a]	–0.06
	(0.042)	(0.081)	(0.054)
PRHISP	0.06	0.04	–0.03
	(0.047)	(0.075)	(0.052)
PRAMIN	0.09	0.61[a]	0.27
	(0.100)	(0.306)	(0.193)
CATHOLIC	–0.14[a]	–0.01	–0.04[b]
	(0.025)	(0.034)	(0.022)
OTHAFFIL	–0.18[a]	–0.02	–0.08[a]
	(0.038)	(0.055)	(0.035)
R-squared	0.30	0.20	0.10

NOTE: Standard errors are in parentheses. Omitted categories are high school, principal is white, and rural. Coefficients for state dummies are not shown. Coefficients on PCTLEP and PEXP are not shown (all were 0 or not significant).

[a]Significant at 95 percent confidence level.

[b]Significant at 90 percent confidence level.

dummies. In general, most of the coefficients on the independent variables were significant and had the expected sign. Some variables, however, had a surprising effect.[11]

Grade Level and Size of School

On average, principals in public elementary, combined, and middle schools perceived fewer problems than principals in public high schools did. This was true even when we controlled for school enrollment level. This effect is stronger for the individual student problem category, which is logical since one would not expect many elementary students to become pregnant or to drop out of school. On average, principals' ratings of individual student problems in elementary schools were 1.08 points lower (on a four-point scale) than those of principals in high schools. This is over two standard deviations of the individual student problem score variable. Public elementary school principals perceived close to one-half (40 percent) of a standard deviation fewer poverty and family-related problems and fewer school conflict problems than high school principals did. Public combined and middle school principals also reported fewer problems of all types compared with high school principals, but the magnitude of the differences was smaller than that for high school and elementary school principals.

In private schools, there was a similar relationship between grade level and principals' perceptions of school problems. On average, private elementary, combined, and middle school principals perceived more problems than their counterparts in private high schools did. The magnitudes of parameter estimates for the elementary, combined, and middle school dummy variables in the regression analysis using the individual problems mean score as the dependent variable (–0.49, –0.41, and –0.35, respectively) imply that these private principals' perceptions of individual problems were more than one standard deviation lower than those of principals in private high schools.

Principals in private elementary and combined schools also perceived fewer poverty and family-related problems than principals in private high schools did, an effect close to one-half of a standard deviation. The coefficient for middle schools in this case was not significant. With respect to school conflict, principals in private elementary and combined schools perceived less conflict than principals in private high schools did, with an effect close to one-third of a standard deviation.

Enrollment is related to principals' reports of problems in both the public and the private sector, even after controlling for the schools' grade levels. With some exceptions, principals at larger schools perceived more problems, although the relationships differed for the sectors.

---

[11]We ran the same model using data from the 1990–1991 SASS to check for result robustness. The model could only be run for the individual problem and conflict variables, since most of the questions included in the poverty and family-related factor were not asked in the 1990–1991 SASS wave. Still, many of the relationships we found for the 1999–2000 and 1993–1994 data also held for the 1990–1991 data.

In public schools, principals' perceptions of individual student problems increased with student enrollment over the range of data and there was a nonlinear relationship between perceptions of poverty and family-related problems and school conflict problems and student enrollment. For perceptions of poverty and family-related and school conflict problems, ratings increased with enrollment up to enrollment levels of about 1,500 (1,430 for poverty and family-related problems and 1,575 for school conflict problems) and then began to decline.[12] The impact of enrollment on school problem ratings relative to very small schools was small for schools of average size (0.05 for individual student problems and poverty and family-related problems, and 0.14 for school conflict problems). However, over the range of the data, differences in enrollment could contribute to differences in problem ratings of up to 0.57 (over one standard deviation) for individual student problems, 0.08 (about one-tenth of a standard deviation) for poverty and family-related problems, and 0.24 (one-half of a standard deviation) for school conflict problems.

In private schools, the relationship between enrollment and problems was positive and linear for individual student and school conflict problems. As with public schools, the impact of enrollment on problem ratings was small for the average-sized private school (0.02 for individual student problems, 0.04 for school conflict problems). However, the difference between the smallest and largest schools could be quite large. For individual student problems, the larger schools, compared with the smaller schools, were rated up to 0.28 point higher (three-quarters of a standard deviation); for school conflict problems, they were rated up to 0.56 point higher (one and one-half of a standard deviation).

The relationship between enrollment and poverty and family-related problems in private schools was nonlinear and opposite to that found for public schools. Poverty and family-related problems were greatest in small private schools and decreased as enrollment grew to levels of about 1,500 students. At that point, problems began to increase with enrollment. Again, enrollment had only a small effect on poverty and family-related problem ratings for the average-sized private school (–0.08 for individual student problems, 0.04 for school conflict problems), but it could make a large difference between the smallest schools and schools with about 1,500 students, reducing the mean score by 0.31 (just over one-half of a standard deviation).

Overall, both grade level and enrollment related to principals' reports of school problems in a way that suggests working conditions are worse in high schools and in large (although perhaps not the largest) schools.

Minority Enrollment and Student Diversity

In public schools, the percentage of minority students enrolled related to principals' perceptions of individual student problems in a nonlinear way, but the magnitude of the effect was small. Individual student problem scores increased (worsened) as the

[12] The largest public school in the sample had 5,380 students; the largest private school had 2,270.

percentage of minority students increased up to minority enrollment levels of 64 percent; thereafter, these scores decreased with further increases in the percentage. However, the effect of minority enrollment on the individual student problem score was quite small: Relative to a school with no minority students, the average school was rated 0.09 point higher, and a school with the critical value of minority enrollment—64 percent—was rated 0.12 point higher. In other words, the minority enrollment percentage contributed at most only one-quarter of a standard deviation to differences across schools in the principals' reports of individual student problems. There was no relationship between minority student enrollment and principals' perceptions of poverty and family-related or school conflict problems in public schools, or between minority student enrollment and principals' perceptions of any of the three types of school problems in private schools.

To measure diversity more precisely, in terms of heterogeneity of racial groups, we included the normalized integration index (DIVINDEX) and the normalized integration index squared (DIVINDSQ) in the model. In the case of public school principals, the only statistically significant relationship was for the poverty and family-related problems variable. The coefficient of DIVINDEX on the poverty and family-related problems variable was negative (–0.04), and the coefficient of DIVINDSQ was positive (0.27), suggesting that there is a nonlinear relationship between student diversity and these problems. Principals' perceptions of poverty and family-related problems decreased as school diversity increased up to levels of 0.07 (a quite nondiverse, or homogeneous, school).[13] Beyond that level, as the school became more diverse, principals' perceptions of poverty and family-related problems began to increase considerably. Principals with completely diverse, or heterogeneous, schools (DIVINDEX = 1) rated their schools 0.23 point higher (worse) than principals at a completely homogeneous but otherwise comparable school. This is slightly over one-third of a standard deviation.

The results for private schools were quite different. The coefficients on the diversity index were significant in the regressions using perceptions of poverty and family-related problems and school conflict problems as dependent variables. The effect was much larger than that for public school principals. The regression analyses suggest that principals in completely homogeneous, or nondiverse, private schools perceived the fewest poverty and family-related problems. Principals in the most heterogeneous, or diverse, private schools perceived the most poverty and family-related problems, rating their schools 0.45 point (close to three-quarters of a standard deviation) worse.

Principals' perceptions of school conflict problems were lowest for moderately diverse (DIVINDEX = 0.22) schools. Above that level, ratings of school conflict problems worsened, with principals in completely diverse private schools rating their schools 0.31 point (over three-quarters of a standard deviation) worse.

---

[13]However, the effect on the poverty and family-related problems rating was only –0.001, an almost negligible improvement on the average ratings.

Low-Income and LEP Students

In both the public and the private sector, principals at schools with higher proportions of low-income students (i.e., students enrolled in free and reduced-price lunch programs) perceived all three categories of problems to be greater in their schools. Although the effect of a one percentage point increase in the proportion of low-income students was quite small, the overall difference in problems perceived between low- and high-income schools could be substantial. In both private and public schools, the relationship was strongest for perceptions of poverty and family-related problems—up to 0.91 rating point in public schools and 0.66 point in private schools—when we compared schools that had all students in free and reduced-price lunch programs with schools that had no students in the programs. The magnitude of this maximal relationship was over one standard deviation in both sectors.

More surprisingly, the percentage of low-income students was also related to principals' perceptions of individual student and school conflict problems. For principals' perceptions of school conflict problems, the percentage of low-income students could account for differences of up to about one-half of a standard deviation among public schools, and well over one standard deviation among private schools.

The percentage of limited English proficient (LEP) students had a statistically significant relationship with principals' perceptions of school conflict problems in public schools. We identified no significant relationships between this variable and perceptions of the other two types of problems in the public sector or between this variable and perceptions of any of the three types of problems in the private sector. Public schools with a higher proportion of LEP students had fewer perceived school conflict problems, with the difference between schools with no LEP students and 100 percent LEP students equal to –0.22 (nearly half of a standard deviation).

Urbanicity

The regression results suggest that urbanicity is not strongly related to principals' perceptions of school problems.[14] Principals in public schools in rural areas perceived more individual problems on average than principals in cities or large towns did. The effect was slightly over one-tenth of a standard deviation.

In the case of public school principals, none of the coefficients on the SUBURBAN dummy variable was statistically significant. For private schools, none of the coefficients on the rural and suburban variables was statistically significant.

Charter and Bureau of Indian Affairs Schools

On average, and holding all else equal in the model, principals in charter schools perceived fewer problems in all three categories. The effects were close to one-fifth

[14]The urbanicity variable was taken from the SASS coding of "locale." It is a three-category grouping that lumps together large and mid-size cities in "city," urban fringe of large or mid-size cities or large towns in "suburban," and rural or small towns in "rural." Here, rural is the omitted category.

of a standard deviation in the individual student and school conflict problem categories, and close to one-tenth of a standard deviation in the poverty and family-related problems category.

Principals in Bureau of Indian Affairs (BIA) schools perceived more individual student and school conflict problems than principals in non-BIA schools did. These effects were slightly over one-quarter of a standard deviation, holding all else equal.

Religious Orientation of School

We found a statistically significant relationship between a private school being Catholic or of another religious affiliation and principals' perceptions of all three types of school problems. Principals in Catholic private schools perceived fewer individual student problems than principals in nonsectarian schools did. This effect was slightly over one-third of a standard deviation. Principals in private schools of other affiliations perceived fewer individual student problems and more school conflict problems than did principals in nonsectarian schools. This effect was close to one-half and one-fifth of a standard deviation, respectively.

Characteristics of Principals

We used variables to control for a principal's characteristics and to see whether they had a significant effect on the principal's perceptions of school problems. A principal's experience as a principal had a statistically significant relationship to his or her perceptions of school problems in public schools only, and even there, the effect was quite small.

We included dummy variables to account for a principal's race/ethnicity to see whether this had any relationship to his or her perceptions of school problems. We thought this would be an interesting variable to analyze, given the growing demand for more diversity among principals as a way to reflect the school population and provide role models who look more like the students themselves (Shen, Rodriguez-Campos, and Rincones-Gomez, 2000).

In the public sector, minority principals perceived fewer school problems on average than white principals did. These effects were not very large but were statistically significant. Compared to white principals, Asian, black, and Hispanic principals perceived close to one-fifth of a standard deviation fewer individual student problems; black and Hispanic principals perceived roughly one-sixth of a standard deviation fewer poverty and family-related problems; and Hispanic principals perceived one-sixth of a standard deviation fewer school conflict problems. In contrast, Native American principals perceived roughly one-sixth of a standard deviation more school conflict problems than white principals did.

In the case of private schools, a principal's race/ethnicity had significant effects on the poverty and family-related problems variable. Asian and black principals perceived roughly one-third of a standard deviation fewer of this category of problems than white principals did. And Native American principals perceived close to one standard deviation more of this category of problems than white principals did.

Apparently, in both public and private schools, minority principals other than Native American principals seem to perceive their working conditions more favorably than white principals do. Since minority principals work mostly in high-minority, lower-income, and larger schools, we found the negative coefficient on the black, Hispanic, and Asian principal dummy variables to be quite surprising.

There are two possible explanations: (1) minority and white principals have different standards regarding what constitutes a problem, or (2) minority principals have better working conditions—at least in their opinion—or are more successful at managing their schools and thus perceive fewer problems compared with white principals in similar schools.

We investigated the hypothesis that even under similar circumstances, minority principals would perceive fewer problems than their white counterparts would. The SASS asks public school teachers only two questions that can be crossed with school problems to assess how perceptions may differ under similar circumstances: "How many times have you been threatened by a student?" and "How many times have you been physically attacked by a student?" We added the responses given to both of these questions by teachers in the principals' schools. Then we looked at minority and white principals' ratings of all the items included in the problem variables—including, "To what extent is student disrespect of teachers a problem?" We wanted to investigate whether these perceptions significantly differed for black and white principals in schools with the same number of attacks and threats.

The results are presented in Table C.9. We found that all principals in schools where teachers reported the larger numbers of attacks and threats gave worse ratings on the school conflict variable—regardless of their race/ethnicity. In schools with similar numbers of attacks and threats, black principals gave worse ratings on school conflict and poverty and family-related problems than white principals did. In other words, in "similar" circumstances, black principals rated their schools as having more problems in these two categories.

Hispanic principals, in contrast, rated their schools better than white principals did even under "similar" circumstances. This was true for all three categories of problems and could be an important reason why the coefficient on the dummy variable for Hispanic principals was negative. The negative coefficient on the black principal dummy variable for poverty and family-related problems is more complicated to explain.

The descriptive statistics in Table C.9 help in understanding the context in which minority principals work. We can see that black and Hispanic principals on average worked in public schools with more minority, LEP, and free and reduced-price lunch students than their white counterparts did. In addition, black and Hispanic principals ran larger schools and had fewer years of experience in their current school. The average non-white principal had 10 percent black or Hispanic students in his or her

Table C.9

Public School Principals' Responses on School Conflict Variable, by Race/Ethnicity

	Black Principals		Hispanic Principals		White Principals	
	Mean	Std. Dev.	Mean	Std. Dev.	Mean	Std. Dev.
Schools with similar numbers of attacks and threats[a]						
Individual student problems	0.48	0.71	0.45	0.89	0.57	0.77
Poverty and family-related problems	1.56	0.83	1.33	0.96	1.36	0.77
School conflict problems	0.91	0.71	0.65	0.69	0.73	0.51
Possession of weapons	0.41	0.71	0.27	0.55	0.32	0.51
Disrespect of teachers	1.40	1.18	0.81	0.96	1.14	0.77
Physical conflict among students	1.32	1.18	0.77	0.96	0.99	0.77
Valid N (listwise)	140		47		661	
All schools						
Individual student problems	0.45	0.32	0.47	0.83	0.54	0.90
Poverty and family-related problems	1.49	0.95	1.41	0.83	1.18	0.90
School conflict problems	0.74	0.63	0.63	0.62	0.63	0.90
Possession of weapons	0.29	0.63	0.22	0.41	0.27	0.90
Disrespect of teachers	1.13	0.95	0.92	1.24	0.95	0.90
Physical conflict among students	1.06	0.95	0.85	1.03	0.84	0.90
Percent minority students	73.8		69.2		25.3	
Percent black students	54.0		12.0		10.0	
Percent Hispanic students	11.0		46.0		10.0	
Percent students on free and reduced-price lunch	59.8		59.0		33.4	
Percent LEP students	5.5		18.3		4.2	
Experience in this school (years)	4.8		4.4		5.1	
School size	590		660		520	
Valid N (listwise)	993		428		8,105	

[a]Schools included had teacher reports of more than one student attack and one student threat.

school, while the average black principal worked in a school having 54 percent black students. Hispanic principals worked in schools where 46 percent of students were Hispanic. Clearly, minority principals tend to work in schools in which higher proportions of students share their race/ethnicity.

When we controlled for these context variables, our regression results showed that black and Hispanic principals perceived fewer problems on average than white principals did.

CONCLUSIONS

We found that schools' observable demographic characteristics are significantly related to principals' perceptions of school problems. Overall, private school principals perceived their schools as having fewer problems than did public school principals. Most of the independent variables in the regression analyses were statistically significant. The independent variables having the strongest relationship with principals' perceptions of problems were school grade level, percentage of students in free and reduced-price lunch programs, and student enrollment. Independent variables reflecting the type of school (e.g., charter or BIA; Catholic or nonsectarian) had negligible effects on principals' perceptions of school problems. Variables such as a principal's experience in the school and the urbanicity of the area in which the school is located seem to have had minor or nonsignificant effects on principals' perceptions of school problems, all other things being equal. Large increases in a school's proportion of students in free and reduced-price lunch programs had very large effects on principals' perceptions of poverty and family-related problems and school conflict problems. Where LEP students were a very high proportion of the school, the number of LEP students had a moderate effect on principals' perceptions of school conflict. Minority principals perceived fewer problems on average than their white counterparts did, even though they had more-challenging working conditions.

Using this information, we were able to cluster schools according to the variables that have the largest negative and the largest positive effects on specific dimensions of principals' perceptions of their working conditions—again, defining working conditions in terms of the job's complexity as measured by the amount of problems the principal perceives.

For example, high schools and large schools seem to have more difficult working conditions. Religious private, public elementary, and charter schools with very homogeneous populations—no matter what race/ethnicity—can be clustered as having less-difficult working conditions. A principal's job in a large, very diverse high school, where he or she is of a race/ethnicity different from that of most of the students, could be labeled as more-difficult working conditions. These perceptions could translate into reputations, discouraging potential principals from entering certain schools or forcing certain schools to hire individuals with lower qualifications.

Appendix D

USING CURRENT POPULATION SURVEY DATA TO EXAMINE SCHOOL ADMINISTRATORS' CAREERS

The Current Population Survey (CPS) is a monthly household survey conducted by the Bureau of the Census for the Bureau of Labor Statistics (BLS). Approximately 60,000 households are interviewed each month. One adult in each household is asked to provide information for all adult members of the household; the data file generated contains an individual record for each adult person in each interviewed household. Sample weights are provided so that nationally representative tabulations can be made.

Households that enter the CPS are interviewed for four consecutive months, ignored for the subsequent eight months, then interviewed again for four additional consecutive months, and then dropped from the sample. With the eight-month break between interview spells, each household is interviewed over the same four-month period in two consecutive years. As a result, individuals can be matched across the two years they are included in the sample. However, the survey follows dwelling units, not specific people, so if people move out of a household during its time in the CPS interview sample, the new occupants are interviewed in subsequent months. This raises issues that must be considered when attempting to match individuals across years.

Different sets of questions are asked in different interview months. In the fourth and eighth month interviews, called the Outgoing Rotation Group (ORG) interviews, detailed employment-related questions are asked in addition to those about standard demographics. In these months, the data include information on weekly earnings and usual hours worked. Each year the BLS generates the Merged ORG file, which contains all ORG interviews in a given year. Because of this construction, an individual is observed only once in the Merged ORG file for a given year.

We obtained the data for our analysis from the National Bureau of Economic Research, which has compiled the Merged ORG files for 1979 through 2000. The variable definitions and response categories in the CPS vary across the years for which we had data, so we coded the data to make the variables we used consistent across all years. In doing so, we were constrained by the variable definitions with the least amount of detail. For example, the pre-1994 CPS questions on educational attainment asked for the highest grade attended and whether that grade had been completed. The responses for highest grade attended were then topcoded at 18 years or more, making it impossible to distinguish between a master's degree (18 years of schooling) and a doctorate (20 or more years). Beginning in 1994, the CPS asked about the highest degree awarded. Thus, to have a consistent time series, we collapsed the later, more detailed data into the broader categories we are able to identify in the pre-1994 data.

ANALYSIS OF TRENDS IN AVERAGE EARNINGS

We used the Merged ORG files to analyze trends in compensation for school administrators and for several other categories of professional occupations. Lawyers and judges, medical professionals, managers, and teachers are the other occupational categories we considered in our analysis.[1] We defined school administration rather broadly for this analysis: an individual is said to be in school administration if he or she is in a managerial occupation and reports elementary and secondary education as his/her industry.[2] We chose this broad definition because the occupation measures in the CPS appear to be rather noisy. Although there is a specific occupational category called "Administrators, education and related fields," we felt that it was not clear exactly which jobs would fit into this category. In analyzing the data, we found a lot of movement between managerial occupations within the elementary and secondary education industry. Although the broad definition brings in many people who are not principals and superintendents, we feel it is more important to have a clear understanding of who is truly included in the category.

Our sample was limited to full-time workers (people working 30 or more hours per week)[3] and excluded people who moved into or out of school administration from administrative support or service occupations. We made the latter restriction because we expected that such cases reflect a misreporting of occupation in one period. In addition, we restricted the sample for our analysis of trends in earnings to people we were able to match across years. Thus, we used a consistent sample across all analyses of CPS data reported here. Finally, we used data from 1983 through 2000 because CPS occupational categories changed in 1983 and there is no clear mapping between the two measures.

We used the consumer price index (CPI) for all urban consumers to convert the earnings measures to constant 1998 dollars. The conversion to real dollars allowed us to make comparisons over time that reflect changes in the purchasing power of an

---

[1]As defined by the 1980 Census of Population three-digit occupational classification, the occupational categories and associated codes are as follows: education administration ($3 \le occ \le 37$ and industry = 842), lawyers and judges (occ = 178 or 179), medical professionals ($84 \le occ \le 89$), managers ($3 \le occ \le 37$ and ind $\cong 842$), and teachers ($155 \le occ \le 159$).

[2]Examples of managerial occupations in the education industry are financial managers, personnel and labor relation managers, purchasing managers, and accountants and auditors.

[3]We limited the sample to full-time workers to purge any differences in compensation across occupations that are attributable to differences in the share of part-time workers.

occupation's compensation. We used the edited earnings per week variable, a continuous variable that is topcoded.[4]

Although the CPS is large and nationally representative, sample sizes can become relatively small when the analysis focuses on a specific occupation. Each year, the Merged ORG file contains between 250,000 and 300,000 observations, but only about 500 people report their occupation as education administration. When the yearly sample size for populations of interest is relatively small, descriptive statistics can be somewhat volatile, as the means are more sensitive to outliers. To address this issue, we constructed a three-year moving average for each of the outcome variables of interest for each occupation group.[5] The moving average smooths the observed trends by dampening the effects of extreme outliers on the year-to-year changes in the outcome variable.

Level of compensation is the primary determinant of how much labor is supplied to an occupation. Changes in compensation over time for a particular profession thus help to explain variations in the number of people willing and qualified to work in that area. We used CPS data to analyze trends in the compensation of school administrators between 1980 and 1999. We also compared the wages of school administrators with those of other professional occupations. These comparisons served two important purposes: (1) they allowed us to disentangle changes in compensation specific to educational administrators from broader trends seen throughout the labor market; (2) they allowed us to see whether the number of people entering or leaving positions in school administration was affected by any differences in compensation between school administrators and other, similar professionals.

It is important to note that the set of similar, or substitute, occupations that are relevant for comparison is determined by the definition of the career field boundary within the career flow model. For example, if the career field is defined very broadly to include all administrative positions in elementary and secondary education, then occupations such as lawyers, medical professionals, and managers are outside the career field and can be used for comparison. However, if the career field is defined more narrowly and the focus is on public education, then positions in private schools are outside the career field and can be considered as relevant occupations for comparison. In our analysis, we considered the career flow model from both of these perspectives. We defined the career field broadly and compared all school administrators to lawyers, medical professionals, and managers, and we then turned to the narrower definition and compared public school administrators to their counterparts in private schools. It is especially important to note that teachers—perhaps the

[4]Topcoding changed twice during the period we looked at. From 1983 to 1988, weekly earnings were topcoded at $999 per week (in nominal terms). From 1989 to 1997, they were topcoded at $1,923 per week; from 1998 on, they were topcoded at $2,884 per week.

[5]The three-year moving average for a particular year is calculated by taking the average of the mean value of the outcome variable over the three-year period surrounding the year of interest. For example, to calculate the moving average of weekly earnings for 1996, we took the average of mean weekly earnings for the years 1995, 1996, and 1997. Since three years of data are needed to calculate the moving average for a particular year, we were unable to calculate values for 1983 and 2000, the first and last years of the sample period.

most relevant career alternative for school administrators—are defined as outside the administrative career path. As a result, the results of our compensation comparisons between teachers and school administrators are given separately at the end of this section.

Comparison of School Administrators and Other Professional Occupations

To avoid interpretation problems related to differing contract lengths (school administrators typically have 11-month contracts, whereas other professionals tend to have 12-month appointments), we used real weekly earnings as a measure of compensation rather than annual income. Figure D.1 displays the average real weekly earnings for each profession between 1984 and 1999. The data show that while the level of compensation for school administrators grew by 11 percent over the two decades, the earnings gaps between school administrators and lawyers and between school administrators and medical professionals widened. In contrast, the earnings gap between school administrators and managers—the occupation most similar to school administration—remained relatively constant. In addition, the results show that the earnings of school administrators were subject to less cyclical variation than were the earnings of medical professionals and lawyers.

Even though school administrators typically are not paid by the hour, it is instructive to decompose the weekly earnings into the number of hours worked and the hourly wage. The decomposition is useful because the total weekly earnings may mask changes in hours worked and wages earned that may be of interest. Figure D.2 presents data indicating that school administrators earned on average 10 percent more

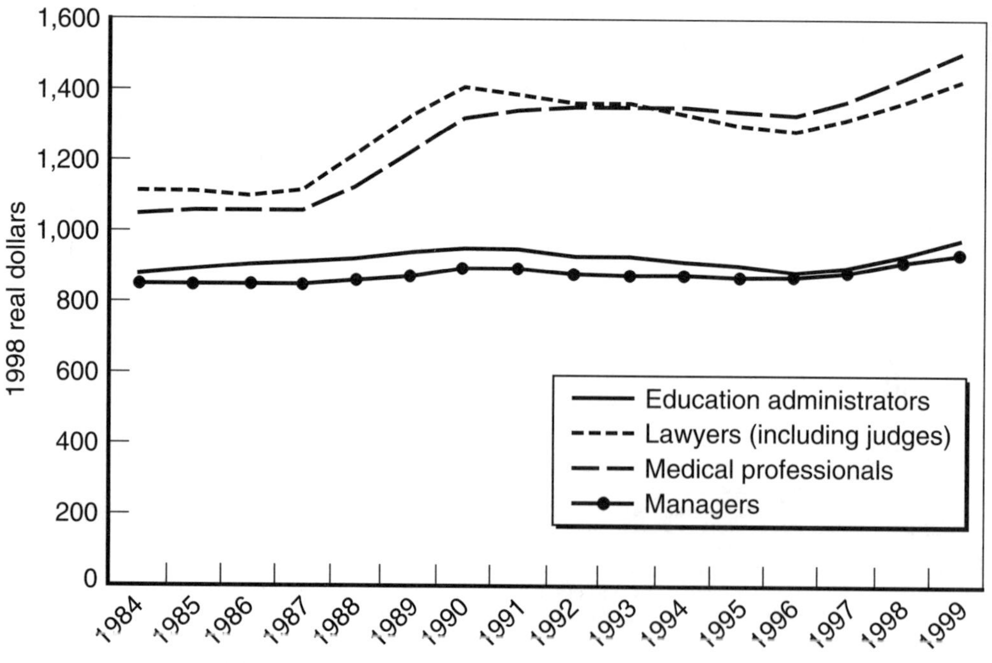

Figure D.1—Average Real Weekly Earnings Across Professions, 1984–1999

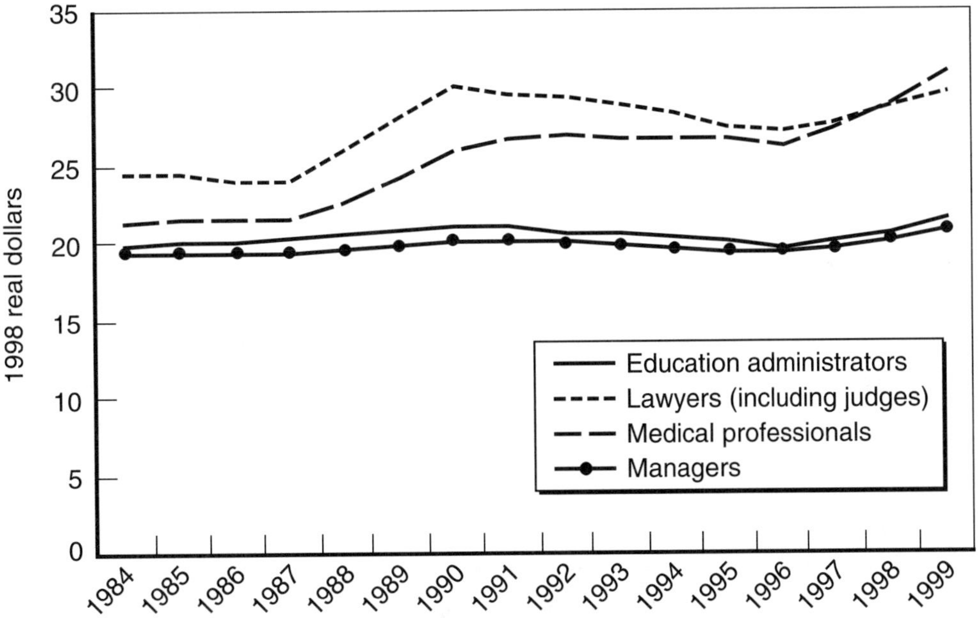

Figure D.2—Average Real Hourly Earnings Across Professions, 1984–1999

per hour in 1999 than they did in 1984. This growth in the hourly rate is slightly less than the observed growth in total weekly earnings, suggesting that the hours worked per week must have remained relatively constant during this time. Figure D.3's results show that this is the case: school administrators worked an additional hour per week in 1999 compared with 1984 (44.5 versus 44.6).

It is interesting to note that the gap between school administrators and lawyers is somewhat smaller for hourly wage rates (Figure D.2) than for weekly earnings (Figure D.1). The strong growth in earnings for lawyers during the late 1980s and early 1990s appears to have been driven in large part by an increase in the number of hours worked rather than an increase in the wage rate. Moreover, the hourly rate gap between school administrators and medical professionals was quite small until 1989, when the hourly rate for medical professionals began to grow relatively quickly. In this light, the changes in relative compensation between school administrators and other professional occupations are not as striking as the initial comparison of total weekly earnings suggested they would be.

Based on this examination, the compensation data do not suggest that the labor market for administrators is in a state of crisis. As evidence, the real value of compensation for school administrators has grown since 1980. Furthermore, the results from the comparisons across occupations indicate that although earnings have deteriorated for school administrators relative to some of the other professional occupations, the average weekly earnings of school administrators relative to managers have remained constant. Of the alternative professional occupations considered, the managerial ones are perhaps the most relevant to the choices potential school administrators make. The lower compensation of school administrators relative to

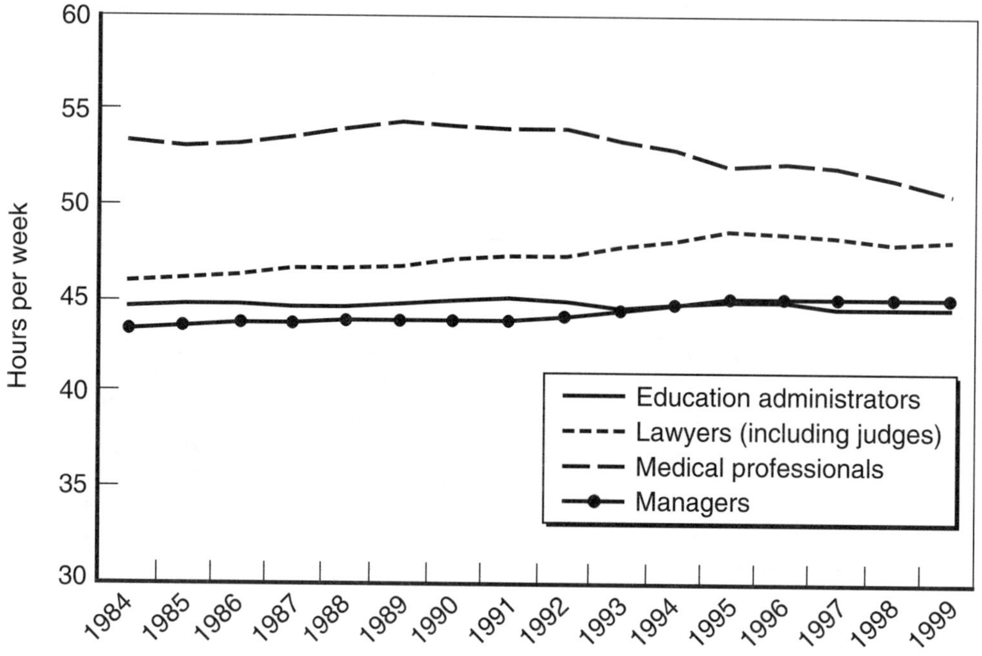

Figure D.3—Average Weekly Hours Worked Across Professions, 1984–1999

medical professionals and lawyers likely affects a person's choice of which occupation to enter originally, but the different schooling requirements among these professions make it unlikely that the compensation difference will spur many school administrators to leave school administration for careers in medicine or law. In contrast, the skills and training required for school administration and other managerial occupations are quite similar, making it relatively easy for someone to move between these two occupations. Thus, in this case, relative compensation is an important consideration.

Comparison of Public and Private School Administrators

A somewhat different picture emerged when we defined the career field more narrowly. Although public school administrators consistently earned more than their counterparts in private schools did, over the past two decades, the differential fell significantly. Figure D.4 shows that in 1984, public school administrators earned on average approximately 40 percent more per week than private school administrators did. By 1999, this earning gap had fallen to 12 percent. Average real hourly earnings saw a similar pattern, as shown in Figure D.5. If working conditions in the two sectors are assumed to have remained relatively constant, these findings suggest that private school administration has become more attractive relative to public school administration. Consequently, we might expect to see people moving out of public and into private school administrative positions.

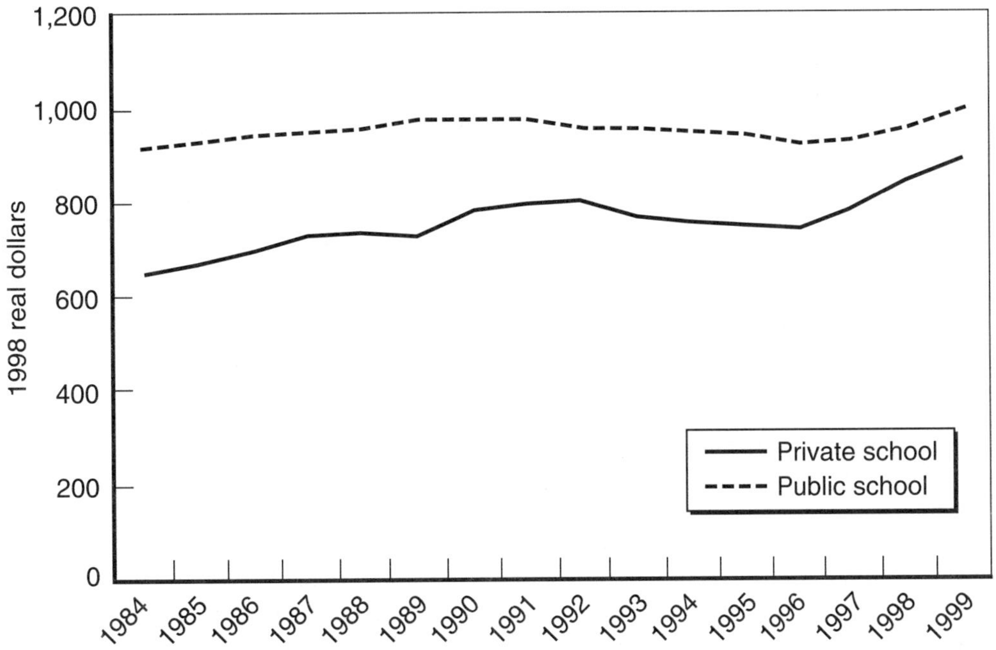

Figure D.4—Average Real Weekly Earnings of Public and Private School Administrators, 1984–1999

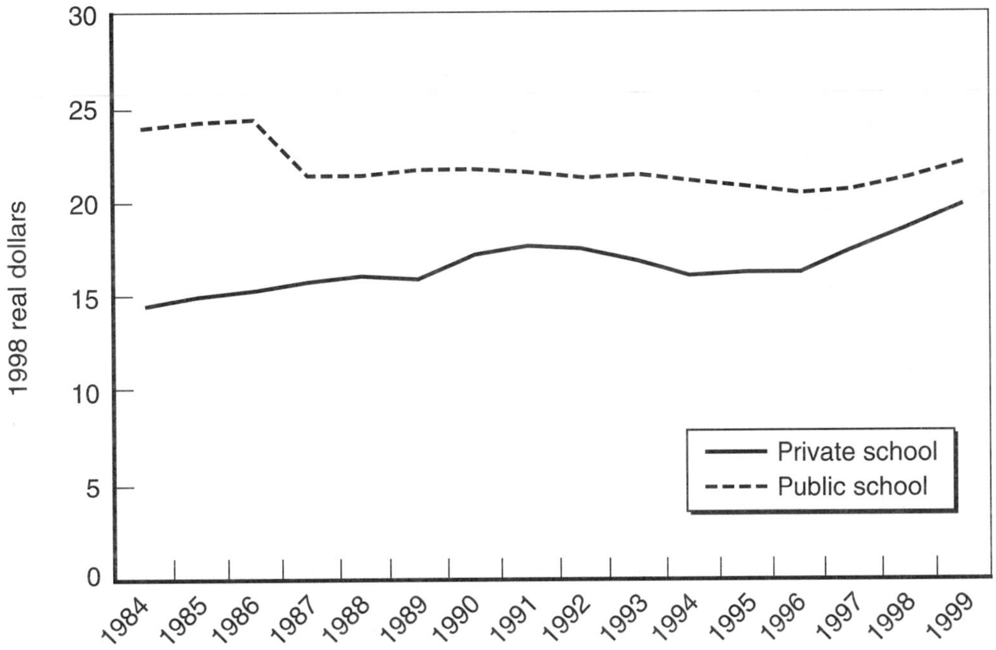

Figure D.5—Average Real Hourly Earnings of Public and Private School Administrators, 1984–1999

Taken together, the results from these analyses raise some interesting issues. Within elementary and secondary school administration, compensation changes may have led school administrators to move between the public and private sectors. However, the compensation for public school administrators remained higher than that for similar positions in the private sector. More broadly, compensation for school administrators did not deteriorate, and their work hours did not increase dramatically over time relative to the work hours of other professionals. It thus appears that other factors affecting labor supply would have to have been changing in order for a reduction in the number of people willing and qualified to fill school administrative positions to occur. One likely candidate is a change in the relative working conditions of the occupations.

Comparison of School Administrators and Teachers

The changes in relative compensation between school administrators and teachers over time can help to explain the movement between these two occupations. Although school administrators earned more than teachers from 1984 to 1999, the size of the earnings gap varied, as shown in Figure D.6. In 1984, the real weekly earnings of school administrators were 31 percent higher than those of teachers. This gap then narrowed until 1996, when it hit 15 percent. After 1996, the trend turned, and the earnings of school administrators grew relative to those of teachers. By 1999, school administrators were earning 24 percent more than teachers.

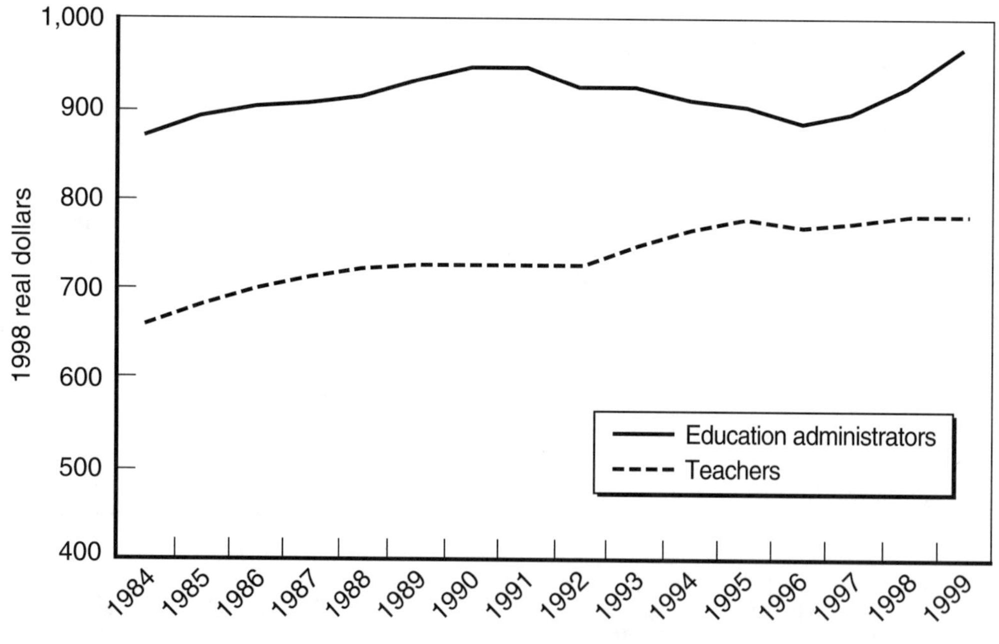

Figure D.6—Average Real Weekly Earnings of School Administrators and Teachers, 1984–1999

This change in weekly earnings between school administrators and teachers appears to have been driven primarily by changes in the hourly wage rate, which, as shown in Figure D.7, followed the same pattern seen for weekly earnings. The gap in hourly wages fell between 1984 and 1997 from 23 to 7 percent. By 1999, however, it had risen: the wage of school administrators was 16 percent greater than the wage of teachers. On average, school administrators reported working more hours per week than teachers did. The difference in hours worked for the two groups fluctuated within a narrow range over time, moving between 2.5 and 1.8 hours per week.

The narrowing of the compensation gap between 1984 and 1996 suggests that school administrative positions may have been becoming less attractive relative to teaching positions. If this were true, we might expect to see fewer teachers willing to move into school administration during this period. After 1996, however, when compensation for school administrators was growing relative to compensation for teachers, we might expect to see more teachers willing to move into administrative roles. This is where it is important to keep in mind that compensation is only one determinant of labor supply. If the working conditions for the two jobs were also changing over time, the effects of the compensation changes on the labor supply might not be observed. Anecdotally, we have heard that the job of school administrator has become more difficult over time. If it has become more difficult relative to the difficulty of a teacher's job, then the increases in the labor supply associated with the compensation increases of the late 1990s could have been canceled out by decreases in the labor supply because of worsening working conditions.

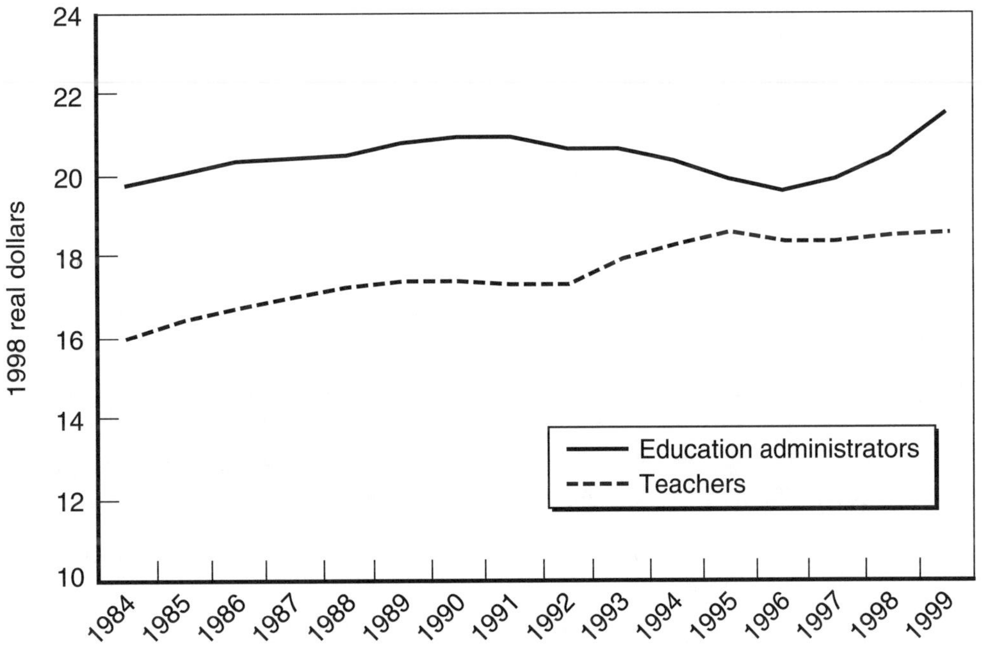

Figure D.7—Average Real Hourly Earnings of School Administrators and Teachers, 1984–1999

ANALYSIS OF ENTRY INTO AND EXIT FROM SCHOOL ADMINISTRATION

An analysis of entry into and exit from school administration requires that individuals in the CPS be matched across years. As noted above, the CPS follows dwelling units, not individuals, so matching is only possible among individuals who remain in the same dwelling unit across years. This aspect of the matched sample is important to keep in mind, since people who move, potentially for a new job, are not included in the sample. As a result, our estimates of entry and exit may serve as a lower bound for the true rates of entry and exit. The match rate for the sample is approximately 80 percent.

Of those people who were school administrators in the first year we observed them, anyone who in the second year has either a non-managerial job or a managerial job outside the elementary and secondary education industry is said to have left his or her school administration occupation. Similarly, anyone who was not in school administration in the first year and then is observed in school administration in the second year is defined as a new entrant to school administration.

Entries

The rate of entry into school administration is calculated as the percentage of people in school administration in the second year who were not in school administration in the first year. As Figure D.8 shows, for the sample period (1983–1999), the entry rate varied significantly from year to year, ranging from 19 to 29 percent. The entry rate becomes somewhat more stable (ranging from 22 to 26 percent), however, when the years are grouped into four time periods.[6] This result is consistent with the earlier

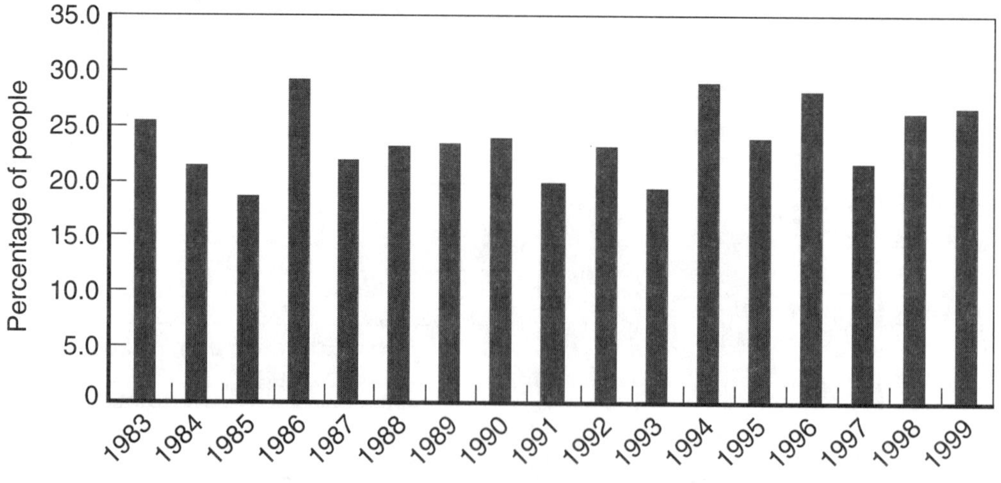

Figure D.8—Rates of Entry into School Administration, 1983–1999

[6]The groupings are: 1983–1984, 1985–1989, 1990–1994, and 1995–1999.

finding that the real value of compensation for school administrators has not changed substantially over time. If we had seen large increases in the compensation for this occupation, then, to the extent that positions in school administration were available, we would have expected to see increased entry into the field.

To characterize where new entrants to school administration are coming from, one must look at their previous occupations. Entrants came primarily from management occupations outside education and from teaching occupations.[7] The largest share of entrants, nearly 50 percent, had been teachers in the previous year, and people entering from managerial occupations in other professions/industries made up about 20 percent. Only about 7 percent moved into the labor force to take positions in school administration. This category appears to comprise people coming out of retirement and people coming directly from an academic program, because the group's age distribution is very wide.[8]

Typically, one expects to see increases in earnings for people switching jobs, and we did see increases, albeit relatively small ones, in real weekly earnings for people entering the field. On average, we found a $20 increase in real weekly earnings among individuals moving into administration from another job. The move into school administration was also associated with an increase in wage rate ($0.25 per hour) and in the reported number of usual hours worked per week (0.9 hours). No differences in the changes in earnings, wages, or hours were found when we compared entrants from teaching positions with entrants from other occupations.

If we focus solely on the school administrative field, then movements from private to public school administration must also be considered as new entries. We found that the percentage of people moving from private to public school administration was approximately equal to the percentage moving in the other direction. Slightly under 3 percent of the people in public school administration in the second year had been in private school administration the previous year.

Exits

As Figure D.9 shows, estimates of the percentage of people leaving school administration fluctuated between 15 and 33 percent during the sample period. When looking at the year-to-year changes in the figure, no consistent trend emerges; but when several years are grouped together, as was done for entries into the field, the exit rates produced are relatively constant, ranging from 22 to 25 percent over time.[9] And, as was the case for entries, this result is consistent with the finding that compensation for school administrators remained relatively steady over the period.

---

[7]Teaching occupations are defined as including pre-kindergarten, kindergarten, elementary, and secondary education teachers and school-based counselors.

[8]The mean age across this group is 54 and the standard deviation is 16. Moreover, the interquartile range is 25. These descriptive statistics indicate that the age distribution across this group is relatively wide.

[9]As for the entries, the years are grouped as follows: 1983–1984, 1985–1989, 1990–1994, and 1995–1999.

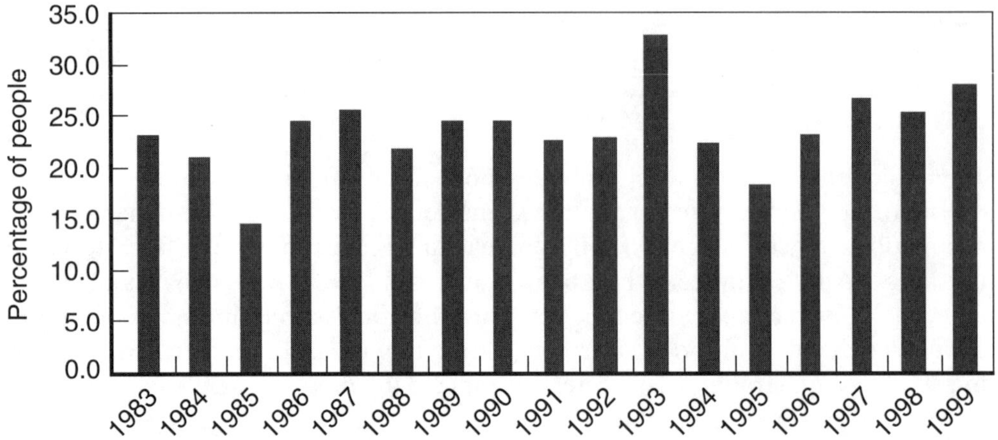

Figure D.9—Rates of Exit from School Administration, 1983–1999

To understand the flows out of school administration, knowing where people are going is important because it can shed light on why people leave. From the results, it appears that people left school administration either to get out of the labor force, primarily through retirement, or to go to a new occupation. Movement out of the labor force accounted for slightly over 18 percent of the exits, and this type of exit appears to have been through retirement, because the average age across this group was 60 (median age, 63). Of all the people leaving school administration, many remained in the labor force. Of those, 22 percent moved into a management position in another industry, and 37 percent moved into teaching occupations. Interestingly, approximately 23 percent of exits were to a wide array of other occupations, none of which accounted for more than 1 or 2 percent by itself.

Compensation and working conditions are factors that might affect an individual's choice to leave an occupation. Among the people leaving school administration for another job, weekly earnings fell on average by $40. This reduction in weekly earnings included both a reduction in hours worked per week (approximately one hour) and a reduction in the hourly wage rate (approximately $0.30 per hour). This result at first seems somewhat counterintuitive, since, as noted earlier, one generally expects to see increases in compensation for job switchers. However, it may be that working conditions and job requirements, rather than compensation, are driving the decision to leave school administration. In addition, many of those leaving returned to teaching occupations, a move for which a reduction in compensation might be expected. To address this issue, we looked at the change in compensation for two groups of people who left: those who left for teaching occupations and those who left for non-teaching occupations. We found greater reductions in weekly earnings for those who left for teaching (–$50), but there were reductions for the other group as well (–$29).

If we define the population of interest as public school administrators, then a move from the public to the private sector would be considered an exit. From 1983 to 1999, only 3 percent of school administrators left public schools for private schools. This movement was relatively small given how the compensation for private school administrators grew relative to that for public school administrators during the same period.

BIBLIOGRAPHY

Archer, J. (2002a). Novice Principals Put Huge Strain on N.Y.C. Schools. *Education Week*, 5/29/02.

Archer, J. (2002b). Leadership Groups Hope to Launch Advanced Certification. *Education Week*, 6/12/02.

Asch, B., and Warner, J. (1999). *Separation and Retirement Incentives in the Civil Service: A Comparison of the Federal Employees Retirement System and the Civil Service Retirement System* (MR-986-OSD). Santa Monica, CA: RAND.

Bell, C., and Chase, C. (1993). The Underrepresentation of Women in School Leadership. In C. Marshall, ed., *The New Politics of Race and Gender: The 1992 Yearbook of the Politics of Education Association*. London: Falmer, 140–154.

Biddle, J., and Roberts, K. (1994). Private Sector Scientists and Engineers and the Transition to Management. *Journal of Human Resources, 29*(1), 82–107.

Biklen, S. K., and Brannigan, M. (1980). *Women and Educational Leadership*. Lexington, MA: DC Health.

Bobbitt, S., Leich, M., Whitener, S., and Lynch, H. (1994). *Characteristics of Stayers, Movers and Leavers: Results from the Teacher Follow Up Survey, 1991–1992*. Washington, DC: National Center for Education Statistics.

Boehlert, L., and O'Connell, R. W. (1999). Where Are the School Leaders for the New Millennium? A Study of Reasons Cited by Incumbent Administrators Who Have Decided Not to Apply for Another Administrative Position. Mimeo.

Boyd, D., Lankford, H., Loeb, S., and Wykoff, J. (2001). Teacher Sorting and the Plight of Urban Schools: A Descriptive Analysis. Mimeo.

Brewer, D. J. (1993). Principal and Student Outcomes: Evidence from U.S. High Schools. *Economics of Education Review, 12*, 281–292.

Brewer, D. J. (1996). Career Paths and Quit Decisions: Evidence from Teaching. *Journal of Labor Economics, 14*(2), 313–339.

Bureau of Labor Statistics (1999). Union Membership by State. *Monthly Labor Review On Line, 122*(6). Available on-line at http://www.stats.bls.gov/opub/mlr/1999/06/regtrend.htm.

Business Week (2002). Executive Pay: Special Report. April 15. Available on-line at http://www.businessweek.com/magazine/content/02_15/b3778012.htm.

Carroll, S., Reichardt, R., and Guarino, C. (2000). *The Distribution of Teachers Among California's School Districts and Schools* (MR-1298.0-JIF). Santa Monica, CA: RAND.

Celis, W. (1993). Heads of Big City Schools Need Political Skill to Last. *New York Times,* 1/17/93.

Chase, S. E., and Bell, C. S. (1994). How Search Consultants Talk About Female Superintendents. *School Administrator, 51*(2), 36–38,40,42.

Colvin, R. (2000). A Premium on Principals. *Los Angeles Times,* 6/28/00.

Cooper, B., and Nakamura, R. T. (1983). *The Unionization of School Administrators: A Study of Public Policy-Making and Labor Relations.* Hanover, NH: Dartmouth College.

Cooper, B. S., Fusarelli, L. D., and Carella, V. A. (2000). *Career Crisis in the School Superintendency? The Results of a National Survey.* Arlington, VA: American Association of School Administrators.

Council of Chief State School Officers (1996). *Interstate School Leaders Licensure Consortium: Standards for School Leaders.* Washington, DC: Council of Chief State School Officers.

Council of the Great City Schools (2001). Urban School Superintendents: Characteristics, Tenure and Salary, Third Biennial Survey. Washington, DC: Council of the Great City Schools. Available on-line at http://www.cgcs.org/reports/supers2001.pdf.

Crow, G. M., Mecklowitz, B., and Weekes, Y. N. (1992). *From Teaching to Administration: A Preparation Institute.* Lancaster, PA: Technomic.

Daniel, C., and Sofer, C. (1998). Bargaining, Compensating Wage Differentials, and Dualism of the Labor Market: Theory and Evidence for France. *Journal of Labor Economics, 15*(3), 546–575.

Dewhirst, H. (1991). Career Patterns: Mobility, Specialization, and Related Career Issues. In R. Morrison and J. Adams, eds., *Contemporary Career Development Issues.* Hillsdale, NJ: Lawrence Erlbaum Associates, 73–107.

Doud, J. L., and Keller, E. P. (1998). The K–8 Principalship in 1998. *NAESP Principal.* Available on-line at http://www.naesp.org/comm/p0998d.htm.

Earley, C. P., and Mosakowski, E. (2000). Creating Hybrid Team Cultures: An Empirical Test of Transnational Team Functioning. *Academy of Management Journal, 43*(1), 26–49.

Eberts, R. W. (1987). Union-Negotiated Employment Rules and Teacher Quits. *Economics of Education Review, 6*(1), 15–25.

Eberts, R. W., and Stone, J. A. (1988). Student Achievement in Public Schools: Do Principals Make a Difference? *Economics of Education Review, 7*(3), 291–299.

Education Writers Association (2002). *Overview: What Is Good Leadership? Searching for a Superhero: Can Principals Do It All?* Washington, DC: Education Writers Association.

Educational Research Service (2000). *The Principal, Keystone of a High-Achieving School: Attracting and Keeping the Leaders We Need.* Arlington, VA: National Association of Elementary School Principals and National Association of Secondary School Principals.

Educational Research Service (2002). *Salaries and Wages for Professional and Support Personnel in Public Schools, 2001–2002.* Arlington, VA: Educational Research Service.

Farkas, S., Johnson, J., Duffet, A., Foleno, T., and Foley, P. (2001). *Trying to Stay Ahead of the Game: Superintendents and Principals Talk About School Leadership.* New York: Public Agenda.

Ferrandino, V. L., and Tirozzi, G. N. (2000). The Shortage of Principals Continues. *NAESP Principal Online,* 10/18/00. Available on-line at http://www.naesp.org/misc/edweek_article_10-18-00.htm.

Fiore, T. A., and Curtin, T. R. (1997). *Public and Private School Principals in the United States: A Statistical Profile, 1987–88 to 1993–94.* Washington, DC: National Center for Education Statistics, U.S. Department of Education.

French, M. T., and Dunlap, L. J. (1998). Compensating Wage Differentials for Job Stress. *Applied Economics, 30,* 1067–1075.

Gewertz, C. (2002). Several City Districts in Hunt for New Leaders. *Education Week,* 7/10/02.

Glass, T., Bjork, L., and Brunner, C. (2000). *The Study of the American School Superintendency: A Look at the Superintendent of Education in the New Millennium.* Arlington, VA: American Association of School Administrators.

Grissmer, D. W., and Kirby, S. N. (1992). *Patterns of Attrition Among Indiana Teachers: 1965–1987* (R-4076). Santa Monica, CA: RAND.

Gruber, K., Wiley, S., Broughman, S., Strizek, G., and Burian-Fitzgerald, M. (2002). *Schools and Staffing Survey, 1999–2000: Overview of the Data for Public, Private, Public Charter, and Bureau of Indian Affairs Elementary and Secondary Schools*

(NCES 2002-313). Washington, DC: National Center for Education Statistics, U.S. Department of Education.

Haffner, A., and Owings, J. (1991). *Careers in Teaching: Following Members of the High School Class of 1972 in and out of Teaching.* Washington, DC: National Center for Education Statistics.

Hallinger, P., and Heck, R. (1996). Reassessing the Principal's Role in School Effectiveness: A Review of Empirical Research, 1980–95. *Education Administration Quarterly, 32*, 5–44.

Hammer, C., and Rohr, C. (1994). *Public and Private School Principals: Are There Too Few Women?* (NCES Issue Brief 94192). Washington, DC: National Center for Education Statistics.

Hanushek, E., Kain, J., and Rivkin, S. (2001). *Why Public Schools Lose Teachers* (NBER Working Paper #8599). Washington, DC: National Bureau of Economic Research.

Henke, R. R., Chen, X., Geis, S., and Knepper, P. (2000). *Progress Through the Teacher Pipeline: 1992–93 College Graduates and Elementary/Secondary School Teaching as of 1997* (NCES 2000-152). Washington, DC: National Center for Education Statistics, U.S. Department of Education.

Henke, R. R., Choy, S. P., Chen, X., Geis, S., Alt, M. N., and Broughman, S. P. (1997). *America's Teachers: Profile of a Profession, 1993–94* (NCES 97-460). Washington, DC: National Center for Education Statistics, U.S. Department of Education.

Henke, R. R., Choy, S. P., Geis, S., and Broughman, S. P. (1996). *Schools and Staffing in the U.S.: A Statistical Profile, 1993–94* (NCES 96-124). Washington, DC: National Center for Education Statistics, U.S. Department of Education.

Herzberg, F. (1987). One More Time: How Do You Motivate Employees? *Harvard Business Review*, September-October, 109–117.

Hoff, K. (1999). Leaders and Managers: Essential Skills Required Within Higher Education. *Higher Education, 38*(3), 311–315.

Hord, S. (1992). *Entering and Exiting the Superintendency: Preparation, Promises and Problems.* Paper presented at the annual meeting of the American Educational Research Association, San Francisco, CA.

Houston, P. D. (2000). Not a Great Job But a Wonderful Calling. *AASA Online: School Administrator*, 6/28/00.

Hurd, M., Smith, J., and Zissimopoulos, J. (2002). The Effects of Subjective Survival on Retirement and Social Security Claiming. Mimeo. Santa Monica, CA: RAND.

Illinois State Board of Education (2000). *Educator Supply and Demand.* Available online at http://www.isbe.state.il.us/research/SupplyDemand/Educator%20Supply%20%20Demand.pdf.

Jencks, C., Perman, L., and Rainwater, L. (1988). What Is a Good Job? A New Measure of Labor-Market Success. *American Journal of Sociology, 93*(6), 1322–1357.

Johnson, M. C., and Douglas, J. R. (1990). Grow-Your-Own—A Model for Selecting Administrators. *NASSP Bulletin, 74*(526), 34–38.

Joy, L. (1998). Why Are Women Underrepresented in Public School Administration? An Empirical Test of Promotion Discrimination. *Economics of Education Review, 17*(2), 193–204.

Kim, M. (1999). Where the Grass Is Greener: Voluntary Turnover and Wage Premiums. *Industrial Relations, 38*(4), 584–603.

Kimball, K., and Sirtonik, K. A. (2000). The Urban School Principalship. Take This Job and . . . ! *Education and Urban Society, 32*(4), 536–543.

Kirby, S., Berends, M., and Naftel, S. (1999). Supply and Demand of Minority Teachers in Texas: Problems and Prospects. *Educational Evaluation and Policy Analysis, 21*(1), 281–292.

Kirby, S., and Grissmer, D. (1993). *Teacher Attrition: Theory, Evidence, and Suggested Policy Options* (P-7827). Santa Monica, CA: RAND.

Lamotey, K. (1987). Black Principals for Black Students: Some Preliminary Observations. *Urban Education, 22*(2), 173–181.

Lee, T., Mitchell, T., Wise, L., and Fireman, S. (1996). An Unfolding Model of Voluntary Employee Turnover. *Academy of Management Journal, 39*(1), 5–36.

Loeb, S. (2000). *How Teachers' Choices Affect What a Dollar Can Buy: Wages and Quality in K–12 Schooling.* Albany, NY: Education Finance Research Consortium.

Murnane, R., and Olsen, R. (1989). The Effects of Salaries and Opportunity Costs on Duration in Teaching: Evidence from Michigan. *Review of Economics and Statistics, 71*, 347–352.

Murnane, R., Singer, J., and Willett, J. (1988). The Career Paths of Teachers: Implications for Teacher Supply and Methodological Lessons for Research. *Educational Researcher, 17*(6), 22–30.

Murnane, R., Singer, J., and Willett, J. (1989). The Influences of Salaries and "Opportunity Costs" on Teachers' Career Choices: Evidence from North Carolina. *Harvard Educational Review, 59*(3), 325–345.

Murnane, R., Singer, J., Willett, J., Kemple, J., and Olsen, R. (1991). *Who Will Teach? Policies That Matter*. Cambridge, MA: Harvard University Press.

National Association of Elementary School Principals (2000a). Profiling the Principalship: New 1999–2000 Salary Statistics. *NAESP Principal Online*, 8/25/00. Available on-line at http://www.naesp.org/prinpro.htm.

National Association of Elementary School Principals (2000b). Study Confirms Powerful Link Between the Principal and School Success. *NAESP Principal Online*, 8/16/00. Available on-line at http://www.naesp.org/news/05.html.

National Association of Elementary School Principals and National Association of Secondary School Principals (1998). *Is There a Shortage of Qualified Candidates for Openings in the Principalship? An Exploratory Study*. Arlington, VA: Educational Research Service.

National Center for Education Statistics (1996). *Teachers' Working Conditions. Findings from the Condition of Education, 1996*. Washington, DC: U.S. Department of Education, Office of Educational Research and Improvement.

National Center for Education Statistics (1999). *Projections of Education Statistics to 2009*. Washington, DC: U.S. Department of Education, Office of Educational Research and Improvement.

National Center for Education Statistics (2000). *Strengths and Limitations of Using SUDAAN, Stata and WesVarPC for Computing Variances from NCES Data Sets* (Working Paper No. 2000-03). Washington, DC: U.S. Department of Education, Office of Educational Research and Improvement.

National Defense Research Institute, Defense Manpower Research Center (1994). *Future Career Management Systems for U.S. Military Officers* (MR-470-OSD). Santa Monica, CA: RAND.

National Institute on Educational Governance, Finance, Policymaking, and Management (1999). *Effective Leaders for Today's Schools: Synthesis of a Policy Forum on Educational Leadership*. Washington, DC: U.S. Department of Education, Office of Educational Research and Improvement.

Neff, T., and Ogden, D. (2001). Anatomy of a CEO. *Chief Executive*, February 2001. Available on-line at http://www.chiefexecutive.net/depts/routetop/anatomyofaceo. html.

Nelson, F. (1991). An Interstate Cost-of-Living Index. *Educational Evaluation and Policy Analysis, 13*, 103–111.

Nelson, F., Drown, R., and Gould, J. (2000). *Survey and Analysis of Teacher Salary Trends, 2000*. Washington, DC: American Federation of Teachers. Available on-line at http://www.aft.org/research/survey00\salarysurvey00.pdf.

Olson, L. (2000a). New Thinking on What Makes a Leader. *Education Week*, 1/19/00.

Olson, L. (2000b). Principals Wanted: Apply Just About Anywhere. *Education Week*, 1/12/00.

Papa, F., Lankford, H., and Wyckoff, J. (2002). *The Attributes and Career Paths of Principals: Implications for improving Policy*. Albany: State University of New York.

Parsons, D. (1996). Retirement Age and Retirement Income: The Role of the Firm. In E. Hanushek and N. Maritato, eds., *Assessing Knowledge of Retirement Behavior*. Washington, DC: National Academy Press, 149–194.

Pickler, N. (1999). School Unions Bill Clears House Panel. *Detroit Free Press*, 10/21/99.

Portin, B. (2000). The Changing Urban Principalship. *Education and Urban Society, 32*(4), 492–505.

Portin, B., DeArmond, M., Gundlach, L., and Schneider, P. (2003). *Making Sense of Leading Schools: A Study of the School Principalship*. Seattle, WA: Center on Reinventing Public Education, University of Washington.

Pounder, D. G., and Merrill, R. J. (2001). Job Desirability of the High School Principalship: A Job Choice Theory Perspective. *Educational Administration Quarterly, 37*(1), 27–57.

Prince, C. (2002). The Challenge of Attracting Good Teachers and Principals to Struggling Schools. Arlington, VA: American Association of School Administrators. Available on-line at http://www.aasa.org/issues_and_insights/issues_dept/challenges_teachers_principals.pdf.

Principals' Executive Program (2002). *PEP 2001–2002 Annual Report*. Available online at http://www.ga.unc.edu/pep/pp/index.html.

Public Schools of North Carolina, State Department of Public Instruction, Division of Human Resource Management (1998). Administrator Supply and Demand Study. Available on-line at http://www.dpi.state.nc.us/school_personnel_support/supply_and_demand/attachment_a.html.

Purkey, S. C., and Smith, M. S. (1983). Effective Schools: A Review. *The Elementary School Journal, 83*(4), 427–452.

Reardon, S. F., and Firebaugh, G. (2002). Measures of Multi-Group Segregation. *Sociological Methodology, 32*(1), 33–67.

Resnick, L., and Glennan, T. (2002). Leadership for Learning: A Theory of Action for Urban School Districts. In A. Hightower, M. Knapp, J. Marsh, and M. McLaughlin, eds., *School Districts and Instructional Renewal*. New York: Teachers College Press.

Richard, A. (1999). Pay Soars for School Chiefs in Big Districts. *Education Week*, 10/3/99.

Richard, A. (2000). L.A. Board Taps Romer for Top Job. *Education Week*, 6/14/00.

Riehl, C., and Byrd, M. (1997). Gender Differences Among New Recruits to School Administration: Cautionary Footnotes to an Optimistic Tale. *Educational Evaluation and Policy Analysis, 19*(1), 45–64.

Rosen, S. (1986). The Theory of Equalizing Difference. In O. Ashenfelter and R. Layard, eds., *Handbook of Labor Economics*, vol. 1. Amsterdam: Elsevier, 641–692.

Roza, M., Hill, P., Celio, M., Harvey, J., and Wishon, S. (2002). A Problem of Definition: Is There Truly a Shortage of School Principals? Mimeo. University of Washington.

Sahagun, L. (2000). Critical Shortage of Principals Seen in L.A. *Los Angeles Times*, 8/27/00.

Shen, J., Rodriguez-Campos, L., and Rincones-Gomez, R. (2000). Characteristics of Urban Principalship. A National Trend Study. *Education and Urban Society, 32*(4), 481–491.

Sinatra, A. (2000). Tough Shoes to Fill: Fewer Educators Willing to Take on Pressures of Being Principal. *ABC News*, 01/12/00. Available on-line at http://www.abcnews.com.

Snowden, P. E., and Gorton, R. A. (1998). *School Leadership and Administration: Important Concepts, Case Studies and Simulations*. Chicago: McGraw Hill.

Stecher, B., and Bohrnstedt, G., eds. (2002). Class Size Reduction in California: Summary of Findings from 1999–00 and 2000–01. Sacramento, CA: California Department of Education.

Steinberg, J. (2000). Nation's Schools Struggling to Find Enough Principals. *New York Times*, 9/03/00.

Stinebrickner, T. R. (1998). An Empirical Investigation of Teacher Attrition. *Economics of Education Review, 17*(2), 127–136.

Strauss, R., Bowes, L., Marks, M., and Plesko, M. (2000). Improving Teacher Preparation and Selection: Lessons from the Pennsylvania Experience. *Economics of Education Review, 19*, 387–415.

Stricherz, M. (2001). Groups Pushing for Measures to Attract, Retain Principals. *Education Week*, 7/11/01.

Succi, M., and Alexander, J. (1999). Physician Involvement in Management and Governance: The Moderating Effects of Staff Structure and Composition. *Health Care Management Review, 24*(1), 33–44.

Tallerico, M., Poole, W., and Bursyn, J. (1994). Exits from Urban Superintendencies: The Intersection of Politics, Race and Gender. *Urban Education, 28*(4), 439–454.

Teske, P., and Schneider, M. (1999). *The Importance of Leadership: The Role of School Principals*. Arlington, VA: The Price Waterhouse Coopers Endowment for the Business of Government.

Tryneski, J. (2000). *Requirements for Certification of Teachers, Counselors, Librarians, Administrators* (64th edition). Chicago: University of Chicago Press.

Walden, M. L., and Sogutlu, Z. (2001). Determinants of Intrastate Variation in Teacher Salaries. *Economics of Education Review, 20*, 63–70.

White, M. J. (1986). Segregation and Diversity Measures in Population Distribution. *Population Index, 52,* 198–221.

Widaman, K. F. (1993). Common Factor Analysis Versus Principal Component Analysis: Differential Bias in Representing Model Parameters? *Multivariate Behavioral Research, 28,* 263–311.